SHE'S A KNOCKOUT!

SHE'S A KNOCKOUT!

A History of Women in Fighting Sports

L. A. Jennings

ROWMAN & LITTLEFIELD
Lanham • Boulder • New York • London

Published by Rowman & Littlefield
A wholly owned subsidiary of The Rowman & Littlefield Publishing Group, Inc.
4501 Forbes Boulevard, Suite 200, Lanham, Maryland 20706
www.rowman.com

16 Carlisle Street, London W1D 3BT, United Kingdom

British Library Cataloguing in Publication Information Available

Library of Congress Cataloging-in-Publication Data

Jennings, L. A.
She's a knockout! : a history of women in fighting sports / L. A. Jennings.
p. cm.
Includes bibliographical references and index.
ISBN 978-1-4422-3643-1 (cloth : alk. paper) — ISBN 978-1-4422-3644-8 (ebook) 1. Sports for women—History. 2. Hand-to-hand fighting—History. 3. Women athletes. 4. Women wrestlers. 5. Women martial artists. 6. Women boxers. I. Title.
GV709.J45 2015
796.83—dc23
2014025171

Printed in the United States of America

For Mike, who is always in my corner

CONTENTS

PREFACE

The Origin Story

In 2006, I was training for my first fighting event, a submission grappling tournament, at the local mixed martial arts (MMA) gym in Tallahassee, Florida. The gym was a steamy and pungent warehouse with no air-conditioning or windows. Sweaty, shirtless men sparred, hit focus mitts, wrestled, lifted weights, and jumped rope to blaring radio rock, and stuck their heads under the water cooler when the heat threatened to overtake them. These men, my teammates, were professional and amateur MMA fighters, some of whom would go on to fight in the International Fight League and Ultimate Fighting Championship (UFC). On a fall day, a young man who worked for the local university newspaper arrived at the gym to write a story about the fighters. Inevitably, he saw me, the only female, training with a coach and asked to speak to me as well. We talked briefly about why I trained, which was to compete in the next month's North American Grappling Association tournament in Atlanta. I mentioned that my boyfriend, now my husband, Mike, was training for the same event. He then asked if I thought MMA was good for self-defense, to which I replied, not really, because it was a sport with rules. He said good-bye, and the following week, my teammates and I eagerly opened the newspaper to read the story about our gym.

In a paragraph near the end of the article, the reporter describes me as standing "barely over five feet tall," which, at a firm five feet, four inches tall, seemed an insult to my stature. Then the article explains that I was training because my boyfriend was and mentions that he was training for a grappling tournament. No mention was made of my plans for competition. In fact, the author explains that this young woman, me, was training for self-defense purposes and that all women should train for self-defense. In the space of a paragraph, I was diminished. My fighting goals were replaced with the more acceptable, at least to this young man, pursuit of women's self-defense. Moreover, my training suddenly became in support of my boyfriend, rather than myself. Journalistic integrity be damned.

During the time that this interview took place and the subsequent article was printed, I was also in my first year of a master's program at Florida State University. My scholarly focus was on cultural studies and feminism, in particular. Frustrated and angered by the demeaning nature of the article, I began to research what feminists have written about fighting sports. To my surprise, the only texts I could find were about the feminism of self-defense. There was nothing about women fighters.

The women's self-defense movement is concerned with protecting women's bodies from physical harm and has become increasingly popular during the past thirty or so years. The connection between feminism and the self-defense movement stems from feminist goals of freedom for women from oppression and objectification of the body. In "The Fighting Spirit: Women's Self-Defense Training and the Discourse of Sexed Embodiment," feminist scholar Martha McCaughey states, "In feminist discourse, the body is often construed as the object of patriarchal violence (actual or symbolic), and violence has been construed variously as oppressive, diminishing, inappropriate, and masculinist."[1] Many feminists find that self-defense is the physical practice of a philosophical and ethical prerogative to protect women from violence and harm. McCaughey states that self-defense is more than a "set of fighting tactics. Self-defense transforms what it means to have a female body."[2] She defines the female body as one that is considered passive and therefore under attack by men who are gendered aggressive.

I find this definition problematic. If men are inherently violent, does that not make women inherently passive? And if so, what does that mean for me, a woman who delights in training to punch and choke my opponent? In addition, I wondered why it was more acceptable for me to train for self-defense than competition in a fighting sport. McCaughey claims that gendered perceptions of men as aggressive make it seem inevitable for men to be violent and that their sexual assault of women is a biological consequence of aggressiveness. She believes that self-defense is important because it alters the ways that women are seen as victims and makes them active in defending themselves. The language used by McCaughey and other self-defense advocates to discuss the training of women in self-defense classes is based on gender binaries. Women are gendered to be passive; self-defense courses train them to be aggressive. McCaughey claims, "When women train to fight back, they defy gender norms. It's manly, but not womanly, to protect and fight."[3] This assertion rests on the belief that women should train to fight back against male aggression, but it makes no concessions for the competitive fighter. I felt constricted, once again, by the assumption that fighting is always a male prerogative.

Since 2006, I have continued to train, fight, and learn. I have finished my doctoral degree and written feminist articles on female fighters. I have read articles from other fighting enthusiasts that celebrate the growing popularity and general acceptance of women's fighting sports. In 2012, women's boxing was included in the Olympics for the first time in recorded history. The UFC featured its first female bout between Ronda Rousey and Liz Carmouche to an astonishingly large pay-per-view audience in 2013. As a martial arts enthusiast, I was elated to see women's fighting sports come out of the margins and into the limelight. Yet, I noticed that many of the corresponding articles and news reports are fixated on the idea that this was the first time in history that women were being taken seriously as fighters, and I knew that this was simply not the case. If fighting is as old as man, then it is as old as woman, too.

The purpose of this book is to illuminate the rich and storied history of women's fighting sports. In the twenty-first century, it can feel as though the image of a woman in a boxing ring, in a MMA cage, or on the mat during a wrestling match is incredibly new and evolutionary, and it is exciting to see women moving to the forefront of fighting sports; however, the false narrative that women have never been taken seriously as fighters ignores the incredible women who fought bravely long before the UFC, television, the automobile, and even the sewing machine.

WOMEN'S FIGHTING HISTORY

There is, in fact, a legacy of women who participated in fighting sports prior to the twenty-first, and even the twentieth, century. Many of these women are not only unknown, they are discounted by boxing and wrestling historians. Women have undoubtedly competed in fighting sports at varying levels, from country fairs to elite events, for thousands of years. This book leaves conjecture and myth aside by focusing on the history of female fighters throughout the past three hundred years, or, since the concomitant growth of the news media in the eighteenth century. It can be argued that sports journalism began when printing capabilities made it possible for newspapers to print stories that did not revolve around the major cultural and political issues of the time. In the sixteenth century, printed materials were innovative and highly valuable, so newspapers and tracts centered on religion and politics. There would not have been space in these precious papers for stories about boxing or wrestling. Nonetheless, by the eighteenth century, the print media proliferated as the art of printing became more streamlined, and the reading population demanded entertainment, as well as news. Scholars have found records of boxing matches in newspapers beginning in the early eighteenth century in England. Of course, people throughout the world were competing in sports far earlier than this, but it was not until the eighteenth century that sporting news became part of the English publishing industry.

To be specific, historically accurate, and concise, this book traces the history of female fighters in Britain and the United States starting in the early eighteenth century. Although there are numerous women who may have learned to box or wrestle during the course of history, this text specifically examines female athletes, which creates a distinction between people who compete in fighting as a competition and those who train for or practice a sport. Certainly, women have struggled merely to train in a fighting art, and there exists a history of restricting women from even learning the art of boxing or wrestling. This book analyzes the history of female fighters within the structured confines of a clearly delineated sport; therefore, the history of female fighters, for the purpose of this volume, is limited to women who have competed in fighting sports at an amateur or professional level.

This particular history looks at fighting sports, not fighting in a military setting. There are numerous excellent scholarly and historical texts that research female warriors, from ancient Spartan fighters to female pilots in World War II, and they are a fascinating study of women in the military. Possibly the most interesting female army was the "Amazons" of eighteenth- and nineteenth-century Dahomey, who comprised the elite force of the king's guards and fought on the front lines of battle. The Amazons underwent grueling training that included wrestling matches, running, calisthenics, and a general hardening of the body beyond anything the male army had to endure. A song of the Dahomey female warriors, handed down through oral tradition, boasts,

> We are men, not women
> Whatever town we attack
> We must conquer,
> Or bury ourselves in its ruins.

The Dahomey warriors were deemed "Amazons" by the many European visitors who saw them in person. The women remained guardians of the king of Dahomey during his wars with France in the late nineteenth century. Although the French eventually defeated the Dahomey kingdom, early hostilities ended in heavy French losses at the hands of the Amazon warriors. The last remaining female Amazon died in 1970.[4] While the history of female warriors like the Dahomey Amazons is a rich facet of women's history and scholarship, this book does not detail women in military combat or tribal warfare. Instead, it focuses solely on women who have competed in fighting sports, whether sanctioned or, as was often the case prior to the end of the twentieth century, unsanctioned.

Our cultural perceptions of the past often anachronistically cast women as perpetually subjugated and constrained figures, and while women were certainly marginalized for most of history, there were times, places, and situations where they participated in decidedly unfeminine behaviors. The women featured in this volume, from England's "Championess" Elizabeth Stokes in the 1720s to America's female wrestler Cora Livingstone in the 1930s and early women's MMA great Debi Purcell in the early 2000s, tell a story of individuals seeking their place within the ring (or mat or cage). This book does not relate the narrative of large social movements, but rather the fight of individual women whose stories come together to substantiate the reality of female fighters in history.

The introduction to *She's a Knockout!*, "Why We Fight," explores the history of fighting within the context of sports and competition. This section defines the concept of sport and examines the history of the three largest subsets of fighting sports: striking, grappling, and mixed discipline fighting. It also analyzes the cultural position occupied by sports, specifically the way that male athletes dominate the sports media, while women are pushed to the periphery. Female athletes, whatever their sport, have experienced discrimination from many corners of society. Women have been restricted from playing sports based on inaccurate medical claims, including the fear that a woman's uterus might fall out of her vagina if she runs, as well as social fears that women who move around more than necessary might become sexually aroused.[5] Women interested in boxing or wrestling were subjected to even more vitriolic discrimination because pugilism was a contentious subject in its own right. But despite the blatantly sexist critics of their participation, many female fighters persevered to compete in the sports they loved. Many historical texts discuss women who took part in combative training as a necessary precaution for times of war. In this volume, the female fighter is defined as a woman who participates in pugilistic competition as an athlete rather than a warrior.

The first chapter of *She's a Knockout!* is an extensive history of women in fighting sports in Britain and the United States. Entitled "Fighting in the Georgian and Victorian Eras," this chapter begins with the story of Elizabeth Wilkinson Stokes, the prolific British boxer of the early eighteenth century. This section centers on British fighters spanning from Elizabeth's victories in the 1720s to the female wrestlers of the late nineteenth century. Although fighting was not a respectable pursuit by any means, boxing and wrestling were both considered British pastimes, and some English were particularly delighted by their female fighters.

Americans also fought competitively, despite the social restrictions against prizefighting. Chapter 2, "American Women Join the Fight," details how fighting women in the United States were treated with contempt not only because of their sex, but due to the social aversion to boxing in general; however, by the twentieth century, there was a tremendous growth in the popularity of fighting sports in the United States. Beginning with the evolution of the traveling circus and burlesque theaters, the third chapter, "Fighting as Spectacle," reveals how fighting became a more mainstream entertainment in the United States in the early twentieth century. Female wrestlers and boxers performed alongside strongmen, bearded ladies, and Chinese acrobats at carnival events, and were celebrated by fans. Pinup-style photographs of female wrestlers were turned into trading cards, and a lady boxer was crowned beauty queen by her local police force. But by the middle of the century, sports of all kinds had come under the jurisdiction of such athletic institutions as the Boxing Commission, which routinely sought to exclude women from participating.

"The Fight to Fight," the fourth chapter of this book, focuses on the latter half of the twentieth century and the numerous court cases and lawsuits that sought equality for women in the ring. This chapter also examines how Title IX, from 1972 through the 1990s, allowed women to legally enter the arena of combative sports and how that new participation was often criticized from multiple cultural ideologies. Although women were now allowed to compete in historically male sports, they were still considered trespassers and unwelcome by all into the world of combative sports.

Chapter 5, "MMA Goes Mainstream," investigates the new sport of mixed martial arts and the increasing population of women competing in amateur and professional fights. In the 2000s, several women were, at various times, named the "face" of women's MMA. Sports media promoted the idea that one woman would, somehow, embody the sport in its entirety and thus bring women's MMA (WMMA) into the mainstream. Ronda Rousey is, undoubtedly, the most famous fighter in WMMA history, but she was not the first woman considered to be the "face" of the sport. As a consequence, this idea has, at times, pushed other fighters into the background, with the media concentrating on one female fighter at a time. This chapter not only reveals the history of women's involvement in the sport of MMA, it explores the way that fighters were praised or criticized based on the social construction of idealized femininity.

MMA may be the fastest-growing sport today—and possibly of all time. And while throughout the past decade it has been frustrating to locate women within the extreme machismo of the sport and its promoters, MMA has been a conduit of change for female fighters. This book reveals how women have not been excluded, but rather forgotten and ignored, by the annals of fighting sports history. It includes numerous women who fought both inside and outside the ring to participate in the sports they love. And while it was not possible to identify every female fighter in history due to time, space, and other logistical restrictions, I hope *She's a Knockout!* sheds some light on the fantastic history of wom-

ACKNOWLEDGMENTS

I owe thanks to a great many people in both the academic and pugilistic worlds.

First, many thanks to my friend and mentor, Dr. Adam Rovner, who guided me through my academic career, as well as University of Denver librarian Peggy Keenan, who answered my numerous and obnoxious questions with enthusiasm. Truly, she is the librarian of librarians. I also want to thank William Mays, *National Police Gazette* archivist, who had what seems to have been a delightful time searching this historic tome for female pugilists.

My sincere thanks go to Sue Fox of the Women's Boxing Archival Network for her assistance and inspiration. I am also grateful to Mary Ann Owen, who provided me with stunning photos, as well as Jack Pokress, boxing photographer, who graciously allowed me to use his photos in this book.

Thank you to Debi Purcell and Lana Stefanac, fighters and my personal heroes.

Many thanks go out to Christen Karniski, the editor who believed in this project.

To my tribe at Train.Fight.Win. Denver, which continues to provide me with inspiration and drive, thank you.

Thanks to my mom and dad for the support, love, and fantastic editing. To my siblings, Caroline and Scott, thank you for keeping me on my toes.

And to my husband, Mike, thank you for everything.

INTRODUCTION

Why We Fight

Boxing, wrestling, and running are the most primal of human sports. Although it seems unthinkable by our current standards of high-priced running flats and designer fight shorts, none of these activities, at their most basic level, require any equipment. Unlike snow skiing or mountain climbing, activities that require certain geographical features, or American football, a sport that necessitates a great deal of people and equipment (and thus, money), boxing, wrestling, and running are sports that are practiced in almost every culture throughout the world. The fascinating aspect of fighting sports is that they pit two people against one another and ask them to prove who the better athlete is. Fighting is often associated with drunken brawls or personal vendettas in film and television, but when organized and regulated by rules and structure, fighting is also a sport.

DEFINITION OF SPORT

In the academic lexicon, sports are often defined in strange and rather obtuse ways. For instance, this definition from Cesar A. Torres in the *Routledge Companion to Sports History* makes the activity of sport almost unrecognizable: "Sports are artificial tests established by rules that not only prescribe the use of less efficient means to achieve the goal stipulated, but also require the implementation of physical skills to do so."[1]

University of California, Berkeley professor Roberta Park recognizes the difficulty of defining sport as a universal term, given that sports have various social and historical implications depending on the culture. Prior to the nineteenth century, sporting events were comprised of a multitude of activities, from riding and jousting to bear-baiting and hunting. In fact, some theorists relate the concept of sport to the word *disport*—"to divert oneself," which is how Michael Mandelbaum describes the emergence of sports as a "diversion" during the increasing amount of free time in the industrial world.[2] The industrial revolution and standardization of the forty-hour work week gave people more free time, but there were few entertainment outlets to fill the void. Prior to the Industrial Revolution, any "free time" was spent in religious endeavors, from reading liturgical works to spending time at church. Mandelbaum claims that the twentieth century "intensified the informal division of the arts into high and low or 'mass' forms."[3] Sports could be categorized as an activity of the masses, since anyone could, in theory, participate, although it is highly unlikely that the blue-collar worker in the city had as much time as an aristocrat to play sports.

In modern American and European cultures, sports are practiced by a spectrum of people of varying ages, ethnicities, economic levels, and, of course, genders. There are levels of competitors in the sports arena, from the casual practitioner to the Olympic-level athlete. As anyone who has ever trained and competed in a sport knows, there is a monumental differ-ence in the fitness workout of a layperson and the rigorous training of an athletic competitor. Hitting the heavy bag for a calorie burn at the local YMCA and competing in the Golden Gloves, while both are based on the sport of boxing, reveals two versions of a sport. To maintain focus and for the sake of being definitional, this book is concerned with sports at the highest level: the competitive athlete. This is not to diminish the more casual versions of boxing, but rather to focus on the cultural and social implications of the amateur and professional athlete.

SPORTS IN AMERICAN MEDIA

But sports are more than just a set of rules. Sports bring people together as fans and athletes in a community bound by the love of a particular activity. In the United States, the "big three" of men's sports—football, basketball, and baseball, with hockey making an appearance as the fourth in some parts of the country—are the center of sports news coverage. These sports are large team sports, generate enormous sums of money, and dominate the sports media coverage. In a 2009 study, researchers found that these "big three" sports dominated 68 percent of combined (main, plus ticker) local TV sports news and *SportsCenter*, with men's football at 21 percent, men's basketball at 23 percent, and men's baseball at 24 percent.[4] Of the remaining 32 percent, women's sports were covered only 3 percent of the time. In addition, the longitudinal study found that coverage of women's sports has actually declined since 1989: In 1989, women accounted for 5 percent of news coverage, and 8.7 percent in 1999, but in 2009, women's sports news coverage plummeted to a shocking 1.9 percent.[5]

Various factors contribute to the dominance of the "big three" male sports in the United States, including the aforementioned economic aspect and prevalence of those three sports in youth sports. Outside of the center of American sports, in the periphery, various men's sports, including soccer, golf, tennis, and various Olympic sports, combined to generate 20 percent of the *SportsCenter* and local sports news coverage, according to the 2009 study. Women's sports, again, generated only 3 percent of total televised sports news stories. Thus, men's sports outside of the "center" are not necessarily marginalized, but they do not have the power and ascendancy of men's football, basketball, and baseball.

Fighting sports have a long and storied history that far surpasses the new sports that dominate American culture. And while they may not make up the majority of sports news coverage, the community of fighting fans and athletes is large and much more international than the "big three" American sports. The most revealing aspect of Cooky, Messner, and Hextrum's study, however, is that the media's interest in women's sports is on the decline. Women have always held tenuous connections in the sporting world in the United States and Europe, depending on the time in history and specific location.

GENDER IN SPORTS

Female athletes are always defined by that qualifier of female. Male athletes are simply athletes, while women are defined first and foremost, by their sex. Professor Michael Kimmel said it best when he related an anecdote about two women at a feminist conference discussing how they self-define. The white woman explained that when she looks in the mirror, she sees a woman. The other speaker explained that when she looks in the mirror, she sees a black woman, revealing that race is a qualifier as important as sex. But Kimmel realized that when he looks in the mirror, he sees a human, because, in a way, gender is invisible to men because they have the privilege of centrality. Such qualifiers as race, class, and gender are steps away from the center. The more qualifiers one has to contend with, for example, a poor black woman, the further she moves away from the central, the position of power. Kimmel explains, "When you are the dominant power in the world, everyone else has to be named." And in the sporting world, where men remain the center, women must always be qualified, or named, before they can be called athletes.[6]

Sports are gendered male for two primary reasons. First, men are, again, the cultural center. Second, and more importantly for the sake of this book, women have been involved less in sports throughout history than their male counterparts. While we explore the history of female athletes during the past three hundred years in the body of this book, suffice it to say that women have not always been welcome in the world of sports. They have always participated in sports, albeit in varying levels through both time and place, but never as extensively as men; however, the idea that women did not participate in sports prior to the twentieth century neglects historical truths. Women have taken part in sports and play throughout the globe and at various times in history. Although women's sports have not generated (and still do not generate) the same amount of interest as men's sports, the news media started publishing articles and stories about female athletes beginning in the eighteenth century. Female athletes were largely treated as anomalies, being depicted in humorous or scandalous examples of what women could do outside of the normative female role. While not all historical accounts pass judgment on female athletes, those that do either criticize them for being too masculine or poke fun at them for being physically inept.

WOMEN'S SPORTS IN THE MEDIA

Unfortunately, this trend continues today, as Professor Michael Messner has identified, with sports coverage that makes jokes about female athletes. In his qualitative study of *SportsCenter* and the astonishingly sparse amount of coverage of women's sports, Messner and his colleagues identified two types of approaches to female athletes. Broadcasts might present a segment on what would be considered a "nonserious" sport, for instance, bungee jumping or professional wrestling, to make fun of women. Or, oftentimes, a segment will cover a serious sport but sexualize the female athletes. In Summer Olympic coverage, networks have dedicated an inordinate amount of time to discussing the rear ends of beach volleyball players Kerri Walsh and Misty May-Treanor. Tennis player Anna Kournikova famously received a great deal of media coverage about her looks and an equal amount of critcism, often from the same news source, about her inability to play. Kournikova may not have been as good as some of the other women on the professional tennis circuit, but she was still an elite tennis player who did not deserve to be called "awful." Yet, this is how much of the commentary regarding female athletes has progressed. Women who are skilled and not stereotypically beautiful are insulted and even referred to as men by some commentators. That insult reveals part of the fear that remains embedded in women's sports, even today: that the women who play sports could, in some way, become masculine.

Historically, sports have been a decidedly male practice. The Victorian era introduced the notion of exercise for both men and women. Although Victorian ladies were still constrained, both socially and sartorially, with long skirts and corsets remaining normative attire, women participated in competitive sports like archery. In the 1920s, the American flapper girl defied normal gender behavior through a "debaucherous" lifestyle consisting of drinking, smoking, dancing, and, of course, the famous short hair and even shorter skirts.

As Babe Ruth made a name for himself on the baseball field, another babe, Mildred Ella "Babe" Didrikson, trounced the conception of the weaker female sex by excelling in multiple sports, including track and field, basketball, swimming, boxing, and tennis. In a famous interview with a sports journalist, Didrikson was asked if there was any sport she did not play. She responded, "Yeah, dolls." Didrikson epitomized the cultural fear that surrounded this new, modern woman. She was considered masculine and unnatural to her sex. *New York World-Telegram* journalist Joe Williams remarked that, "it would be much better if she and her ilk stayed home, got themselves prettied up, and waited for the phone to ring." Williams's sentiments were echoed by some, although many fans and journalists praised Didrikson's athletic prowess and skill in a multitude of sports.

THE FEMALE BODY IN SPORTS

It is no secret that the female body is one of the most reproduced figures in cultural history. Because of this deep obsession with the female form, it can be hard for women to escape stereotypes regarding the body, whether they are scientists, athletes, writers, or mothers. When a woman participates in an activity, even one as gender-neutral as politics or writing, the body is always present. Hillary Clinton and Sarah Palin were both judged on their looks in the 2008 presidential campaigns at a much higher rate than their male opponents. Elizabeth Angell, an editor for *Allure* magazine, complains in her article "Sex and Female Politicians" that a "female politician should never be judged for her physical attributes or her sexuality."[7] Many people would agree with Angell's sentiments. Yet, beauty remains at the forefront of nearly any discussion involving a prominent and powerful woman.

American culture is obsessed with the female body. The female form is used to market a variety of products, including clothing, cosmetics, food and alcohol, cleaning products, household goods, automobiles, hotels, and lifestyle products. Our cultural conception of the female body is largely driven by the presentation of women in the media, but our personal experience also provides a broader definition. Part of defining a woman is taking into account the way the female body functions in society as a mother, sister, wife, and daughter, but also as a lawyer, student, doctor, army captain, or fighter. Sadly, a preoccupation with appearance often makes women feel like their ability to perform their jobs, activities, and hobbies well is subsumed by the initial (and continual) judgment based on their looks.

THE "CENTERFOLD IMPERATIVE"

Historically, teenage girls who participate in sports have been deemed tomboys whose femininity, and often sexuality, is questioned. According to Lawrence Wenner's book *MediaSport*, female athletes in the twentieth century sought to assert their heterosexuality by promoting traditional feminine practices, assuring "themselves and others that sport can (and should) be highly consistent with what this culture deems to be womanhood."[8] Any deviation from socially normative female behavior endangered the female athlete's public persona.

There is a point for most female athletes in their rise in popularity where a photo shoot in *Maxim, Sports Illustrated*, or even *Playboy* is required. These pictorials are always sexualized and often eroticize the sport of the athlete or simply put the woman in a bathing suit. A female athlete who is talented in her sport and fulfills current ideals of beauty creates media frenzy, often overshadowing the sport and focusing solely on the athlete's appearance. There is a silent requirement, which I have dubbed the "centerfold imperative," where an athlete must eroticize her image to garner media attention. Tennis stars Maria Sharapova and Anna Kournikova are both famous for their looks; Kournikova's beauty quickly surpassed any expectations of her as an athlete. As a result, she was never taken seriously as a tennis player. This critique is often applied to female athletes who are celebrated and highly publicized for their beauty. As chapter 5 of this book reveals, in 2011, Miesha Tate complained that the upstart fighter Ronda Rousey was only creating headlines because of her looks. Although Tate's argument was proved wrong, Rousey's beauty has absolutely helped her achieve the media zeitgeist necessary to promote and arrange the fight with Tate.

Gina Carano was considered the face of women's mixed martial arts (MMA), but most people commented on her beauty before detailing her skill as a fighter. In 2009, Carano faced off against Cris "Cyborg" Justino for the Strikeforce championship title. The match was referred to as "Beauty versus the Beast" by certain sports media outlets. Cris was an incredibly talented fighter, but she was given the unfortunate title of the "Beast" in this matchup. Internet pundits and commentators alike seemed disgusted by the Cyborg because she apparently looked "too masculine" and did nothing to promote her femininity. Even after a devastating defeat by Justino, Carano's popularity far exceeded that of her former opponent.

In 2012, Justino tested positive for performance enhancing drugs, prompting many "I knew she was a man!" conversations, and it may have ultimately ended her career. Still, beyond the confirmation of drug use, MMA fans seemed most displeased by Justino's physical appearance.

Although her promoters attempted to follow the centerfold imperative, Justino did not make the same "hot" lists as Carano. Unfortunately, a female athlete *must* be beautiful to receive publicity and subsequent endorsements. In fact, female athletes must not only be beautiful, they should be sexy as well. Many female athletes pose for risqué and sexualized photography to promote their image as an athlete and a woman. For many women, their popularity as an athlete is invariably tied to the presentation of their sexuality. Auto racer Danica Patrick received little public attention until famously posing for *Playboy* magazine in 2009. For women who participate in historically male sports, posing in bikinis for men's magazines is a way to reassure viewers that while they are competing in a male arena, they also fulfill the expectations of conventional femininity. The fifth chapter of this book continues to explore the issue of the centerfold imperative within the context of MMA and the digital world.

Female athletes walk the line between hiding their sexuality and embracing or even exploiting it. In a 1919 Wimbledon match between Mrs. Lambert Chambers of England and Suzanne Lenglen of France, both women were assessed and compared based on their appearance rather than their skills on the court. Mrs. Chambers wore traditionally feminine and respectable garb, ostensibly overheating in long woolen skirts on the court and wearing a blazer in her off-court appearances. Mademoiselle Lenglen, meanwhile, played in short silk dresses and wore extravagant flapper-era fashion and makeup off the court. Critics praised and decried both women for their individual infractions, much like the media in the twenty-first century. Women cannot get it right: They are too feminine or too masculine, too fashionable or too dowdy, too attractive or not attractive enough.

While male athletes can be recognized for their athletic endeavors only, a female athlete must also be judged on her appearance. In 2013, Wimbledon winner Marion Bartoli was criticized by British radio commentator John Inverdale, who concocted an imaginary conversation where Bartoli's father informed her that she had to be a good athlete because she was "never going to be a looker." Bartoli's father seemed astonished by this presumption, but other media sources were quick to criticize Inverdale's claim while simultaneously supporting it. An article in the *Los Angeles Times* compares Bartoli's style of play to her "stocky, not tall and lithe" figure, claiming that "her serve is anything but smooth" and that she "pounds the ball with two hands from both sides."[9] The author even belittles Bartoli's victory by arguing that "Bartoli's path was easier" because higher seeds in the tournament lost early matches.

Another interesting aspect of 2013 Wimbledon was the seemingly delightful reality that Britain finally had a champion when Andy Murray won seventy-seven years after the last British champ; however, numerous media outlets and tennis resources failed to recognize that Britain already had a more recent Wimbledon champ, but that the champ was a woman. In 1977, Virginia Wade won the Wimbledon singles title, but her legacy has disappeared from history.

FIGHTING SPORTS

Fighting sports have long been considered primitive, and to a certain extent, this is true. Fighting may be one of the most primal of human activities after eating, sleeping, and sex. It is easy to imagine the earliest species of hominids swinging at one another over leftover meat or a closer proximity to the fire. But although we can only speculate as to the validity of this scenario, there is historical evidence that fighting was indeed considered sport in the ancient world. Wall paintings in Egypt from 2000 B.C.E. depict groups of men practicing various wrestling techniques. Poets and prose writers alike celebrated athleticism in ancient Greece. Nearly every society, existing and extinct, has a martial art or folk fighting style practiced by certain portions of its citizenry. It would be impossible for me to accomplish the purpose of this book, which is to explore the history of female fighters, and fully cover the history of fighting arts throughout the world. There are a number of excellent scholarly texts that have already accomplished that great feat. Instead, I will briefly outline the history of striking and grappling arts as they pertain to the history of female fighters.

For the purpose of clarity, this section focuses on defining the primary fighting sports discussed in this book. Although nearly every culture can boast a unique fighting style, most hand-to-hand fight sports can be classified in three basic groups: striking, grappling, and a mixture of the two.

There are numerous subgenres that fit within each of these broad spheres, and, of course, there is some overlap; however, to be concise, I present fighting sports that fall into these three categories. It is important to note that I do not analyze fighting styles that include weapons, for instance, fencing or Kali. When used in this book, the term *fighting sports* refers to striking and grappling in all of their cultural arts and iterations. Furthermore, most ancient historical accounts of fighting arts feature male athletes, so this historical section focuses on defining the various arts using male examples. We shall save the stories of women fighters for the bulk of the book and rely on the men to help define the particulars of striking, wrestling, and mixed discipline fighting sports.

Striking Sports

Striking sports are those in which one fighter hits his or her opponent with fists, forearms, elbows, knees, or shins. The most common striking sport is boxing, which has the restriction that fighters must hit solely with the hands to the upper portion of the body. There are numerous other popular sports that fall under the general heading of striking sports, including kickboxing and Muay Thai, and even more striking arts that, while not necessarily sport, provide foundational movements for MMA (discussed later in this section). Kickboxing incorporates kicks, along with blows to the lower body, into the sport of boxing. Muay Thai, the traditional sport of Thailand, adds elbow and knee strikes to its striking practice. Arts like Kenpo, tae kwon do, karate, and kung fu are also striking arts, and have their own realm of competition. While these martial arts, as well as kickboxing and Muay Thai, came to greater prominence in the Western world during the twentieth century, boxing is the more widely practiced striking art in the West.

Boxing is often considered one of the world's oldest sports, but it was not until the last few decades that women's boxing became an officially sanctioned sport in the United States and abroad.[10] Social views of boxing vacillate greatly throughout the history of pugilism, from the noble discipline of Spartan warriors to the vile practice in the grimiest streets of eighteenth-century London. And although the sport of boxing continues to raise eyebrows and turn the stomachs of some fragile citizens, the sweet science has a history that unites the lives of noblemen and poor workers.

The *Oxford English Dictionary* (*OED*) defines boxing as "The action of fighting with fists." This is boxing in its most basic form. *OED* continues by adding that boxing is "now usually applied to a pugilistic encounter in which the hands are covered with well-padded leather gloves." But historical accounts of boxing suggest that the earliest practitioners of the sport fought bare-knuckled and sometimes to the death. Boxing was not the only striking fight style practiced in antiquity, but since most sources define it as punching rather than kicking, modern historians tend to place all ancient fighting styles under the "boxing" umbrella.

Ancient Boxing History

One of the earliest written accounts of an organized boxing match occurs in Homer's *The Iliad*, a text considered a historical reference by ancient Greeks rather than our current classification as a literary masterpiece. The funeral games for the recently slain Patroclus included a prizefight in the "painful art of boxing."[11] The first contender, Epeus, took the challenge (the prize being a mule) with a loquacious display, setting a precedent for the type of bravado that is now standard for any fighter. The man swaggered and declared,

> Let the man who is to have the cup come hither, for none but myself will take the mule. I am the best boxer of all here present, and none can beat me. Is it not enough that I should fall short of you in actual fighting? Still, no man can be good at everything. I tell you plainly, and it shall come true; if any man will box with me I will bruise his body and break his bones; therefore let his friends stay here in a body and be at hand to take him away when I have done with him.[12]

Epeus' boasting scared all the soldiers except for Euryalus, and the two prepared for the fight. Homer describes the match as follows:

> The two men being now girt went into the middle of the ring, and immediately fell to; heavily indeed did they punish one another and lay about them with their brawny fists. One could hear the horrid crashing of their jaws, and they sweated from every pore of their skin. Presently Epeus came on and gave Euryalus a blow on the jaw as he was looking round; Euryalus could not keep his legs; they gave way under him in a moment and he sprang up with a bound, as a fish leaps into the air near some shore that is all bestrewn with sea-wrack, when Boreas furs the

top of the waves, and then falls back into deep water. But noble Epeus caught hold of him and raised him up; his comrades also came round him and led him from the ring, unsteady in his gait, his head hanging on one side, and spitting great clots of gore.[13]

Homer then explains other funereal contests in running and wrestling, which I examine in the following section on the history of wrestling. But this literary passage established boxing as a legitimate sport, practiced and celebrated by the heroic Greeks.

Other early accounts of boxing exist in artwork and pottery. A beautifully preserved sixteenth-century B.C.E. fresco dubbed *Boxing Boys* from the island of Santorini shows two young men with long, dreaded hair and small loin cloths punching one another at close quarters. A fragment of a Mycenaenan pot circa 1300–1200 B.C.E. found in Cyprus features two stylized male figures striking at one another with extended arms.[14] Ancient sports reached the zenith in 776 B.C.E., with the inaugural Olympic Games, and in 688 B.C.E., boxing became an official sport. Ancient Olympic boxing matches had no ring, no rounds, no rests, and few rules. Boxers could strike while their opponent was down, and they fought until one of the fighters could not continue. Emperor Augustus apparently loved boxing matches and preferred them to all other gladiatorial events featured in the Colosseum. Seutonius claimed that while the emperor's "chief delight was watching boxing," he especially loved amateur bouts, "slogging matches between untrained roughs in narrow city alleys."[15]

Modern Boxing History

The English Restoration released the puritanical restrictions on public entertainment lingering from the Middle Ages and allowed for various types of spectacles to be performed in designated areas in London and other cities. Boxing emerged as a popular spectacle, along with cockfighting, bear-baiting, and the theater. The *Protestant Mercury*, a British newspaper, was the first to report a boxing match in 1681, with the Duke of Albemarle in attendance.[16] The aristocratic support of the sport hit an apex in 1723, when King George I ordered the construction of a ring in Hyde Park. The king's support of boxing fostered an environment in which fighters received patronage from wealthy nobles, who supported their training and made heavy bets on the pugilists.

The late eighteenth and early nineteenth centuries constituted Britain's golden age of boxing, during which the sport became both a "science" and a manly art. Of course, the manliness of the sport did not restrict women from participating in the cultural surge. During a stay in London in 1768, historian William Hickey watched two "she-devils" "engaged in a scratching and boxing match, their faces entirely covered with blood, bosoms bare, and the clothes nearly torn from their bodies."[17] Street fights were common in the back alleys and barrooms of cities, but women also participated in boxing in the public arena the same as many men in the eighteenth century. Chapter 1 is dedicated to the early modern female fighters who became darlings of the British media, and chapter 2 focuses on the sensations of early American tabloid culture.

The American boxing obsession began in the early nineteenth century, with the 1816 fight between Jacob Hyer and Tom Beasley. Although there was no formal governing body established to enforce rules, it was said that there was "some attempt" at maintaining structure during the bout. New York was the home of the American boxing craze, and numerous individuals from all classes trained and sparred in new gyms that sprouted up throughout the city and state. Although upper-class and working-class men alike practiced boxing in the 1820s, a mere decade ended the gentlemanly involvement in the "manly art of self-defense," as the sport was first titled. Critics deemed the sport violent; in a letter to the *New York Post* in 1826, the writer declares, "Such practices are brutal and detestable in themselves and disgraceful to the country in which they are suffered to take place. What is called by its advocates the science of defense, is only the commission, always of horrible violence, and sometimes murder."[18]

While this recriminative letter may seem hyperbolic, the dangerous reality of boxing made itself known in the 1842 bout between Thomas McCoy and Christopher Lilly. At this point in the history of American boxing, regulation existed only on a peripheral level, and bouts often went dozens or even hundreds of rounds. In the 120th round of the McCoy–Lilly fight, McCoy collapsed dead in the ring after receiving more than eighty direct blows. The inquest revealed that his lungs were filled with fluid, and he drowned in his own blood. McCoy's death, the first in the American boxing arena, sparked outrage and provided prizefighting critics with new ammunition to use in their quest to outlaw the sport.[19] But boxing would persist in American culture, and in the late nineteenth century, fighters like John L. Sullivan reinvigorated interest in fighting. The twentieth century introduced the many greats of boxing in the United States, for example, Joe Louis, Jake LaMotta, and Muhammad Ali. And alongside the men, every step of the way in both the United States and England, women fought, sometimes in the shadows and other times in the limelight. This volume introduces many of these women, who were champions in their own right and often recognized as such by their male cohorts.

Grappling Arts

Like the striking category, grappling includes numerous popular subsets, from freestyle and Greco-Roman wrestling to Brazilian jiu-jitsu (BJJ) and catch-as-catch-can wrestling. For the purposes of this book, grappling is a contest between two individuals who seek to control one another through submission holds and dominant positions. Grappling can take place standing, which is how most folk-style wrestling was practiced by workers who enjoyed wrestling recreationally but did not wish to soil their clothing in the dirt or mud. Grappling on the ground, which is part of catch wrestling; all styles of Olympic wrestling; and Brazilian jiu-jitsu mark the separation from the recreational standing style of country folks. These styles of grappling are practiced in a gym space, rather than on the grass after a long day in the fields. But all grappling styles are predicated on using strength and leverage to move or supplant an opponent.

I use the term *grappling* because the Western conception of wrestling, which is based on Olympic rules, does not include the type of joint manipulations and choke holds found in BJJ and catch-as-catch-can wrestling. Also, the term *wrestling* often elicits the idea of professional wrestling, which, in its current format, is not a competitive sport, but a staged performance. There are numerous iterations of wrestling; however, the word *wrestling* has a connotation that points to either the Olympic sports or theatrical "professional wrestling." Hence, it seems fitting to place these individual martial art subsets under the heading grappling, which can be summed up as gripping or controlling an opponent without strikes.

Many traditional martial arts have a grappling component. Numerous small tribes in Africa and South America continue to compete in local wrestling events, and some martial arts, for instance, Japanese jiu-jitsu, use small joint manipulations to throw an opponent a great distance using a small movement. Thus, grappling is, in a way, an all-encompassing fighting art. In this book, the primary grappling sports explored are Olympic-style wrestling, BJJ, submission wrestling (also known as catch-as-catch-can or no-gi wrestling), and judo. These are the four primary subsets of grappling in which there exists a large competitive community and a primary governing body.

Ancient Wrestling History

Like boxing, the earliest literary account of wrestling occurs in Homer's *The Iliad*. This seminal match was between two famous characters, Ajax and Ulysses.

> Forthwith uprose great Ajax the son of Telamon, and crafty Ulysses, full of wiles, rose also. The two girded themselves and went into the middle of the ring. They gripped each other in their strong hands like the rafters which some master-builder frames for the roof of a high house to keep the wind out. Their backbones cracked as they tugged at one another with their mighty arms—and sweat rained from them in torrents. Many a bloody weal sprang up on their sides and shoulders, but they kept on striving with might and main for victory and to win the tripod. Ulysses could not throw Ajax, nor Ajax him; Ulysses was too strong for him; but when the Achaeans began to tire of watching them, Ajax said to Ulysses, "Ulysses, noble son of Laertes, you shall either lift me, or I you, and let Jove settle it between us."
>
> He lifted him from the ground as he spoke, but Ulysses did not forget his cunning. He hit Ajax in the hollow at back of his knee, so that he could not keep his feet, but fell on his back with Ulysses lying upon his chest, and all who saw it marvelled. Then Ulysses in turn lifted Ajax and stirred him a little from the ground but could not lift him right off it, his knee sank under him, and the two fell side by side on the ground and were all begrimed with dust. They now sprang towards one another and were for wrestling yet a third time, but Achilles rose and stayed them. "Put not each other further," said he, "to such cruel suffering; the victory is with both alike, take each of you an equal prize, and let the other Achaeans now compete."
>
> Thus did he speak and they did even as he had said, and put on their shirts again after wiping the dust from off their bodies.[20]

A great deal of ancient art worldwide depicts men (and sometimes women) wrestling in various formats. Egyptians, Etruscans, Spartans, Vikings, Mayans, and other tribes practiced wrestling for sport.

Modern Wrestling History

Boxing may have had some semblance of respectability due to the promotion of the sport by British aristocrats, but wrestling was considered more of a country bumpkin activity. In the eighteenth and nineteenth centuries, wrestling was primarily practiced in rural areas amongst farm workers and other laborers. Wrestling, even more so than boxing, became a source of entertainment and spectacle in Britain and the United States in the twentieth century, but it has a rather grand history.

In 1520, the twenty-nine-year-old King Henry VIII of England challenged fellow monarch King Francis of France, to a wrestling match at the historic "Field of the Cloth of Gold" meeting. Although Francis was able to throw the older and larger Henry to win the match, the two left the meeting as friends, despite Henry's historic bad temper. Folk wrestling, in fact, was regularly practiced by young country girls in the seventeenth, eighteenth, and nineteenth centuries. There are numerous examples of young women competing in wrestling, which we will explore in this book, although wrestling was not as popular as boxing.

The twentieth century saw wrestling emerge as a popular form of entertainment in traveling circuses. One result of this popularity was that by the middle of the century, grappling became bifurcated into entertainment-style wrestling that was primarily staged and sport wrestling practiced in schools and universities, as well as the Olympics. Men can compete in Greco-Roman wrestling, which is actually French folk wrestling dubbed Greco-Roman in the nineteenth century during a furious revival of all things Greek. The other wrestling style offered in the Olympics is freestyle wrestling, and in 2004, women's freestyle wrestling entered the Olympic Games. Wrestling continues to be one of the most widely practiced sports in the world by numerous cultures and subcultures, despite the 2012 attempt by the International Olympic Committee (IOC) to remove the sport from the Games' roster. The immediate uproar incited by celebrities, athletes, and fans of wrestling helped reverse the IOC's decision, and wrestling returned to its rightful place in the Olympic Games.

Brazilian Jiu-Jitsu, Judo, and Submission Wrestling

Submission wrestling is often identified as the ground game for MMA. Like sport wrestling, submission wrestlers wear shorts or a singlet instead of the gi (also called a kimono) seen in Brazilian jiu-jitsu and judo. The Japanese throwing art of judo became popular in the United States after World War II, when GIs returned home from battle. But judo has long captivated the West. Famed fictional sleuth Sherlock Holmes practiced judo, and in his wake, several other literary detectives declared to be proficient at the art. Judo is an offshoot of Japanese jiu-jitsu created by Kano Jigoro to teach to school children in the early twentieth century.[21] The art concentrates on throwing or taking down an opponent. Once on the ground, judo players fight to pin their opponent to the mat or submit him or her in a joint lock or choke.

In addition to practicing wrestling and boxing, President Teddy Roosevelt enjoyed judo and installed a small training space in the White House, where he was joined by his wife and sister-in-law. Judo officially became an Olympic sport in 1972 for men, and in 1992, women were added to the program, making it the first Olympic fighting sport to include female practitioners. The most famous judo player today, at least to the general public, is Ronda Rousey, the current Ultimate Fighting Championship (UFC) women's bantamweight champion. Her involvement in the art has probably helped increase its practice in the MMA world.

BJJ has a fascinating history; in the late nineteenth century, many Japanese men immigrated to Brazil and taught their country's art of jiu-jitsu. One man, Carlos Gracie, who learned jiu-jitsu from Master Esai Maeda Koma when he was fifteen years old, is responsible for the origin of the Brazilian version of the art. Gracie and his family morphed the Japanese art, which primarily concentrated on takedowns and throws, into a more ground-based fighting system. Practitioners wear the traditional Japanese gi, or kimono, and can use the jackets and pants to help manipulate their opponents into takedowns, sweeps, submissions, and chokes. One of Gracie's nephews, Royce Gracie, was in the first UFC event, sparking the zeitgeist of MMA in the United States and abroad; however, BJJ and judo were not the only "traditional martial arts" that helped generate the new sport of MMA.

THE GLOBALIZATION OF MARTIAL ARTS

Boxing and wrestling were the most dominant forms of fighting sports in Western history prior to the 1970s, but that changed when the twentieth century witnessed a rise in other types of martial arts competition. Martial arts legend Bruce Lee popularized Eastern fighting styles when his films were released internationally beginning in 1971, with *The Big Boss*. The following year, the popular *Kung Fu* television series aired on ABC, creating a cultural fervor for all things from the Orient, to use the parlance of the time. Martial arts schools sprung up throughout the United States, offering, amongst others, Chinese kung fu, Korean tae kwon do, the Japanese arts of jiu-jitsu and judo, the Okinawan art of karate, and Muay Thai (the martial art of Thailand). These martial arts were already being taught in some parts of the United States prior to the Bruce Lee phenomenon, but Lee's films and cultural influence heightened the American populace's interest. Thus, martial arts schools proliferated in the 1970s. As a result of this concomitant growth, options for fighting sports events expanded beyond the two primary sports of boxing and wrestling.

TRADITIONAL FIGHTING ARTS

The globalization of martial arts in the postmodern era led to an explosion of martial arts schools throughout the world, but certain arts remained as dominant as the cultures from which they originated. For many years, and even today, karate and tae kwon do were the primary martial arts taught in the English-speaking world. In the Western world, both arts center on technique, discipline, tradition, and spirituality. Tae kwon do uses swift, high kicks to generate points against an opponent, but there is little use of hands and little defense.[22] In 1988, tae kwon do was introduced as an exhibition sport in the Summer Olympics, and in 2000, it became a full medal sport. When tae kwon do became an Olympic event, both men and women were included in the sport, a historic moment for women's equality in the fighting world. There are four weight classes for both men and women, and the attire and basic equipment are the same.

It may seem surprising to some martial artists that tae kwon do, and not kickboxing, Muay Thai, or karate, became an Olympic sport. Karate, which some people unfamiliar with martial arts use interchangeably with tae kwon do, is a style of fighting that originated in Okinawa. Karate is an all-encompassing martial art that includes striking with hands, feet, elbows, and knees, as well as throws and ground fighting. Like many fighting arts, karate began as a self-defense style but eventually evolved from techniques and katas (forms) into the sparring practice of kumite. The kumite has many different iterations, from point sparring to full-contact, bare-knuckle fighting, seen most famously in the 1988 Jean-Claude Van Damme film *Bloodsport*. While it may seem a bit hyperbolic to claim that the kumite evolved into the sport of MMA in the 1990s, there is no doubt that karate is one of the many fighting styles that generated the idea of an anything-goes venue. Such early UFC fighters as Chuck Liddell and Bas Rutten have as their foundations traditional, Eastern martial arts. Today, some professional MMA fighters have returned to traditional martial arts to set themselves apart from the standard MMA style that has proliferated during the last few years.

KICKBOXING AND MUAY THAI

The term *kickboxing* is a new one, although fighting styles worldwide include striking with hands and feet. Many accounts of early boxing, before the institution of the Queensbury rules, tell of boxers kicking one another in frustration. The French art of boxing, savate, has many of the same rules as kickboxing, and in the twentieth century, savate fighters often fought using other styles in early MMA bouts.[23]

Muay Thai is one of the most popular martial arts in the world, despite its humble beginnings in the rural areas of Thailand. Most MMA fighters today train in some form of kickboxing, but oftentimes it is assumed that MMA is comprised of kickboxing and Brazilian jiu-jitsu simply because of the prevalence of both styles in the martial arts world. Muay Thai allows kicks, punches, elbows, and knees, which makes it a solid foundation for MMA fighters. Kickboxing and Muay Thai remain popular today and have enjoyed more than thirty years of grounding in American and European cultures. Surprisingly, however, neither kickboxing nor Muay Thai are Olympic sports.

Women participate in all of these martial arts in the United States, although limitations, of course, continue because of various gender biases. In some of the countries of origin, women are dissuaded from competing. Thailand's Lumpini and Ratchadamnoen stadiums, for example, do not allow women to enter the sacred fighting ring. In the countryside and other rural environments, such rules are relaxed and women do indeed fight, but women's Muay Thai is practiced more outside of Thailand. These cultural biases against women will undoubtedly change in the future as the culture becomes less conservative regarding these issues, but for now, women have a limited role in practicing and competing in Muay Thai in Thailand.[24]

Different types of fighting sports other than the traditional boxing and wrestling expanded in the twenty-first century. Many people have expressed concerns in the twenty-first century that boxing may be on the decline, although fighters like Manny Pacquiao have reinvigorated interest in the sport globally. The sport of wrestling was endangered in 2012, when the IOC decided to eliminate wrestling from future Olympic Games for lack of popularity or interest. There was a tremendous outcry from the international wrestling community and general public. Not only was wrestling an original sport in terms of the ancient Grecian games, it was also one that included women. Luckily, the IOC overturned the change, and wrestling was returned to its rightful place in the Olympic pantheon before the start of the next Games.

MIXED MARTIAL ARTS

Although the term *mixed martial arts*, or MMA, as it is more commonly known, is relatively new to the pugilistic lexicon, the idea of a mixed fighting sport is an ancient one. It has been called many things throughout the years: mixed martial arts, anything goes, no-holds-barred, *vale tudo*, as well as the UFC, the business now functioning metonymically for the sport. The history of MMA, in its current iteration, deserves a book of its own; however, I provide a brief examination of the history of MMA to facilitate the entrance of women in the sport in chapter 5.

The Pankration

The best-known historical version of a MMA format occurred in ancient Greece. The Greeks competed in the Pankration, which translates to "complete strength" or "complete victory."[25] The Pankration was an amalgamation of boxing and wrestling, with the added techniques of leg sweeps, kicks, and knees; the only prohibited techniques were biting and eye-gauging. Other martial arts elsewhere in the world ranged from standing techniques to those carried out on the ground, although none appeared to have risen to the same level of competition as the Pankration.

As the Roman Empire rose to prominence, the bare-fisted Pankration was made more violent by the addition of caestus, "hard leather gloves that covered the hands, wrists, and forearms and into which metal studs, teeth, and spikes were inserted."[26] The caestus morphed the Pankration from a brutal but technical art into a violent spectacle that exhibited little technical proficiency. These gladiatorial bouts ceased with the fall of the Roman Empire, but the Pankration's "anything goes" fighting style is said to have influenced martial arts worldwide, from karate and the Chinese shuai jiao to the eventual cultural phenomenon of the UFC. Nonetheless, the MMA format did not become popular again until nearly two thousand years after the Roman Pankration events.

It seems fair to say that any group that fought regularly in history, whether in large military battles or small tribal warfare, evolved a fighting style that went beyond sport. No tribesman in South America would resort to his sport of wrestling and forgo striking if faced with an enemy. But most sport fighting styles, including the varied wrestling arts of small villages throughout the world and the boxing matches in Europe, had rules, of sorts, that restricted that type of "anything goes" contact when it came to competition.

MIXED DISCIPLINE FIGHTING

In the late nineteenth century, several highly publicized fights occurred between boxers and wrestlers seeking to prove the superiority of their sport. American heavyweight world boxing champion John L. Sullivan fought his trainer, William Muldoon, a former Greco-Roman wrestling champion, in 1887. Muldoon reportedly threw Sullivan to the ground twice within the first two minutes, and the fight was over. A few years later, Japanese jiu-jitsu star Mitsuyo Maeda moved to Brazil and helped found the new sport of Brazilian jiu-jitsu. At the same time, no-holds-barred matches, known as *vale tudo* in Portuguese, were held at carnivals throughout Brazil, with fighters from multiple disciplines competing in a ring. The history of *vale tudo* is a bit murky, but suffice it to say that when the Gracie family, who learned under Mitsuyo Maeda, entered the fray, the sport changed forever.

In the United States, men who had learned the art of judo while abroad returned home and grew the sport in their own country. In 1963, famed judo player Gene LaBell fought Milo Savage, a light-heavyweight boxer, in what would be the first televised MMA fight in the United States.[27] Thirteen years later, LaBell refereed an exhibition match between boxing legend Muhammad Ali and Antonio Inoki, a skilled grappler who learned from the famous catch wrestler Karl Gotch.[28] Although the match did not include any wrestling, Inoki kicked Ali's legs so savagely that the boxing champion never had another knockout win after this fight, although it is unclear if his decline was due to the debilitating leg strikes. Inoki spent most of his time on the ground, while Ali stood over him and called for him to stand up and fight. The fight was a spectacle, but when it was over, fans and journalists were disappointed rather than clamoring for more mixed discipline fighting events. In fact, some fans reportedly threw objects into the ring in disgust when the fight ended in a draw.[29]

These exhibition-style matches continued in the United States, but MMA did not become part of the zeitgeist until the 1990s, with the UFC in the United States and the Japanese PRIDE Fighting Championships. The first wave of "mixed martial arts" fights were not between two MMA fighters, but rather two different fighting styles; however, as the UFC gained popularity, MMA became a style in itself. Fighters now train in all facets of MMA, which allows punches, kicks, knees, elbow strikes, takedowns, throws, chokes, and submissions of all kinds. Chapter 5 outlines the cultural impact of MMA fighting and how women literally fought to be allowed to compete in the UFC, the largest MMA promotion in the world.

MMA is undoubtedly the fastest-growing sport in the world, both in its practice by individuals in gyms throughout the world and in viewership. MMA may not appear on *SportsCenter* as much as football or even men's golf, but this is probably due to the proprietary viewing platform of pay-per-view. There have been recent concerns regarding diminishing pay-per-view numbers, undoubtedly due to increased illegal streaming or, on a more positive note, the communal aspect of watching the UFC in groups at home or in bars. Despite the decrease in pay-per-view customers, the cable-network televised events have greatly increased in number; the UFC 156 preliminary bouts, held on February 1, 2013, and televised on FX, drew a record-breaking 1.897 million viewers. This number pales in comparison to the big three sports; the NFL pulled in an average of 34.7 million viewers per game during the playoffs in January 2013, but it was a significant increase for the UFC.

THE HISTORY OF FEMALE FIGHTERS IS IGNORED

The popularity of MMA and the growing number of women competing in the sport has undoubtedly been supported by women competing in other types of martial arts. When I began my research for this book, I was surprised to find that certain claims about female fighters have remained constant throughout the decades and centuries. During the past three hundred years, detractors have claimed that women do not belong in fighting sports because they are male-dominated activities. Some critics have asserted that the female body is not fit for fighting. Others argued that boxing and wrestling had always been male sports and that women should stay away from those arenas. And today, many fighting commentators and Internet pundits continue to suggest that there is something unnatural or deviant about women in fighting sports, yet the history simply does not bear out that assertion. Women have been competing in fighting sports for thousands of years, despite the perpetual claims by opponents of female fighters that they do not belong in the ring, on the mat, or in the cage. The convenient forgetfulness or misremembering of the past is a way to erase the history of female fighters and substantiate the inaccurate belief that women have never, and will never, belong in certain male spaces.

The history, then, of female fighters has been conveniently forgotten by those who wish to deter women from participating in official fighting sports. The girl who will be told that she cannot box in 2015 because she is a girl will be receiving the same message that was conveyed to women during the last decade and last century. Articles published in the mid-1980s proclaim that women would demean the sport of boxing by participating because it had always been a manly endeavor, but the truth is that women have a rich history in fighting sports, one that can be substantiated by archival evidence. This book explores the history of women who

I

FIGHTING IN THE GEORGIAN AND VICTORIAN ERAS

In the mid-eighteenth century, Englishman William Hickey composed his collected memoirs, which include numerous descriptions of the tawdry British underbelly. Hickey had a proclivity toward seedy drinking establishments and seemed to delight in recounting the stories of his poor and lower-class countrymen and women. He recalled watching a barroom brawl between two women in particularly colorful language:

> Two she-devils, for they scare, had a human appearance, were engaged in a scratching and boxing match, their faces entirely covered with blood, bosoms bare, and the clothes nearly torn from their bodies. For several minutes not a creature interfered between them, or seemed to care a straw what mischief they might do each other, and the contest went on with unabated fury.[1]

While fighting sports appear to have been carried out regularly enough that inhabitants of a particular town were not shocked by seeing two women in the ring, accounts of female pugilists in the seventeenth and eighteenth centuries are rare.

Although it is difficult to know the extent to which women competed in boxing, wrestling, and other pugilistic arts, various sources indicate that women in the United States and Europe were indeed part of the spectacle of fighting. Prior to the seventeenth century, it appears that pugilism was practiced, but not necessarily as a competitive sport, perhaps due to the restrictions of the church; however, considering that bear-baiting and dog fighting operated alongside Shakespeare and Marlowe in the theater houses, the church must have turned a blind eye to a variety of entertainments.

The reality is that men, and possibly women, were performing some type of fighting as entertainment prior to the Georgian era, which extended from 1714 to the mid-1800s. The availability of print media proliferated in eighteenth-century England, and newspapers became the popular mode to supply news to the reading public. Most written evidence of fighting events is from the eighteenth century, when newspapers and bulletins became more abundant. It makes sense that during a time when printed media were new and most precious, sports news was not regularly published. Additional historical records may become available in the future detailing the history of fighting as a spectator sport prior to the seventeenth century in the North-Western Hemisphere, and when that occurs, it is likely that we will discover that women were part of the action.

Historical records currently provide scarce data with which to piece together the history of early modern female combatants. Many of the records from the seventeenth and eighteenth centuries rely on anecdotal evidence from travelers and historians relating the stories of brawls between women. Zacharias Conrad Uffenbach, a German citizen, published the narrative of his 1710 travels to London, where he took in a boxing match. He was informed by a female spectator that she "had fought another female in this place without stays and in nothing but a shift." The woman claimed that "they had both fought stoutly and drawn blood," and von Uffenbach notes with apparent distaste that this "was apparently no new sight in England."[2] Interestingly, an English traveler around the same time period recalled watching two women fight topless in Paris. It seems that the spectacle of fighting, to these men of leisure, was more interesting abroad than in their own home countries.

Boxing and other fighting sports remained fringe activities for women in the United States and Europe throughout the seventeenth, eighteenth, and nineteenth centuries. Female fighters intermittently appeared in the media and then disappeared until another woman would arrive a few decades later. Although records in eighteenth- and nineteenth-century print media are surprisingly abundant, there is no clear guide on which we can rely that includes all female boxing or wrestling contestants. It is the very nature of history that, unfortunately, excludes the commonplace and the everyday. Based on current documentation and resources, there are prominent examples of female fighters prior to the mid-twentieth century. Undoubtedly there were more women competing outside of the eye of the media, and hopefully more female fighters will be uncovered in the future. For now, however, we must focus on the more famous examples of female pugilists in the United States and Europe.

The nearly two hundred and fifty years between the days of the most famous female pugilist, Elizabeth Wilkinson Stokes, and the signing of Title IX in the 1970s were a period of spotty yet vigorous matches between female fighters. Although it appears that the boxing world treated many of these women, including Stokes, as legitimate and skilled fighters, the new print media sensationalized these bouts. In several cases, we have only the names of the women, along with a note that reinforces the gender of the two fighters. And in numerous instances, books and articles reference a particular historic match but do not provide a citation of the original source material. For example, numerous authors relate the anecdote of an 1876 boxing match between Nell Saunders and Rose Harland at the Hills Theater in New York City. These books and articles reveal that the winner received a silver butter dish as her prize. This quaint, domestically oriented prize may seem sexist by today's standards, but at the time, a silver butter dish would have been a highly desired and worthy object. Still, the butter dish was not the typical prize offered to male fighters at the time; male winners of boxing matches received money or, depending on the venue, free beer. The butter dish given to the winner of the Saunders–Harland fight may have been a promotional tactic, but while little else is known of the bout, the feminine nature of the prize has remained a solid piece of pugilistic history in many historical accounts. While there is no original source material for the Saunders and Harland match, it most likely did occur. Sadly, the lack of original documentation makes the story, with its fascinating detail of the silver butter dish, seem unsubstantiated and perhaps only anecdotal.

Although the 1876 fight lacks original source material, there are records of multiple other early bouts between women. Female fighters were a source of entertainment and spectacle for early fighting fans and the print media, just like today. This chapter delves into the extensive period of pugilism in Britain from the eighteenth century to the early twentieth century, when women who fought in striking and grappling arts were a source of entertainment sensationalized by the new print media.

Although enthusiasm for female pugilists waned in the Victorian era, as concerns regarding the female body and motherhood grew in the scientific community, there have always been females who defied social conventions to compete in these historically masculine sports. While these women may haven been treated with scorn by the majority of the population, some praised their tenacity and skill. And so this chapter begins with the story of Elizabeth Wilkinson Stokes, the championess of boxing.

ELIZABETH WILKINSON STOKES: THE CHAMPIONESS OF EUROPE

Fighters, by necessity, are champion self-aggrandizers. In the history of athletic trash talking, such boxers as Muhammad Ali and Mike Tyson unabashedly asserted their own skill and prowess. Self-aggrandizement, in tandem with insulting ones opponent, is both a defensive and offensive strategy for fighters outside of the ring. A fighter can praise himself and assuage any fears of inadequacy, while simultaneously degrading his opponent. Ali and Tyson may epitomize the trash-talking boxer of the late-twentieth century, but both men would probably bow to the incredible discursive skills of Elizabeth Wilkinson, self-styled "Championess of America and of Europe" in the early eighteenth century.

Wilkinson fashioned herself the "European Championess" of boxing in the early eighteenth century, a title she undoubtedly earned. Her first bout, in 1722, was the result of a challenge to Hannah Hyfield, a woman Wilkinson would soundly beat after twenty-two minutes of solid fighting. The *London Journal* published Wilkinson's original challenge, admitting that the paper did so because it was unfamiliar with female pugilists:

> Boxing in publick at the Bear Garden is what has lately obtained very much amongst the Men, but till last Week we never heard of Women being engaged that Way, when two of the Feminine Gender appeared for the first Time on the Theatre of War at Hockley in the Hole, and maintained the Battle with great Valour for a long Time, to the no small Satisfaction of the spectators.[3]

The paper then produces the following textual exchange in which Wilkinson challenges Hyfield prior to the fight:

> I, Elizabeth Wilkinson of Clerkenwell, having had some Words with Hannah Hyfield, and requiring Satisfaction, do invite her to meet me on the Stage, and Box me for Three Guineas, each Woman holding Half a Crown in each Hand, and the first Woman that drops her Money to lose the Battle.

Hyfield responded in kind, declaring, "I Hannah Hyfield of New Gate Market, hearing the Resoluteness of Elizabeth Wilkinson, will not fail, God-willing, to give her more Blows than Words, desiring home Blows, and from her no Favour."[4]

Wilkinson reportedly beat Hyfield after twenty-two minutes and then went on to compete for the next six years, when her name disappears from the records. In fact, Wilkinson's name has been the subject of much debate amongst historians because she is listed as both Elizabeth Stokes and Elizabeth Wilkinson. Some boxing historians tie her to the recently executed murderer Robert Wilkinson, who, in addition to being a killer, was apparently a prizefighter. In 1927, Arthur L. Hayward edited the lengthily named *Lives of the Most Remarkable Criminals Who Have Been Condemned and Executed for Murder, the Highway, Housebreaking, Street Robberies, Coining, or other Offenses*, an anthology of biographies of eighteenth-century British criminals from a 1735 collection of original papers that has since been released as an e-book by Project Gutenberg. This compilation includes the story of Robert Wilkinson, the infamous murderer and pugilist. Curiously, the piece ends with a reprint of the Wilkinson and Hyfield challenges. The author provides no further commentary but instead insinuates a connection between the murderer Robert Wilkinson and the pugilist Elizabeth Wilkinson.[5]

Boxing history enthusiasts have read into this connection extensively, making suppositions about whether Elizabeth and Robert were blood relations or husband and wife. Others questioned if Elizabeth's adoption of the last name Wilkinson was a sort of bloody tribute to the former prizefighter cum murderer. The former theory is based on evidence that the names Elizabeth Wilkinson and Elizabeth Stokes do not appear in any records prior to her public challenge to Hannah Hyfield; thus, her absence from public record as Elizabeth Wilkinson must indicate that she changed her name. Nonetheless, it is not unlikely that a young woman in eighteenth-century Britain could have existed without her name appearing in written records. And even if her name did, for some reason, appear in print prior to the 1722 challenge, those documents may not have survived.

Following her victory over Hyfield, Wilkinson became a fixture in James Figg's boxing venues, where she continued to dominate the ring. Although she certainly defied eighteenth-century gender roles through her pugilistic activities, Wilkinson was not condemned by English society. She was the heroine of the eccentric British Isles. Nineteenth-century English sports journalist Pierce Egan published a series of tomes on the boxing phenomenon in British culture. Egan ties the popularity of boxing to English nationalism, citing the relationship between the inherent "manliness" of boxing and the pugilistic prowess of men born on British soil, but he notes that national pride in boxing extended beyond male citizens. In a small section entitled "Female Pugilism," Egan quotes an exchange between Wilkinson and Hyfield, exclaiming, "Even heroines panted for the honours of pugilistic glory!"[6] Egan does not complain about Wilkinson's involvement in the sport but instead celebrates her pugilistic skill as evidence of the superior nature of British stock in the ring.

Sometime between 1722 and 1726, Elizabeth Wilkinson became known as Elizabeth Stokes, the wife of fellow pugilist James Stokes. Stokes was Elizabeth's promoter and an associate (and later opponent) of legendary boxer James Figg. Figg was the most prominent promoter and male boxer of the early eighteenth century, but Elizabeth, at the time, was the more famous fighter. In his essay "Disappearance: How Shifting Gendered Boundaries Motivated the Removal of Eighteenth-Century Boxing Champion Elizabeth Wilkinson from Historical Memory," Christopher Thrasher argues that "society" purposefully erased Elizabeth Wilkinson Stokes from boxing history in favor of a male contemporary. Figg is currently cited as the "father of boxing" by the International Boxing Hall of Fame, but according to Thrasher, Stokes was the more popular of the two. Using a scan of the Google Books database from the eighteenth through the twenty-first centuries, Thrasher reveals that while Stokes was more popular during the nineteenth century, Figg far surpassed her in the twentieth century, as Stokes fell into obscurity.[7] Perhaps the late Victorian era return to masculinity led historians to put Figg on a pedestal and Stokes in the corner.

The *British Gazetteer* announced on Saturday, October 1, 1726, the upcoming bout between the British Elizabeth Wilkinson Stokes and the Irish Mary Welch. The bout was to take place at the Stokes amphitheater, which was owned by Elizabeth's husband James. A note at the bottom of the advertisement explains, "They fight in cloth Jackets, short Petticoats, coming just below the Knee, Holland Drawers, white Stockings, and pumps."[8] The paper also contains the following words from Welch:

> I, Mary Welch, from the Kingdom of Ireland, being taught and knowing the Noble Science of Defence, and thought to be the only Female of this Kind in Europe, understanding here is one on this Kingdom, who has exercised on the publick Stage several Times, which is Mrs. Stokes, who is billed the famous Championess of England; I do hereby invite her to meet me, and exercise the awful Weapons practiced on the Stage, at her own Amplitheatre, doubting not, but to let her and the worthy Spectators fee, that my Judgment and Courage is beyond hers.

Stokes responded to Welch, claiming that she was undefeated in the boxing ring:

> I, Elizabeth Stokes, of the famous City of London, being well known by the Name of the Invincible City Championess for my Abilities and Judgment in the above said science; having never engaged with any of my own Sex but I always came off with Victory and Applause, shall make no Apology for accepting the Challenge of this Irish Heroine, not doubting but to maintain the Reputation I have hitherto established, and (few) my Country, that the Contest of its Honour, is not ill entrusted in the present Battle with their Championess, Elizabeth Stokes.[9]

While advertisements for fights were printed and reprinted throughout Britain, there seems to be no official or unofficial document detailing the outcome of these bouts; however, it appears that Stokes remained undefeated in her pugilistic career.

On July 1, 1727, Elizabeth and James Stokes were jointly challenged by the aforementioned (and assumed defeated) Mary Welch and her training partner, Robert Baker, also of Ireland. Although the husband and wife were challenged as a couple, they fought individually against their Irish opponents. In their challenge, Welch and Baker "invite Mr. Stokes and his bold Amazonian Virago," whom they claim to suffer from vanity based on several "petty successes," to fight on Monday, July 3, 1727. Elizabeth and James responded in what may be one of the most snarky and derisive comebacks in pugilistic history:

We, James and Elizabeth Stokes, of the City of London, were of Opinion that by our former Performances, we had establish'd to ourselves such a Reputation, as would effectively have secur'd us from the Trouble of any Hibernian Challenges, but finding these Concomitants (as they call themselves) in Pursuit of Fame, are not susceptible of any Conviction of their Insufficiency to stand in Competition with us, but what they purchase at a very smart Expense, we shall for this once do them the Favour to comply with their Invitation, and hope they will have the Modesty to impute it more to their own Indiscretion, than to any Enmity of ours, if their imaginary Prospect of being Sharers in Renown, should be chang'd into a real Partnership in a defeated Combat.[10]

In addition to being the European boxing championess, Stokes acted as an instructor to aspiring young pugilists. In the announcement for a fight with Mary Baker (presumably the former Mary Welch, now married to her boxing partner, Robert), there is an endnote announcing that "two of Mrs. Stokes's scholars are to fight six Bouts at Quarter-Staff, between the Womens Bouts." Although the details of these students, including their gender, is lost, the note reveals that Elizabeth's famous reputation as a boxer positioned her apprentices to compete in the same large venue as their teacher.[11] Throughout the course of her career, Stokes primarily fought in boxing matches, although her skills with a short sword and dagger were well-known. Sword and dagger fencing matches were popular in England at the time, although boxing remained a highly practiced sport. The former soon fell out of favor.

In 1728, Stokes responded to her most demanding challenge yet from Ann Field, an ass-driver from Stoke Newington. Historians often cite this challenge, not only because of Field's humorous job description, but because Stokes was so assured in her response. The bout itself, held on October 7, 1728, was easily overshadowed by the clever and funny correspondence in the media:

I, Ann Field, of Stoke Newington, ass-driver, well known for my abilities in boxing in my own defence wherever it happened in my way, having been affronted by Mrs. Stokes, styled the European Championess, do fairly invite her to a trial of her best skill in Boxing for 10 pounds, fair rise and fall; and question not but to give her such proofs of my judgment that shall oblige her to acknowledge me Championess of the Stage, to the entire satisfaction of all my friends.

Field's courageous challenge was met with particularly cutting remarks from Stokes:

> I, Elizabeth Stokes, of the City of London, have not fought in this way since I fought the famous boxing woman of Billingsgate twenty-nine minutes, and gained complete victory (which was six years ago); but as the famous Stoke Newington ass-woman dares me to fight her for the 10 pounds, I do assure her that I will not fail meeting her for the said sum, and doubt not that the blows which I shall present her with will be more difficult for her to digest than any she ever gave her asses. [12]

At this point in time, the British news media published challenges like the ones between Stokes and Field but did not provide coverage of the event, nor of the aftermath of the fight. Sports journalism did not really exist, hence we have no blow-by-blow coverage of any of Stokes's fights; however, based on the many challenges issued and answered by Stokes during her career, we can assume that she went undefeated.

It appears that James and Elizabeth's combative partnership was standard practice amongst the few female pugilists in the eighteenth century. They were often challenged as a pair, with Elizabeth fighting the wife and James the husband. Thomas and Sarah Barret challenged the couple in tandem in December 1728.[13] Elizabeth was once again challenged to fight in public, but this time it was her opponent's husband who called out the famous English pugilist. Dubliner Thomas Barret, who claimed to have fought "six hundred-odd Battles," brought his wife, "the fair Sarah Barret," to face the "profound" talents of Elizabeth Stokes. Speaking of his wife, Thomas said that Sarah "has fought thirty-five Battles in Ireland, Scotland, and England, and was, never yet defeated, and does not in the least doubt but to have as good Success with this European Championess." Elizabeth and James responded coyly, claiming,

> I, James Stokes, and Elizabeth Stokes, of the City of London, thought not to fight in Publick anymore, but being credibly informed both by Scotch and Irish Gentleman of name, of the Bravery of this new Irish Champion and Championess in North Britain; but I am no-ways surprised at this Encounter, and will display the Judgment of the Sword to their Disadvantage, my spouse not doubting but to do the fame and hopes to give a general Satisfaction to all Spectators. [14]

Elizabeth's career continued in the media through 1730. In May 1729, Dubliner Charles Wright and his "Scholar" Mary Waller challenged James, the "renowned City Champion," and Elizabeth, "hitherto accounted Britania's most puissant Heroine."[15] In the most verbose and flowery challenge yet, Joseph Paddon called out the "two impregnable fortresses" of James and Elizabeth Stokes to take on him and his student, whom he "trained from her Cradle to the Toils of War."[16] Soon thereafter, Elizabeth's career ended abruptly, following eight years of combat.

Elizabeth Wilkinson Stokes may be the most venerated female pugilist in British history, but she was not the first, nor the last, woman to defy gender norms and enter the boxing ring. The details of her personal life are, regrettably, constricted by a lack of documentation. Little was written about Stokes outside of the aforementioned public, self-aggrandizing quotes. If we were to base our estimation of the fighter on these documents alone, we may be quick to deem her arrogant, prideful, and snarky, but, as with many professional fighters, the boastful challenges and insults featured in the media were tools to generate interest, and thus money, for her fights. Elizabeth and James Stokes, along with nearly every other noteworthy fighter of the past four hundred years, relied on hype to increase attendance at their matches, which, subsequently, increased their overall earnings. Because of the limited amount of information available about Elizabeth Wilkinson Stokes, the greatest female boxer of the eighteenth century (and perhaps beyond) remains an enigma.

BOXING SCHOLARSHIP

Boxing was undoubtedly a popular activity in Britain after scholarship about the sport emerged hundreds of years ago. A banner year for pugilistic scholarship came in 1813, when Pierce Egan published his famous volumes of prizefighting articles collectively known as *Boxiana*, and an anonymous writer produced the lesser-known but intriguing *Pancratia: A History of Pugilism*. *Pancratia* primarily consists of stories of various pugilistic encounters and is a wealth of information about how fights occurred in the eighteenth century. The author recounts a 1793 bout in Essex in which two women battled for forty-five minutes in a fight that was both violent and skillful. The women, with their caps removed and hair tied back, were eventually separated, but not until one of them had been so thoroughly beaten that the crowd feared for her life. Her husband, apparently more interested in continuing the bout than in his wife's health, encouraged her to continue to fight.

The author confesses that although he was an ardent supporter of the "cause of pugilism," he did not wish to see women fight. He explains that in women, "it is the gentleness of their manners, and their acknowledged inability of defending themselves, that frequently excite [men] to acts of the greatest bravery and gallantry!"[17] Although the author was admittedly discomfited by women boxers, only seven pages later, he relates the story of a "well-fought pugilistic contest" between "two heroic females," Mary Ann Fielding and a "noted Jewess," name not included. The fight lasted an astonishing one hour and twenty minutes, with Fielding, fighting with "great coolness and singularity of temper," declared the victor.[18] It is doubtful that the author changed his mind regarding female pugilists in the span of seven pages. The earlier statement that men are made more gallant by female weakness may have merely been lip service or, perhaps, a method of bolstering his own fecundity. Regardless, *Pancratia* reveals that women continued to box during the eighteenth century, despite social strictures or a patriarchal assertion of machismo.

GENDER POLITICS OF EIGHTEENTH-CENTURY BRITAIN

Elizabeth Wilkinson Stokes may be the most famous female fighter in British history, but there are a multitude of women who were just as tough and vivacious. Stokes figures greatly in the narrative of British nationalism and, thus, has extensive academic and historical texts dedicated to her memory. Other female fighters, including another Brit, "Bruising Peg," and American Gussie Freeman, exist in historical records, but their stories are not as celebrated as the eighteenth century's "Championess" Stokes, but before their stories and those of other female pugilists are told, it is important to establish the historical and cultural context in which these women lived.

Scholars have written extensively on the subject of gender politics in eighteenth-century Britain, but this section provides only a brief overview to contextualize female pugilists. In his book *Women's Sports: A History*, Allen Guttmann explains that some women who practiced sports in the eighteenth century did so at the behest of upper-class men, who enjoyed watching females compete in exploitative athletic endeavors. Young women were encouraged to compete in races wearing thin shifts, in theory to allow for greater mobility, but in reality, to appeal to male spectators. This bucolic pastime was popular in rural environments, but the crowd often included aristocratic men. Country villages and farms would hold days of games, races, and sporting events where the inhabitants could enjoy a day of respite from work while competing in various games and sports. Wealthy young men would attend as spectators and, in their capacity as local lords and men of power, watch young farmhands compete in wrestling or young girls enjoy physical activities denied to the young ladies of their own class.[19]

Although women of the lower echelons of society were able to practice various sports during their free time, aristocratic women, for the most part, did not participate in sports competitions. Poverty-stricken women living in urban areas competed in boxing, wrestling, and other sports activities for money at the expense of their own safety and moral rectitude. Girls in rural environments seemed to participate in sporting activities for their own pleasure, but aristocratic women were unable to practice sports because of various cultural, social, and even medical limitations. Certain activities, for example, hunting or walking, were permissible for upper-class girls; however, the idea of a lady participating in rigorous activity was scandalous and lewd.

In the city, however, these somewhat innocent, if sexually charged, events became seedier, as the participants were excessively poor and, according to many historians, "sexually disreputable."[20] Yet, the women who boxed in the cities, especially London, appeared to have taken pride in their prowess and were duly praised for their skill and valor. In 1793, two women fought in a "pitched battle" for more than forty-five minutes.[21] One of the women was reportedly skilled in the science of pugilism, and she nearly killed her opponent, who was talked into fighting by her rapscallion husband. The newspaper reported this event without opinion and noted that it was the spectators who stopped the fight. It is likely that any random boxing match fought in the streets, whether between women or men, would have quickly generated an audience. Nevertheless, Guttmann notes, while male spectators watched women fight for a multitude of reasons, all of them were titillated by the voyeuristic pleasure of watching the bouts.[22]

The practice and study of sporting activities became mainstream during the eighteenth century in the West (no doubt in the East as well, but that is outside of the parameters of this book). In 1801, Joseph Strutt published his history of British sport with the expansive title (typical of the time period) *The Sports and Pastimes of the People of England, Including the Rural and Domestic Recreations, May-Games, Mummeries, Pageants, Processions, and Pompous Spectacles, from the Earliest Period to the Present Time.* This epically named tome organizes and categorizes sporting practices in England according to the class of people who either played or watched them. Pugilism is listed as a lively spectator activity for gentry and commoners alike. Of course, the inestimable Elizabeth Wilkinson Stokes makes an appearance in the annals of British pugilistic history, as does "Bruising Peg," a lesser-known but no less interesting female fighter discussed later in this chapter. Female athletes were still an anomaly in pugilistic sports, although other athletic activities attracted women from throughout the social strata. Running, walking, dancing, cricket, ice skating, shooting, and even yard games, for instance, blind man's bluff, were popular pastimes for women with free time. But while feminine activities could include these popular pursuits, girls and young women were principally expected to prepare themselves for the prospective role of motherhood.

Education in the eighteenth century, still primarily afforded to the gentry and aristocracy, taught women skills considered to be useful to the wife of an Englishman, which included needlework, music, dancing, and the art of conversation. Literary clubs in England and salons in France provided opportunities for women to enter into intelligent discourse on such subjects as literature, art, music, and education. British ladies, known as the bluestockings, invited men to join in the conversation, although famous literary critic and essayist William Hazlitt rejected the female circle entirely, explaining "I have an utter aversion to bluestockings. I do not care a fig for any woman that knows even what *an author* means."[23] During his life, Hazlitt's dislike of women extended only to these learned female thinkers. He did not anticipate that it would be his landlady, the apparent opposite of a bluestocking, who would be more disruptive to his person than the women of the salon. The landlady stored Hazlitt's dead body under his bed in an effort to drum up interest in letting his former quarters. Although Hazlitt may have decried the intellectual circle of women as "odious," it was he who was "odorous" in the coming years.[24]

Despite the efforts of men like Hazlitt, education for women became a major political issue promoted by both women and men in the eighteenth century. In 1792, Mary Wollstonecraft published her feminist manifesto, "A Vindication of the Rights of Woman," and forever changed the dialogue regarding women's rights. Wollstonecraft's call to arms demands fair treatment for women and encourages women to take part in the inevitable struggle for equality. Wollstonecraft knew that sports and physical fitness would be part of the fight, declaring, "I wish to persuade women to endeavor to acquire strength, both of mind and body, and to convince them that the soft phrases, susceptibility of heart, delicacy of sentiment, and refinement of taste are almost synonymous with epithets of weakness."[25] In fact, Wollstonecraft argues that girls "should take the same exercises as boys,"[26] and with this declaration, the movement to integrate both sexes in sports education was born. Wollstonecraft herself birthed her second daughter, Mary Wollstonecraft Godwin, who later became known as Mary Shelley and author of the famous gothic horror novel *Frankenstein* (1823).

As the eighteenth century came to a close, it seemed that women were closer than ever to reaching some semblance of autonomy within the male-dominated social order; however, the nineteenth century proved that the patriarchy would be bolstered by a new queen obsessed with family, order, and, above all, reticence.

NINETEENTH-CENTURY BRITISH BOXING

Female pugilism continued to be a sensational phenomenon, and boxing remained the primary sport in Britain, although many accounts of boxing in the nineteenth century had little to do with sport. Nineteenth-century British newspapers contain numerous accounts of street fights, typically of the "dirty" variety. In 1832, a Mrs. Hemsted was arrested after biting the thumb of a Miss Thompson, who claimed to have lost feeling in the arm and a good bit of blood from her mauled phalange. Mrs. Hemsted had apparently been charged before with boxing, although it is unclear whether this was a prizefight or another street brawl.[27] The term *pugilism*, by this time, referred not only to boxers in a somewhat organized combat sport, but to street brawlers and toughs as well. Nonetheless, boxing was on its way to becoming a standardized sport with rules and regulations in the nineteenth century.

A September 25, 1805, article in the *Times* entitled "Female Pugilism" relates a fight between "Miss B***r, sister to the renowned 'Champion of England,'" and an antagonist with whom Miss B had argued on an earlier occasion.[28] The *Times* describes the bout as a "fair but severe and well-fought battle that lasted upward of fifty minutes" and ended with victory by Miss B***r's antagonist. The article claims that both women appeared "well satisfied with the total demolition of each other's caps, handkerchiefs, &c, and the scratches and bruises on their necks and faces."[29] Perhaps the most fascinating part of the story is the final line, which states that, "Miss B. was seconded by her mother." The fight between these two women was initiated because of a personal dispute and not because either woman apparently claimed to be a championess of boxing, which explains why their names are withheld. The *Times* was and still is a paragon of the English media; therefore, it is significant that the newspaper reported this fight nonchalantly and failed to comment on the bizarre nature of seeing two women embattled in the public arena. In truth, the article declares the fight "another proof of the heroism of British Amazons, clearly evincing that the courageous blood which flowed through the veins of our ancient countrywomen is not entirely extinct in the fair sex of the present day."[30]

While the *Times* may be complimentary to the female fighters in its account of the 1805 fight, just two years later, on March 24, 1807, the newspaper changed its tone when it reported on an organized bout between two women. The paper says the following about a boxing match between Betty Dyson and Mary Mahoney:

> There were several fights amongst the lower orders, on Sunday morning, near Hornsey wood; but the one which must afford the most disgust, was between two women, Betty Dyson, a vender of sprats, and Mary Mahoney, a market woman. These Amazons fought upward of forty minutes, and were both hideously disfigured by hard blows. The contest was for five guineas.[31]

This description was, perhaps, a premonition of the coming era of strict morality and clear gender boundaries brought forth by the young Queen Victoria. The "disgust" with which the author recounts the fight contrasts sharply with the story of Miss B***r from 1805. Both articles describe the female fighters as "Amazons," but the earlier version delights in the idea of fearless British women, while the 1807 story focuses on their "hideously disfigured" faces after the bout. This two-year period indicates the cultural shift in Britain between the eighteenth and nineteenth centuries, where frailty was prized over female strength. The days of the Amazons, the female pugilists who were heroines of Britain, were in danger.

NINETEENTH-CENTURY MEDICINE

There are brief stories of women's boxing in nineteenth-century England, although none of the figures from this time period approached the dominating appearance of Elizabeth Wilkinson Stokes in the 1720s. In the early nineteenth century, some upper-class women began to practice sports, but these activities were, for the most part, intended to assuage boredom rather than demonstrate physical prowess. Aristocratic women practiced archery, played cricket, and rode horses, but the social norm in the Victorian age was for women to be frail and delicate rather than strong and robust. The literature of the day, coupled with the example from Queen Victoria, promotes the image of the beautiful and fragile heroine. Bram Stoker's *Dracula* contains two female heroines, Mina Harker and Lucy Westenra, who are delicate, pale, and beautiful. Stoker presents these women in opposition to three female vampires, who are described as voluptuous and ruddy. The frailty of Mina and Lucy makes them good, while the vigorous sensuality of the vampires both arouses and repulses the male characters. Many other Victorian-era texts prized delicately pale and weak women, yet viewed strong, healthy women as somehow unfeminine. This taste for weak femininity created a cultural reproof for women who seemed more robust. While the upper classes in Britain and the United States may have admired frailty in women, the lower ones did not share that preference. Obviously, working-class women needed strength to do daily work, and voluptuousness or ruddiness of color indicated to men a wife's potential to both work and reproduce.

Such novels as Gustave Flaubert's *Madame Bovary* (1856), Leo Tolstoy's *Anna Karenina* (1873–1877), and Kate Chopin's *The Awakening* (1899) explore the boredom and ennui common to middle- and upper-class women in the nineteenth century. Many women were described as frail, unable to get out of bed, depressed, and, in the new signifier of the era, suffering from some form of hysteria. Male physicians encouraged their female patients to withdraw from any and all creative pursuits, limiting their daily activities to the rearing of their family and caring for themselves. "Celebrated" female specialist Dr. S. Weir Mitchell told his patient, Charlotte Perkins Gilman, a budding writer and new mother suffering from postpartum depression, to "live as domestic a life as possible. . . . Have but two hours intellectual life a day. And never touch pen, brush, or pencil as long as you live."[32] Gilman claimed that she nearly went crazy and diagnosed herself as suffering from depression because she wanted to be an activist, not a domestic goddess. Gilman went on to write the short story "The Yellow Wallpaper" about her experience with depression and ill treatment via the medical community.

The medical community has been historically obsessed with female bodies, probably because the vast majority of doctors, healers, researchers, and quacks were men. Women were told that their bodies were weak, substandard, diseased, and problematic by the scientific community, which was seemingly bent on disparaging and controlling the female population. Through the guise of science, women were controlled, regulated, and relegated to purely domestic roles. And while we may chuckle at the outdated notions regarding female bodies, a number of these "scientific" notions about women continue to permeate society, especially in the realm of sports. Female athletes continue to be the subject of medical debate, especially in the "bro-sciences" of exercise and nutrition.

FASHIONING THE FEMALE BODY IN THE NINETEENTH CENTURY

Fashion was another insidious, albeit sometimes fabulous, way of controlling women in the nineteenth century. According to the *Survey of Historic Costume*, "women who dressed in the most stylish gowns of the 1830s and 1840s, when sleeves were set low on the shoulder, would not have been able to raise their arms above their heads and were virtually incapable of performing any physical labor."[33] Wide skirts, bustles, and corsets made it difficult for middle- and upper-class women to move, much less breathe. As a result, throughout the century, attempts were made by some women to find a style of clothing that would not restrain them, but allow them to participate in exercise and not destroy their vital organs. Corsets were made to cut higher on the thighs, allowing for better movement, and the hard matter that shaped the garment was changed to a more flexible material. While these changes helped women breathe a little easier, the idea of the cessation of the corset was not popular.

The majority of fashion criticism came from health reformers who believed the corset to be dangerous and deforming of the body; however, most reformers did not call for the end of corseting, but an augmentation of the corset so that it would longer destroy women's vital organs. Historians note that the corset was deemed an essential part of female dress, and while it may have been refashioned to alleviate some of the pressure on major organs, no woman, even those in the lower classes, would agree to stop wearing this staple undergarment.

But dress reform was a prominent issue in the late nineteenth century. Some publications suggested that certain aspects of clothing be reformed, for instance, overly tight corsets, but nothing was advised that would demean women or create a new dress code that was immodest or unbecoming. The Bloomer costume, named after feminist leader Amelia Bloomer, was created by Elizabeth Smith Miller and consisted of a shorter skirt worn over wide pants. The costume was worn by many feminist reformers, and although it did not become a mode of popular dress, it did influence a gymnastics costume for women.

The debates that surrounded the corset and other dress practices of the Victorian period were usually gendered. Some men and women believed that the corset and wide hemlines were restricting for women physically and socially, but many women believed these fashion practices to be necessary and important for a gentlewoman. The main problem for women, however, was the social requirement for middle- and upper-class women to wear the corset. The corset had long been associated with the dress practices of the elite, and tradition had made it improper for bourgeois or upper-class women to wear a garment without a corset underneath. Fashion historian and theorist Valerie Steele explains that the "cultural weight placed on propriety and respectability made it difficult for women to abandon the corset, even if they wanted to."[34] The smooth figure produced by the corset was without any imperfections, and as one fashion writer commented in the late 1870s, "People who refuse to wear any corset at all look very slovenly."[35] Thus, the corset was required not only to create a perfect figure, but also to display a level of wealth, education, and breeding.

While corsets had long been associated with upper-class women, as the garment industry became more industrialized, they and many other clothing items that were previously handmade became readily available to the public at a lower cost. The efficiency of the corset factories, along with the publication of fashion trends in many women's periodicals, resulted in the trickling down of elite trends of the upper and middle classes to the lower, working classes. As the bourgeoisie attempted to differentiate themselves from lower-class women, the newly modernized factories repeatedly imitated the higher-priced corsets and sold them inexpensively. Industrialization not only readily provided inexpensive goods like clothing, it also led to more jobs and, therefore, a rapidly expanding population in the cities. During this time, all women were able to keep up with current fashions by using lesser-quality material and less decorative accents than that used in the clothing worn by the bourgeoisie. The corset and the phenomenon of tight-lacing became more popular as products became more available.

Regardless of social status, the Victorian woman wore a corset to convey a sense of elegance and try to make her waist as small as possible. While the lower classes struggled to keep up with the major fashion trends of the day, middle- and upper-class women attempted to distinguish themselves from their maids. The body of a laborer should, by class standards, be a harder, more callous form than that of a feminine and dainty member of the elite, but a slender waist was a desirable quality that indicated beauty and class. Although the corset was a sign of conspicuous leisure and often physically debilitating for women, many of the working class still toiled while wearing their corsets.

SPORTING LIFE IN THE NINETEENTH CENTURY

In addition to the medical and sartorial customs that restricted the movement of the female body, social hierarchies often determined who could and should practice a specific type of sporting activity. Aristocratic women were limited to walking as exercise, primarily as an activity to improve posture. In Jane Austin's *Pride and Prejudice* (1813), the Bingley sisters are horrified that Elizabeth Bennett would walk three miles through wet fields to visit her ill sister. The sisters display their usual cattiness toward Elizabeth's general appearance, from her windblown hair and ruddy cheeks to her mud-encrusted petticoats, but the true disgust seems to come from her willingness to walk rather than call for a carriage, as any middle- or upper-class lady would do. Yet, later in the evening, Miss Bingley invites Lizzie Bennett to walk around the room with her after dinner, apparently, as Mr. Darcy says, "because you are conscious that your figures appear to the greatest advantage in walking."[36]

But beyond walking and perhaps riding horses, women in the early nineteenth century were not encouraged to exercise. Lower-class and country women were not restricted in the same manner, primarily because they were expected to do some form of manual labor as part of their social position. Women in the lower echelons of society had more freedom to pursue sports than their middle- and upper-class sisters, but the move toward increased education for women, which often included exercise as part of the mission, ignored the women in the lower classes.

SCHOOL ATHLETICS

The educational reforms of the nineteenth century built upon the ideas of Mary Wollstonecraft and other feminists (although the term *feminist* is decidedly anachronistic, since it was not used at that time). Public and private schools existed in England, the new United States, and abroad prior to the nineteenth century, but during that century, exercise became a focus of numerous educational institutions. Each school had its own assortment of calisthenics or exercises that female students performed. Although none were designed to be especially strenuous, many British schools eventually included a "Sports Day" dedicated to footraces, tennis matches, and other games. The inclusion of team sports in the latter part of the nineteenth century led to a period of intense competiveness amongst students.

Jennifer Hargreaves relates in her book *Sporting Females* that girls at the Roedean public school in Sussex practiced so rigorously for their sport that "half the girls could show their heads above the horizontal bar from a hanging position, and nearly every girl could go hand over hand up the sixteen-foot rope."[37] While the acceptance and institutionalization of female athletics grew in British and American schools for middle- and upper-class girls, the lower tiers of society did not receive the same type of benefits. Like the experience of young Jane Eyre, the titular heroine of Charlotte Brontë's 1847 novel, charity schools did not typically provide students with the nonacademic activities found in the institutions of the higher classes. Of course, many families in the country, as well as poverty-stricken families, did not send their children, much less their daughters, to school. Yet, sports thrived in these environments, especially such "low-life" sports as boxing and wrestling, which were practiced by men and women, and thus boys and girls, alike. And it was among the lower classes that the story of "Bruising Peg" became part of boxing history, both in historical documentation and sensationalized fiction.

THE DIARY OF MARGARET "BRUISING PEG" MALLOY

In Britain, the nineteenth century was not a time of prolific female fighting, although several names stand out in the archives. Margaret Malloy, known as "Bruising Peg," is the most frequently cited British female fighter after Elizabeth Wilkinson Stokes. Unlike her predecessor, Peg has not become synonymous with British nationalism and the symbol of early female combatives; however, her story was fictionalized in 1898 by Paul Creswick, who "edited, or rather wrote" the journal of "Bruising Peg" and published it in London. Creswick is primarily remembered for his work on the history of the Robin Hood legend, King Arthur, and other popular culture narratives, with such enigmatic titles as *At the Sign of the Cross Keys* (1896), *The Temple of Folly* (1898), and *The Ring of Pleasure* (1911). A prolific writer who has sadly become lost in the depths of English literary history, Creswick appears to have had a predilection for exploring sensational topics. He concocted the story of Margaret Molloy in *Bruising Peg: Pages from the Journal of Margaret Molloy, 1768–9*.

Like many other literary texts at the time that were advertised as "found documents," a trope more commonly used in detective fiction, Creswick's role as "editor" rather than "author" was meant to lend a sense of authenticity to the novel. While his book is undoubtedly fiction, the framing of the female fighter reveals the muddy Victorian attitude toward such topics. Victorians approached sex, violence, and other issues of morality with a seemingly divided attitude of fascination and disgust. Creswick's portrayal of "Bruising Peg" is simultaneously sympathetic and dismissive; the perfect tone for a sensationalizing Victorian novel about female aberration. Although Peg's journal is fiction, the story is useful for this book. This analysis starts by examining Creswick's rendition of the famous boxer and then explores her position in the historical record in comparison with this narrative.

Bruising Peg begins with the following poem, which reads like a Muhammad Ali rhyme:

> I can dance a minuet, and curtsey as graceful as you please;
> and I know the art of boxing as you know your ABC.
> I will fight a duello with the point one day,
> no doubt—may you be there to mark my victory![38]

Peg's journal includes her intimate thoughts, from her concerns regarding her lover to detailed depictions of her fights based on Creswick's understanding of eighteenth-century pugilism. While describing her first fight against "Hannah," a less experienced woman whom Peg claims she could have killed in the ring but decided not to, Peg reveals that she removed her bodice, slipped her underclothes down to her waist, and hiked her skirt about her knees. In case the reader assumes that this simply meant that the women were still covered in a final layer, Peg describes the breasts and stomach of her opponent.

The idea that women historically fought topless or in the nude is not a revelation. Drawings from the same time period in France depict women boxing with breasts bared and skirts drawn up around the waist, and in many non-European fighting traditions, from Africa to South America, women wrestled and performed other physical activities wearing little to no clothing, although large amounts of fabulous jewelry were often worn. In Britain, however, where the social stigma of a bare ankle, let alone naked thigh or stomach flesh, could start tongues wagging about a highly born woman, the reality of topless women fighting in public was unlikely. In his epically titled tome *The Amusements of Old London; being a survey of the sports and pastimes, tea gardens and parks, playhouses and other diversions of the people of London from the 17th to the beginning of the 19th century* (1901), William Boulton recounts Elizabeth Wilkinson Stokes and her opponent fighting in "close jacket, short petticoats, and Holland drawers, and with white stockings and pumps."[39] Whether Creswick may have furtively fantasized about topless women fighting or simply wished to titillate the reader, the scene described by Peg reads more about class than the sartorial choices of female fighters.

Yet, in the novel, Peg appears nonchalant about the idea of bearing her breasts in public. She recalls that upon her arrival, several men yelled at her to undress, but she declined, preferring to wait until her opponent arrived, not because she did not want to seem unseemly, but because she was concerned that she might be cold. But if Peg and Hannah were indeed cold just prior to their fight, the instant the bell rang, the action inside the ring was hot. Peg describes her mental processes throughout the fight with incredible detail in a manner that would resonate with any modern fighter: "This is what always happens. The world suddenly narrows to one woman, and that woman is battling with me. I swear to you that I see nothing else; I feel nothing but a savage fury of delight. That she hurts me is one of the keen joys that flow exaltingly through my person."[40]

Peg also relates several of her tactics, striking the left abdomen just above the stomach (presumably the liver) with the left hand to make the opponent "shoot his head forward instantly," which sets him or her in perfect range for a "*cout de grace*" with the right hand. Yet, at the moment of victory, when the body of Hannah lay quivering at her feet, "one leg was drawn up over the other, her arms were flung across her face, her breasts were swollen monstrously," Peg claims to feel like a monster herself:

> I hate myself—I execrate the day that I was born. Why do I live that I am so vile? These horrid fits come upon me, and rob me of all reason. There is no good in any part of me. And see, in this hour of victory, what Fate hath in store. The mob's applause? Bah! A purse of guineas, won by beating this poor woman that hath done me no great harm?[41]

Margaret's journal is the narrative of a conflicted woman. She admits her delight in fighting while in the act, but when not in the ring, she feels demoralized and "unsexed."[42]

Throughout *Bruising Peg*, Creswick depicts Peg as a member of a lower class, albeit one who was apparently adept at curtseying with the best of them. Peg's casual attitude toward fighting nude reveals the less rigid social codes outside the aristocracy. Peg describes her large limbs, bleeding hands, and "horrid" face, but her real shame comes from the nature of her profession, which, although popular amongst the people, makes her feel unwomanly. When a younger sister, Anne, comes to visit Margaret, she notes that while she had been able to beat everyone in the neighborhood since she was fourteen and easily defeated Hannah and other fighters in the ring, she would be devastated if Anne found out about "Bruising Peg." She is a heroine to the lower classes, but when she comes into a fortune and elevates herself into the burgeoning bourgeoisie, Peg becomes "Margaret" and attempts to leave behind the inner "beast" that urges her to fight.

The novel progresses in a slow and somewhat convoluted narrative regarding the romantic endeavors of Margaret and her younger sister Anne; however, the interesting moments come when Peg finds herself seething from within, wanting nothing more than to hit someone and release her hidden rage. She hates this desire to fight but delights in the sweet release of beating someone with her hands. The body and conclusion of the novel are, as previously mentioned, bizarrely constructed, but the depiction of Margaret/Peg as a conflicted woman resonates throughout Creswick's novel. The novel, through the voice of Peg, suggests that women "afflicted" with bloodlust must be tormented and, as evidenced by the conclusion of her narrative, in need of a strong husband to restore her femininity. Creswick's novel, while delightful to a modern historian of women's fighting sports, did not garner much attention during the author's lifetime. Whether readers were uninterested in the topic of a female fighter, turned off by the title, or, more likely, unimpressed by the author's writing style, the book was largely ignored and remains out of print today.

The real "Bruising Peg" is remembered only in name from a brief line in Boulton's historical survey of London entertainment, *The Amusements of Old London*. Boulton relates a battle between two women who "fought for a new shift valued at half a crown in the Spa Fields, New Islington," according to a 1768 newspaper source. The winner was a "woman called Bruising Peg, who beat her antagonist in a terrible manner."[43] The real "Bruising Peg" existed in the eighteenth century as a brutal fighter, but Creswick's novel introduces her within the context of Victorian sensibilities. The novelization of her life and experience as a pugilist remains an example of the tendency to define female fighters as troubled yet easily fixed through marriage to an appropriately masculine husband.

A FEMININE TRIAL OF SKILL

Street fights continued to be a method of settling disputes amongst the poorer classes of England. Upper classmen would risk their lives to fight duels with swords or pistols, but the men and women of the lower classes dueled with their fists, probably because their communities needed them to remain alive to help sustain their families. In its April 7, 1822, edition, *Bell's Life in London, and Sporting Chronicle* carefully details the fight between two women of Kent Street.[44] *Bell's* was a weekly publication that covered various types of sports, including boxing. The paper eventually became a staple in most Victorian men's Sunday reading regimen. In this particular issue of *Bell's* was the story of a fight between Sally and Nancy over a lover. The women wore "short jackets, secured at the waist by a handkerchief, their hair cropt expressly for the present purpose." Unlike the disgust of the *Times* fifteen years earlier, this delightful article uses colorful language to expound on the fighting skills of the two women, claiming that the "Ladies, on coming up to the *scratch*, displayed *fine science*, but were *cautious*." Round one went as follows:

> Nan *made play*, but Sal was not *to be had*, and fought rather *shy*. Some maneuvering ensued, when Nan, made a *feint*, Sal Attempted to put in a left-handed hit, which was well stopped by the former, who placed a blow near the place where Sally took her snuff, and which made her *ivories* dance a reel in their box.[45]

While this fight may have originated from of an ordinary quarrel, it was organized like a legitimate bout, with each round ending with a score on either side. Round three began with the following snarky comment from *Bell's*: "This was a good manly—we beg our Readers' pardon, but we had really forgotten that we were speaking of the *softer* sex) a good *womanly* round."[46] As the fight ensued, the women exchanged blows, with Nan landing a "heavy hit" that caused the "*claret* to flow prodigiously from [Sally's] upper lip." After Nancy later managed to throw Sally out of the ring and "spoiled the look of her adversaries *mug*," the paper reports that the skill shown at the beginning of the fight began to decline in the later rounds: "These rounds were more like a pull-cap concern for a *sweet-heart* between two nursery-maids than an exhibit of *science* between *Ladies* possessing *their* abilities—but we must, in justice, acknowledge they were *both* already beaten."[47]

In the thirteenth round, the women primarily clinched, undoubtedly from the same fatigue that affects boxers today, and the author suggests that if their hair had not been cropped short, they would have resorted to hair pulling. The seconds, deemed "Ladies in Waiting" by the paper, suggested that the fighters each drink a glass of "*strip-me-naked*," which was apparently a euphemism for gin. After a twenty-minute break, the fight resumed, although Nancy quickly took Sally down with a "floorer," which knocked the latter out for nearly three minutes. Although Sally attempted to come back with what the paper describes as "*baby-play* rounds" and declared that "she'd die afore she'd give in," the fight was soon over, with Nancy declared the victor. The women were "apparently well pleased with themselves, and with each other," so they removed to a nearby bar to "sign a treaty of peace" over drinks. The tone of this account is a far cry from the disgust expressed by the *Times* in 1807, yet the cheeky language pokes fun at the spectacle of Nancy and Sally's fight.

The general attitude toward women fighting vacillated between antipathy and fascination during the Victorian era. For some men, watching two women wrestle or box was simultaneously humorous and erotic. For other men and women, the distasteful spectacle of female fighters was a source of revulsion. In 1888, there were reports of a woman dying in the ring after a battle of great "vigor and determination."[48] The victor of the fight, Mrs. Christmas, was placed in jail after her adversary, Ellen Noonan, died from injuries received during the fight. And while Britons struggled to reconcile the reality of human life, the body, and sex with strictures of Victorian social codes, across the pond, nineteenth-century Americans were searching for identity in their new, but already troubled, country.

2

AMERICAN WOMEN JOIN THE FIGHT

In 1856, the *Detroit Daily Free Press* reported about a "brutal prizefight between two women" in Gloucester, New Jersey. The women, who punished one another "to such an extent that they were covered with blood from head to foot," were also punished by the law, as they and several onlookers were arrested and taken to Woodbury Jail.[1] Ten years later, in St. Louis, Missouri, Maggie Shoester and Annie Wood, employees of a beer saloon on Market Street, were "barbarously mutilated and disfigured with cuts and bruises and all sorts of fantastic bloodstains and blotches" after a fight.[2] There is no information on whether the women were punished for the bout, but perhaps their position as barmaids gave them some protection against the machinations of the police.

Women in the United States traveled a tougher route to the ring than their British sisters. In the late eighteenth century, the United States was a combination of puritanical ideology and the movement toward Enlightenment. American women were doubly restricted: The strict religious morality and the Enlightenment's ideals of science and reason placed fighting outside the confines of acceptable behavior. Fighting sports were considered barbaric, disruptive, and indicative of a lower moral order. More importantly, most people believed that boxing and other forms of pugilism were vestiges of the old country, and many Americans wished to dissociate completely from British culture. Thomas Jefferson and other leaders of the new republic criticized boxing as violent and morally degrading.[3]

In 1835, New Jersey passed a law banning the "degrading practice of prizefighting," which was quickly adopted by numerous other states in the Union.[4] Without the aristocracy to back them, like their British pugilistic brethren, fighters in the United States risked fines and jail time to practice the art of boxing. But even the law could not stop the world's oldest sport, as boxing matches continued to transpire in back alleys and bars. There is little evidence of boxing matches with female fighters occurring in the United States prior to the mid-nineteenth century, although it is likely that these types of illicit bouts were held without detection by police and escaped media exposure.

While the majority of prizefighters were men, some women became involved in the highly illegal and despised sport. In 1866, a fight in South Brooklyn invited a critique of not only the lower classes, but the immigrant citizens who lived in that part of the city. The October 19, 1866, installment of the *Daily Evening Bulletin* reports that the women living in that part of Brooklyn

> are, as everyone knows, composed of no gentle elements, and make up for the lack of the purring softness of dangerous female women of higher stations in life by the greater length of their nails, greater power of physical endurance, and a super abundance of pugnacity in general, which they are by no means delicate in bringing into requisition on every available occasion.[5]

The paper goes on to make snide remarks regarding the people in the community, even using the designation the "ladies (?)" for the women. According to the account, during an intermission before a prizefight, a Mr. Stackpole bet $50 that his wife Elizabeth, "could whip any woman in the crowd in a square stand-up fight." A Catherine Meisser, with Mrs. Judy Hart acting as her second, engaged in a bloody battle with Mrs. Elizabeth Stackpole, who was seconded by her husband. After some rough and dirty fighting, the seconds became involved as well, and Mr. Stackpole apparently attacked Judy, the result of which was a "general attack of the crowd, armed with haysticks and stones, on Stackpole and his wife." Nearly everyone involved was arrested and charged with felonious assault, although there appear to be no records regarding the aftermath of these cases. Regardless, the melee was attributed to the lower-class status of the individuals, the ferocity of the "ladies (?)," and the nature of prizefighting.

In 1869, Sarah "Sally" Chapman and Mary Ann "Molly" Jones, two women described by the *Chicago Tribune* as being "of questionable repute," each bet $25 that they could best the other in what the *Tribune* dubs the "petticoat championship of America."[6] Men of the roughest and lowest orders attended the fight, which was held at three o'clock in the morning a few miles outside of Boston. Per the *Tribune*, the women wore only a "pair of ordinary drawers, stockings, and women's gaiters." Thus, the women were evidently topless during the fight, in addition to being drunk. The *Tribune* declares that the "scene was one of excitement, as well as of disgust and pity." Neither woman showed signs of having trained in the "semidignified art of self-defense," and at one point, Molly reportedly leapt over the tables that created the "ring" around the fighters after dodging one of Sally's particularly heavy attempts.[7] But she overcame her fears and hopped back in the ring. After round eighteen, Molly's friends tried to call off the fight because they were afraid the women would kill one another. Molly bravely entered the ring again, but she reportedly cried the entire time and begged for someone to take her away. The fight was called in favor of Sally, obviously, after the twenty-first round. The *Tribune* claims that the fight was "probably one of the most brutal and revolting of [affairs] that ever took place in the country." The paper also denounces the city of Boston for allowing this type of event to take place, especially since Massachusetts was supposed to be "so famous for morals"; however, the women were the recipients of the most damage, having their faces "badly disfigured" and their reputations, especially Molly's, forever cemented in the newspaper.[8]

GENDER POLITICS

In the aftermath of the Revolutionary War and the creation of a new country, the eighteenth century was a tumultuous and quickly changing time in American history. Perhaps due to the image of women as the daughters of Eve, they have typically been viewed as weak in morality and self-control. The racial diversity in the burgeoning American culture configured white women as innocent, pure, and prone to victimization at the hands of nonwhite men. Like their European sisters (and women worldwide, it would seem), American women existed under laws and social codes that limited their actions based on their gender.

Education in the British colonies (prior to the revolution) was, as expected, spotty and infrequent. A nascent government fighting for independence had more important things than education to funnel time and resources into. During the seventeenth century, most children in wealthy households were taught by private tutors, although girls typically only learned to read, while boys studied reading, writing, mathematics, and the sciences. By the eighteenth century, more organized schools had been established and teachers, both male and female, hired to instruct young American minds. The puritanical-turned-Victorian middle class in the United States, empowered by their positions as shop owners and traders, pushed a strict moral ideology in politics and social customs. Late nineteenth-century bourgeoisie Americans vilified prizefighting, along with alcohol, obscene language, prostitution, abortion, showy dress, and excessive body ornamentation (for example, cap ribbons). But late nineteenth-century American culture also grew striated, as the excessive politeness of the Victorian age clashed with the growing "cult of manliness."

A CULTURE OF WEAKNESS

The fashion of nineteenth-century American women, like their British counterparts, also included restrictive clothing and such unhealthy dressing practices as wearing corsets and carrying heavy hoop skirts on their hips. Women were undoubtedly exhausted from the restricted lung capacity forced by wearing tight corsets and the weight of carrying dozens of pounds of fabric. In addition to their heavy dresses and fripperies, they wore extensive undergarments, for instance, chemises, drawers, and "safety belts," which functioned as a sort of prototypical adult diaper for menstrual cycles.[9] Crinoline or steel-hoop skirts and corsets helped women manipulate their bodies into the desired form, and underwaists protected expensive and dear fabrics from bodily oils. It was common for women to carry in excess of thirty pounds, although weight estimations vary from source to source. Regardless of the exact number, both the weight and restricting nature of Victorian-era clothing must have made getting and staying dressed an exhausting practice.

Mid-nineteenth century Americans also followed British trends by making a virtue of fragility and weakness. Wan-faced women on fainting couches perceived the almost tubercular state of appearance as a sign of beauty and class. While this pale look may have been popular in the fashionable sets and middle-class households that sought to emulate them, many people regarded this exaggerated ill health as ludicrous. Critics condemned women who put on an air of illness as products of romantic novels that featured feeble heroines. Indubitably, male authors were to blame for promoting illness as beauty, but the young women who followed the trend, especially healthy ladies who contrived to be sick, made themselves useless.

The author of the 1870 *Bazar Book of Decorum* decries contrived illness and states harshly, "We doubt whether any woman who cultivates sickness and weakness has a sound idea of the value of good looks."[10] This type of affected illness was typically only prevalent in the upper and middle classes; people who were poor or lived in rural environments had no time to feign sickness when there were mouths to feed and work to be done. Women in the country were often described as ruddy, buxom, and strong, necessary characteristics for the type of woman living on a farm or in some other rural setting. In the cities, lower-class women also had to be robust and indelicate to survive the rigors of urban life, and it was typically this class of women, the girls who were raised to be strong, that produced the nineteenth-century female fighter.

WRESTLING AND THE ADVENT OF CATCH-AS-CATCH-CAN

Wrestling, even more so than the sport of boxing, has a history as spectacle. Even today, wrestling is often first associated with the staged "professional" wrestling seen on television, in which highly charismatic men and women leap off the ropes and smash one another with chairs, all the while creating a bewildering and mystifying narrative that easily rivals a dimestore detective novel. In the late nineteenth and early twentieth centuries, wrestlers often made up part of the cast of performers in traveling circuses and fairs. Catch-as-catch-can wrestling famously originated in the circus scene as a series of brutal and sneaky techniques meant to ensure victory for the wrestlers, who declared they could take all comers.

Women also performed athletic feats as members of traveling circuses, from acrobats and contortionists to strongwoman performances, as well as boxing, fencing, and wrestling. Jackley's Circus, a popular venue featuring performers from Europe, toured the United States in the mid-1870s and included female wrestlers as part of the entertainment. Large crowds would gather to watch the highly publicized all-female wrestling competition, the prize of which was jewelry, presented in front of the crowd on a pillow. The wrestling competitors, all of whom hailed from Vienna and were "imported . . . at enormous expense," wore white shirts, red trousers, white stockings, and black shoes.[11] The women reportedly wrestled in the catch-as-catch-can style, although it appears from the description of the bouts that it was more of an "anything-goes" style of fighting. These particular women were unschooled in the art of wrestling and, of course, designed to titillate and amuse the men in attendance, which they dutifully did. The final two contestants were described as "stout as stumps and quick as flashes on their legs." The two girls struggled for the advantage, and one of them ripped a large piece of the other girl's skirt off, revealing what the *Cincinnati Enquirer*, that oft-declamatory publication, describes as a "patch of walnut buff as big as a sombrero to the eyes of the gods." As familiar as we may be in the twenty-first century with euphemistic language and double entendres, one can hazard at least one guess as to what the paper was referring. The bout continued despite the destruction to the contestant's habiliment, and when the fight was over from a legitimate throw, the women exited the stage. The paper claims that these particular girls were praised because their fight, unlike the previous soft-core tussles between the beautiful young women, was a genuine display of effort and skill.[12]

In 1880, three hundred people watched a wrestling match between Miss Ida Alb and Professor Charles A. Standbrook at the Theater Comique in St. Louis, Missouri. The event was indeed a spectacle, with prefight entertainment consisting of a contortionist, a professional eater, and a master prestidigitator. Alb was apparently a veteran of wrestling matches at the Comique, although the *Enquirer* notes that her opponent was typically her sister. This was the first time that she would compete against a man. The match consisted of numerous throws back and forth between the contestants, but none were deemed legal in the Greco-Roman style until Standbrook threw Alb over his head and flat onto the mat. That ended the first round, and the two took a break. In the second round, Alb returned the favor, although her opponent was able to keep his shoulders off the floor, preventing a full throw. She was not satisfied with his defense, so she wrestled with him on the floor, trying to get a pin. Although she was unsuccessful in this attempt, she managed to get a full throw, and thus ended the second round. She threw him again in the third round and won the match.

There is again a question of legitimacy in this fight. The paper describes Standbrook as not a large man, but standing nearly a head taller than Alb. In addition, Alb's finishing move was not a hip throw, but the rather astounding feat of tossing Standbrook over her head. The *Enquirer* does not speculate on the performative aspect of the bout, except to say that people booed at the beginning when the two circled one another carefully, and others thought Standbrook was not trying; however, as the bout began in earnest, the crowd seemed to cheer and, perhaps, suspend their disbelief. Because bouts were fought in performance halls, whether wrestling or boxing, they were sometimes choreographed. Venues were not required to disclose whether the fight was theatrical or a true test of skill, so audiences had to use their own judgment. Regardless of the validity of the fight, it made headlines because of the pairing of a man and a woman.[13]

After this bout, there seem to have been no publicized wrestling matches featuring female combatants in the United States, or at least there are no surviving records of any such events for the next decade. There is, however, a dearth of firsthand sources that relate stories of women wrestling in the nineteenth century. Numerous secondary sources might reference a particular article or event, but when hunted down through academic databases and resources, many of these articles do not seem to exist. In many instances, Internet authors will perpetuate the myth of a particular boxing or wrestling match without an attempt to discover the original source material. Consequently, there are several "famous" boxing matches retold by many different authors that do not appear to exist or no longer exist in their original format. For example, numerous writers recount the story of a women-only wrestling tournament held by *National Police Gazette* owner Richard Kyle Fox in 1891. Several secondary and tertiary sources claim that there was an advertisement for this event, in which the combatants, Alice Williams and Sadie Morgan, were required to cut their hair short.[14] It is a fantastic story, and one that Internet authors, in particular, put forth without any careful citation. Yet, the *National Police Gazette* archives have no record of such an event, although their head archivist agrees that it sounds like the type of affair that Fox would have loved to promote. After a great deal of careful research, it appears that most of these Internet sources use incorrect information for source material. It was not Fox who put on the wrestling match, it was Billy Lester of "Billy Lester's Big Show" fame.

In late April 1891, Lester presented "Billy Lester's Big Show" at the Kernan Theater in Maryland. The *Washington Post* wrote that Lester's show contained a number of well-known, talented performers. Alice Williams and Mary Morgan, not the aforementioned Sadie, were predicted to demonstrate excellent skill and strength in their wrestling match, and that prediction was certainly accurate.[15] Two days later, the *Post* reported that during their bout, which was the "most exciting thus far," Williams came off the victor, with three throws to Morgan's one.[16] This event is an important part of the history of female wrestlers, but the fight between Alice Williams and Mary Morgan has been misremembered in many Internet sources. The detail of the women cutting their hair short is not substantiated by the original and correct source material, and the name of the second fighter, Mary Morgan, often referred to as Sadie in other sources, is also incorrect. But the notion that Fox and his *National Police Gazette* would have been fervent supporters of female fighters is, indeed, correct.

THE RISE OF AMERICA'S GOLDEN ERA OF BOXING

In the United States, prizefighting was a popular form of entertainment, but the pugilists themselves remained thoroughly ensconced in the lower classes. Prizefighting was illegal in the nineteenth century in the United States, decried by politicians and religious officials as barbaric. Furthermore, prizefighting correlated directly with gambling, a sin to most religious people. Unlike the boxers in Europe, who were often backed by aristocratic men, just as Shakespeare and other playwrights were once supported by royalty, the fighters in the United States had no upper-class individuals to overrule the prudish morality of the middle-class American "Victorians."[17] Hence, prizefighting was a crime, albeit a rarely indicted one.

The *National Police Gazette*

Fights between women in the United States remained intermittent and ridiculed, just as prizefighting continued to be outlawed in nearly every state in the Union. In the mid-1880s, a group of women arrived on the boxing scene, helped, in part, through the promotion of the American tabloid the *National Police Gazette*. The *National Police Gazette* was founded in 1845, but it would not become the popular purveyor of spicy gossip and grisly gore until Richard Kyle Fox took over the publication in 1877. In the late nineteenth century, the sport of boxing was largely illegal in the United States, and promoters, fighters, and spectators could be arrested for attending illegal fights. Of course, this did not stop boxing matches altogether, it merely created an environment where the lower classes were at risk of arrest, while the upper-class men who enjoyed boxing could attend these illicit events with impunity.[18] Fox felt that prizefighting should be legalized in the United States, and he sought to legitimize the illegal sport by creating fighting events sponsored by the paper and providing coverage of the fight in a somewhat fair, unbiased voice. Of course, Fox's efforts to legalize and legitimize prizefighting were not entirely altruistic. The *Police Gazette* exuded sensationalism on every page, but that is exactly what made it a popular read for Americans. Fox promoted fighters from a variety of backgrounds, from the famous John L. Sullivan, to such female fighters as Hattie Leslie and Gussie Freeman, to African American fighters, but his objective was always to write content that presented sensationalized news to America's reading public, who hungrily devoured the blood, grit, sex, and violence provided by Richard Fox and his *Police Gazette*.

In 1884, the *Police Gazette* published an article on John L. Sullivan and the popularity of pugilism in the United States. The piece glorifies the muscular male physique, embodied, of course, by the highly successful Sullivan. The paper credits Sullivan with the growing popularity of boxing, which was seemingly unknown in the United States until he made headlines, aided, undoubtedly, by the efforts of the *National Police Gazette*. The article claims that because of Sullivan, fights were increasing between various types of pugilists, from heavyweights and lightweights, to child boxers and "women boxers of every degree of size, weight, and color."[19] Two months later, the *Police Gazette* published a photo of Hattie Stewart, presumably the first highly publicized female boxer in America. The paper declares Hattie Stewart a champion, claiming that she was "eager to box any of the many female champions of America," which suggests that other women competed and named themselves champion in 1884, and ostensibly prior to that date.[20] Even if there were female champions prior to Stewart, spectators were still titillated by the presence of women in boxing.

In fact, two years earlier, in 1882, the *Georgia Weekly Telegraph* reported a boxing match between Miss Natelle Lester and Miss Alice Jennings. According to the paper, the assembled fans did not know that the women would participate in the event. Thus, "there was a general craning of necks by the audience."[21] At stake was a silver cup, which "would be presented to the lady who gave her opponent the greatest number of straight hits."[22] The paper declares that female boxers were an "anomaly"; however, it also admits that Lester had "long been the holder of the champion badge for female pugilists." So although the women may be anomalous, they are also part of a growing tradition of female boxers.

Like nearly every other report of female pugilists, the paper details the women's attire and claims in a derogatory tone that "both ladies were arrayed in garments which afforded the audience an opportunity to indulge in a study of the anatomy of the human form."[23] The fight was careful and scientific, with both women landing accurate blows, although it apparently devolved into a "clawing match" by the end. Still, it seems likely that the paper would categorize the tired scuffles typical of any boxing match through feminizing terms like *clawing*, while describing men in a similar situation as merely brawling. Jennings was declared the winner, having landed twenty-one punches, while her opponent, the presumed former champion, landed fifteen.[24] The fight between Jennings and Lester reveals that women were indeed part of the boxing world in the 1880s, even prior to the *Police Gazette*'s public display of women's boxing.

The Art of Self-Defense

The 1880s saw an increase in pugilistic schools throughout the country. Boxing schools popped up in the United States in the early nineteenth century, often under the guise of fencing academies. Unlike prizefighting, which was seen as a debased and lowly form of entertainment, sparring offered gentlemen an opportunity to practice the manly art of boxing without tarnishing their reputations. Sparring while wearing leather boxing gloves provided practitioners with exercise and skill, while simultaneously reinforcing the masculine ideal of boxing. During the Victorian era, a time of prudishness heretofore unseen in Britain and America, men sought to reestablish their masculinity outside the world of dandyism and romantic poetry, but to say that boxing schools gained popularity *only* for men to reassert their masculinity would be false. Women also began training in the science of pugilism, and not because they wanted to increase their femininity or masculinity. In fact, most girls and young women who trained in "self-defense" in the 1880s did so simply because it was fun.

In 1886, several papers published the story of a boxing school where teenage girls learned to box in the Queensbury style. The teacher, an elegant and well-spoken older woman, remarked to the reporter that her charges were sparring for exercise, and not, she emphatically stated, for any type of exhibition or prizefight. This school taught boxing as an art, and the pupils loved it with a fervor that shocked the reporter. Inside the gym, the girls used an early form of a speed bag, made with a football tied to a rope, to train prior to their sparring match. The article describes a sparring match between two girls, who moved with the grace of dancers and the precision of experienced prizefighters. There was no winner, and after the bout, the girls discussed their tactics and mistakes like two military officials.

While it may seem astonishing to find a women's boxing school in 1886, this program was not the first, nor the only, of its kind. The article states that, "sparring is no new exercise for women," and that many famous actresses used sparring to stay in shape. Moreover, in New York, there was a school for society girls to learn the "art grown womanly of self-defense." In 1895, the *Police Gazette* reported on a ten-round bout at a Chicago gymnasium in which two young women fought to a knockout. The paper claims that new members fainted, and the rest of the girls, including the two contestants, cried together in the dressing room; however, they had a seemingly "lovely time," because everyone was "eager for the next bout."[25]

HATTIE STEWART

In 1884, Hattie Stewart, a woman of Germanic descent, was featured in the *Police Gazette* as a champion of boxing who was "eager to box any of the many female champions of America."[26] As previously mentioned, this challenge suggests that numerous women had already claimed to be the championess of boxing, and that Hattie was an up-and-coming fighter. That same year, Anna Lewis, another prominent female boxer, was described by the *Police Gazette* as a "tall, stately woman of masculine bearing" with a "pleasing face."[27] The paper also included details of Anna's measurements, similar to what many Hollywood gossip websites do today. As listed by the *Police Gazette*, Lewis was five feet, six inches tall and weighed 155 pounds, and although she was willing to fight any woman at any weight, she refused to cut below 140 pounds. Lewis trained with a man named Eddy for four months and was waiting for an opportunity to test her skill in the ring.

Unlike today, where promoters and managers arrange bouts between fighters, it seems that most women used the press to find an opponent. Lewis planned to submit a challenge to the *Police Gazette*, which she hoped, like many of her cohorts, would lead to a bout, but at the point when Lewis's description and image appeared in the *Gazette* in October 1884, she had no fight experience and no record with which to assert herself a "championess." Her wish was fulfilled when she met and was defeated by Stewart in the ring. Lewis had irked Stewart by claiming that she was the championess of the world. The women were supposed to fight eight rounds with the standard Queensberry rules for a $200 purse, but Stewart knocked Lewis out in the second round.[28] Hattie claimed that Anna, and the other Hattie, Hattie Leslie, were trying to mimic her game but were unable to live up to the reputation and skill of the great championess, Hattie Stewart.[29]

The *Omaha Daily Bee* interviewed Stewart in December 1887, and titled the article, "She Loves to Fight," a true sentiment expressed by the woman the media would dub the "Female John L. Sullivan."[30] The paper declares that no one would suspect that the attractive Stewart was the female prizefighting champion of the United States. She is described as soft-spoken, yet proud of her accomplishments. Perhaps the most interesting aspect of this interview is the history of Hattie's experience as a fighter in training, the details of which are typically missing from this time period. For historians and scholars, it is frustrating that while we read descriptions of fighters and their various bouts, we have little to no information regarding their training.

Stewart explains that she began to fight early in life while at school in Philadelphia. In 1876, at the age of twenty, she learned "boxing and club-swinging," a typical accompaniment, like fencing, to nineteenth-century boxing lessons. She also taught boxing to other women, apparently making her living from fighting, as well as coaching, much like fighters do today. She married Richard Stewart, who was the swordsmanship master at the gymnasium where Hattie taught boxing. But while Hattie may have trained herself and other women in the art of pugilism, she claimed that her opponents simply should not have been in the ring, saying, "Most of the women I meet in the ring are no good. They won't stand up and give the people the worth of their money. After one or two rounds, if they get a 'straight' in the head, they go off crying."[31]

Her description appears to be apt in some cases, for instance, the 1888 fight between Mary McNamara and Julia Perry, during which technique quickly fell to the wayside after the first round and was replaced by hair pulling and scratching.[32] In fact, McNamara knocked Perry down and then dragged the woman around the ring by her hair until the end of the round. Perry and her second, who was also her brother, were obviously upset. Yet, for some reason, they called on the police to settle the dispute. Instead of siding with the scalp-sore Perry, the policeman arrested them both, along with McNamara and her second.[33] Thus, it appears that Hattie Stewart's claim that many of her female opponents did not belong in the ring was correct.

When asked about a future opponent, Mrs. Alice Robson, Stewart responded in a manner similar to modern fighters; she revealed a detailed knowledge of Robson and her training: "Mrs. Robson, I am told, is twenty-seven years old, is a brunette, five feet six, who fights at 150 pounds. Her husband is a master painter at Crafton, near Pittsburg. She's taking four lessons a week in boxing, I hear, with Tom Connors, the wrestler, as her trainer."[34] This information reveals that many female fighters in the late nineteenth century not only trained to fight, they trained with experienced and well-known male coaches.

Stewart also discussed her fight weight, which was 150 to 160 pounds. She informed the paper that she was currently 190 pounds, but that was because she had not been training. She explained, "I can soon get down to

160 pounds by banging away at the sand bag a few hours each day. I can take off 15 pounds a week if it's for a fight." Prior to discovering this interview, it was unclear if American female fighters underwent "cutting" for fighting. Stewart admits to being able to cut a great deal of weight, and through the use of heavy cardiovascular training that seems so current, so incredibly modern, especially to those of us training today.[35] The image of Stewart working the heavy "sand bag" in an effort to lose fifteen pounds a week seems normal to those who have cut weight for a fight. Of course, the difference for her would have been her attire, which, based on figure 2.1, would have made movement more difficult than if she would have been dressed in the stretchy attire worn today.

In an interview with the *Washington Post* in October 1898, Stewart claimed to have fought several men and beaten them all.[36] Stewart boxed George La Blanche, Hattie Leslie's boxing instructor, and "accidently" stuck her thumb in his eye after six long rounds. She attempted to fight Leslie herself but claimed that the other Hattie preferred to fight through the press rather than with her hands.

Stewart did not limit her pugilistic experiences to professional engagements; she claims to have beaten numerous men in public places for disrespecting her. When trying to set up a fight with another woman's male promoter, the man, Billy Manning, argued with her about the terms of the match, so Stewart "made a roughhouse finish by using Billy's 158 pounds for a feather duster."[37] But Stewart claimed that she was not trying to brag about her immense success. Instead, she wanted to regale the public with some of her more interesting victories.

The article continues with Stewart explaining a rather progressive feminist attitude toward women's rights and women's fights, although the term *feminist* is anachronistic. Interestingly, in 1888, women's rights advocates spoke out against female prizefighters, arguing that women's suffrage would not be helped by physical violence.[38] But Stewart believed that women could gain more independence and agency through empowering their bodies. She explained that boxing was not "too mannish" for women to practice and, in fact, was better exercise than tennis, golf, or bicycle riding because it "exercises every fiber of the body and imparts a certain amount of self-reliance in the woman of today."[39]

Stewart advocated that everyone should exercise for a half an hour daily and try all types of exercise, from calisthenics to fencing, although she thought that boxing was best. Rather humorously, for anyone who has ever been hit with any type of boxing or mixed martial arts (MMA) glove, she claims that a "rap" from a specially made ten-ounce boxing glove would not feel like more than a "straw tickle." She explained to the paper that women were becoming increasingly independent and that part of that freedom required them to learn to protect themselves. Stewart remained the most prolific and famous female boxer of the late nineteenth century, although she shared the spotlight with another Hattie for a short time.

HATTIE LESLIE

Elizabeth Wilkinson Stokes remains Britain's most prized championess, but in the United Sates, the first lady of boxing, Hattie Leslie, has been totally forgotten in the annals of pugilistic history. Born in 1868, in Buffalo, New York, Leslie was, according to the *National Police Gazette*, considered the "champion female pugilist of the world" who "challenge[d] any woman in the world."[40] A veritable Amazon, Leslie weighed 199 pounds and stood five feet, seven and a half inches tall, and she was described as a "good-looking brunette" who "[did] not look tough."[41] Per the *Cincinnati Enquirer*, Leslie was a "boxer of unusual ability" who "knocked out pretty fair fighters in practicing with them."[42] Leslie met Gussie Freeman in the ring in 1882, and the formidable Leslie reportedly frustrated Freeman to no end.

On September 16, 1888, Leslie boxed Alice Leary at eight o'clock in the morning on Navy Island. Both women are described as actresses, but they apparently had enough pugilistic training to be knowledgeable of the Queensbury rules. Leary was described as "very hard with her fists," "more quarrelsome," and "more of a slugger" than Leslie.[43] The bout was highly publicized, although the title of the *Cincinnati Enquirer* article on the upcoming fight on July 11, 1888, proclaims, "Both of them should be arrested."[44] This invective may have been steeped in sexism, since the two fighters were women, but there was legal precedence for arresting prizefighters.

The *Daily Inter Ocean* published the story of the bout, dubbed it a "disgraceful affair" where "Leslie knocked out her opponent—not so good looking now." The women fought seven three-minute rounds for a $250 purse. The article describes the fight in detail, beginning with the women's outfits: "Hattie wore white tights and a sleeveless shirt, and Alice had on black ones."[45] The *National Police Gazette* writes that instead of padded boxing gloves, the women wore "driving kids, lined with a thin coating of flannel . . . the ends of the fingers and thumbs were clipped, and the cording was taken out to avoid cutting the faces of the fighters."[46] While it may be assumed that these early MMA-style gloves would have done less damage to the fighters' skin, most modern fighters would not want to be struck with them.

Although the *Daily Inter Ocean* labels the battle "disgusting" and the competitors "disfigured," it also admits that the women fought well. According to the article, Leslie and Leary "slogged each other in regular male professional style. . . . The women fought like tigresses at times, but hit no foul blows. After the fight both made their toilets, came back to Buffalo, and had their disfigured faces and bodies attended to by physicians."[47] The headline for this bout appeared at the top of the page, directly above a short article about famed boxer John L. Sullivan, who was, says the paper, in ill health at the time. Sullivan, a famous pugilist with a history of debauchery, was often cited in newspaper stories. The positioning of the post on the Leslie–Leary fight above the blurb on Sullivan would have been significant in 1888. They were, in fact, headliners of the fighting world.

The *Cincinnati Enquirer* deems Leslie and Leary "female brutes" in their coverage of the fight.[48] But most surprising were the legal hearings in the aftermath. On October 3, 1888, the New York district attorney brought charges against the men who participated as seconds and the managers of both Leslie and Leary. Per the *Chicago Tribune*, they were charged with aiding in a prizefight, which, while sometimes "tolerated" with men, was never allowed between women. The district attorney did not necessarily blame the women as much as the men, whom he believed incited the women to compete in the violent event. He explained that the men who abetted in this fight

> must have forgotten the mother that bore them. They must have forgotten that their mother was a woman, and I trust as an outcome of this affair that these men shall be severely punished at the hands of the law, and that never again can it be said that men can get together and pollute the honor of womankind.[49]

Everyone involved, including the women, was tried, and their defense was that the fight was a "sham," an event performed as entertainment rather than a true fight; however, the previous descriptions of the bout and the women's bruised and battered faces indicate that the fight was, indeed, a reality. The jury agreed with the district attorney, and the men who seconded the fight were found guilty and instructed to pay $500 in fines. While the district attorney seemed hesitant to blame the "softer sex," he must have mustered up the courage to indict them, because both women spent six months in prison for their wrongdoing.

Nonetheless, this was not the end of Leslie's pugilistic career; in fact, it was just getting started. She would continue to be a source of fascination and disgust in late nineteenth-century American culture. One of the interesting things about Leslie is that her image appeared in various publications from time to time. The September 6, 1890, edition of the *National Police Gazette* includes a full-page layout of pictures of various boxers, including Leslie. Beneath the images of five male boxers, a full-sized profile of Leslie appears on the left, while on the right, there is a picture of two black women facing off before a judge. Leslie, the "handsome female champion pugilist of the world," stands with bare arms in what appears to be fitted breeches, an uncommon outfit for a woman in the late nineteenth century (see figure 2.1).

In the same publication, to the left of Leslie's picture, the *Police Gazette* published a photo and brief snippet of the renowned professor Alf Ball and his "famous colored boxers" (see figure 2.2). The women were "creating such a furor by the scientific display they [made] with the gloves" and could "hit, stop, counter, and upper-cut equal to Hattie Leslie, the female champion of America."[50] Unlike Leslie, they did not receive personal recognition; their names are noticeably absent from the announcement. In addition, it is Ball, the white "professor" of boxing, who is lauded for his skill in teaching the women to fight instead of recognizing their aptitude to do so.

There are several occasions where black fighters are mentioned without their names, as though their identities were tied solely to their skin color. But in 1882, Bessie Williams and Josephine Green, both heavyweight boxers, fought in Salt Lake City.[51] Williams and Green are both described as weighing in at more than 280 pounds and being expert in the manly art of pugilism. The fight was highly anticipated, as both women were reputed to be excellent and brutal boxers. With a $20 purse and the

Figure 2.1.   "She Hits Hard" in the *National Police Gazette*. Courtesy of National Police Gazette Enterprises, LLC.

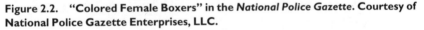

Figure 2.2. **"Colored Female Boxers"** in the *National Police Gazette*. **Courtesy of National Police Gazette Enterprises, LLC.**

title of colored lady champion on the line, the women knocked one another around the ring until Williams succeeded in knocking out Green with a hard right to the nose. The ladies were lauded for their skills, but the majority of nonwhite fighters at the time were routinely ignored and marginalized, both for their sex and skin color.

As a white woman, however, Leslie continually had her name and picture in print. Another portrait of Hattie Leslie, published in the *National Police Gazette* on October 8, 1892, features the recently deceased fighter in a more revealing outfit, legs and arms bare. Posing in the typical boxing stance, her tight-fitting blouse and short skirt are prominent, while her face, partly hidden in the shadows, recedes; however,

Leslie's face is unmistakably beautiful and her features sharp and striking (see figure 2.3).

A year after her bout with Alice Leary, Hattie Leslie was once again in the news with the announcement of an upcoming bout with Ethel Marks. An article published in the *Cincinnati Enquirer* on December 19, 1889, announces that this "novel match" would indeed be novel, because instead of their usual manner of boxing, Leslie and Marks would wrestle in the Greco-Roman style.[52] According to the paper, this would be a first for this type of exhibition, so the fighters and their backers met to agree to terms, which were as follows:

> Articles of agreement entered into by and between Hattie Leslie, party of the first part, and Miss Ethel Marks, party of the second part. Said parties hereby agree to meet in a wrestling match on a day to be named hereafter, under the following conditions: The said party of the first part agrees to throw the said party of the second part four times in an hour, actual wrestling time, or forfeit a purse of $100.[53]

The agreement also stipulates that "all dangerous locks, such as the hang and strangling holds, are hereby barred by mutual agreement."[54] As always with female fighters, the clothing was part of the prefight negotiations: "Both contestants also agree that they will wear costumes appropriate to the occasion, that will be presentable before any kind of an audience." Even more interesting, the weight of the fighters was agreed to before the fight, just as weight classes are contested and settled today. The women simply agreed that neither would weigh in at more than 220 pounds at the time of the match.

Two days later, the *Enquirer* reported that the match was, indeed, a go. The women, described as "mountains of flesh," are both lauded in terms of their beauty, size, and athletic achievements. Writes the *Enquirer*, "The match, aside from the novelty of the participants being women, ought to be a good one from an artistic standpoint."[55] Marks was a weight lifter but also skilled in numerous athletic endeavors. As the newspaper suggests, the bout promised to be entertaining.

However, on December 29, 1889, the *Enquirer* reported that the bout was rather embarrassing, with the two women "rolling about the canvas as graceful as baby elephants in the straw."[56] The newspaper, often changing its opinion of Leslie from beautiful and skilled to fleshy and "elephantine," declares that her fighting ability was "75 percent wildcat

Figure 2.3. Hattie Leslie in the *National Police Gazette*. Courtesy of National Police Gazette Enterprises, LLC.

power."[57] Despite the earlier agreement to arrive at the fight at less than 210 pounds, Marks checked in at a reported 225 pounds, while Leslie came in at 220 pounds. The weight advantage appeared to have worked in Marks's favor, as several of Leslie's attempts to take her down for a pin of sorts were thwarted.

Leslie, on the other hand, managed to get off several good throws, including one in which she picked up her opponent and tossed her onto the mat. Both women were apparently frustrated and angry at various times during the match, resorting to such illegal moves as striking and kicking, even though they were restricted from wrestling, the wager being whether Leslie could throw Marks to the mat four times in an hour. Despite her best efforts and the enthusiasm of the crowd, Leslie failed to meet her goals.

Only a few months later, the women planned to meet again for a wrestling match. The *Cincinnati Enquirer* reported on January 5, 1890, that this second fight was a "female fake," although the women did study with professional wrestlers in preparation for the event. Per the *Cincinnati Enquirer*, fans were dissatisfied with the bout, claiming it to be a "fake."[58] The match reportedly looked as though it had been planned out in advance, with some viewers claiming that the ladies were whispering instructions to one another. The paper concludes that the women's seconds were enraged after the bout and that a subsequent fight between the two men in a catch-as-catch-can style soon followed.[59] Whether the fight was a theatrical performance or arranged to drum up interest in forthcoming events, it remains a historic moment for female wrestling in the late nineteenth century.

On September 25, 1892, Hattie Leslie passed away at the young age of twenty-three from a battle with typhoid fever in Milwaukee, Wisconsin. Her husband, John Leslie, nursed her throughout her illness. Typhoid, an illness born of contaminated food and water, was a prevalent calamity of the nineteenth century; however, by the 1890s, it was largely on the decline compared to previous years.[60] At the time of her death, Hattie was engaged at the People's Theater, where she gave "sparring exhibitions with a male opponent."[61] Her passing was commemorated in the *National Police Gazette* with a full-page image, as well as the headline "Hattie Leslie's Last Round" in Milwaukee's *Sunday Sentinel*.

Leslie remains an enigma in women's pugilistic history. Was she an actress or a fighter? Many of her bouts are labeled "performances," and her career as an actress is often mentioned in articles and press releases. Yet, she undeniably competed in various fighting matches, including the famous bout with Alice Leary, in which both women emerged with bruised faces and bloody knuckles. Her somewhat seedy second wrestling match with Ethel Marks may have been arranged, but their first fight appears to have been genuine. Leslie fought hard to throw her larger opponent, and while she succeeded a few times, she was ultimately unable to achieve the promised four throws. Their second fight may have been fixed, or it may have simply been cleaner than the first because both women knew what to expect and received some training from professional Greco-Roman wrestlers. But if it was rigged, perhaps Leslie and Marks acquiesced to promote their male seconds. Regardless, Leslie died young and would have unquestionably continued her fighting career if not for the fatal disease that took her down.

GUSSIE FREEMAN: SLASHER OF THE ROPEWALKS

Toward the end of the nineteenth century, the American media became more accepting of female boxers, even in large metropolises. In 1891, Gussie Freeman entered the boxing community with a nonchalant attitude regarding gender and social norms that shocked and delighted newspaper outlets and fans alike. An article in the November 22, 1891, edition of the *Brooklyn Daily Eagle* names Freeman the "Slasher of the Ropewalks." "Gus" is described as a "born fighter" who "never cared for the society of people of her own sex, except to meet them at a bout of fisticuffs and to glory in their inevitable discomfiture."

Freeman's prowess in the ring was recognized during her bout with Hattie Leslie, in which the two women apparently set to "bruising" one another in 1882. At the time of the bout, Freeman was twenty-five years old, weighed 175 pounds, and was reported to be "afraid of nothing that walks on the ground."[62] According to the *New Hampshire Sentinel*, more than two thousand spectators, including women, packed into a tiny hall to watch the two women fight for a $25 purse. The winner of the fight was never determined, because the police interrupted the bout, although not until the ladies had "cut and battered" one another and been "covered with their own blood."[63] The sixteen policemen required to separate the women were part of the audience and only jumped in, according to the account, after the crowd went into a frenzy while watching Leslie and Freeman's bloody, yet skillful, brawl. While some people felt uneasy about such brutal contact between women, the media recognized that Freeman was a unique and fascinating woman, worthy of admiration, mixed with condescending pity and scorn.

Female boxers typically did not occupy the higher orders of the American social strata. Most of these women, and men as well, worked with their hands (literally), which set them apart from the middle and upper classes, which feared the elements of hard work. It was the prerogative of the growing American middle class to emulate aspects of the upper crust, while also forming habits and conventions that demonstrated the new respectability of the bourgeoisie, and the term *respectability* was of the utmost importance to middle-class Americans in the late nineteenth century. Men and women avoided any type of behavior linking them to the lower echelons of society. Female pugilists, of course, automatically revealed themselves to be outside the normative middle-class ideology via their participation in fighting; however, many of these women presented themselves as respectable, or at least a simulacrum of Victorian American propriety, outside the ring. Both Hattie Stewart and Hattie Leslie dressed in the appropriate middle-class female garb when not in the midst of fighting. One can imagine that barring any bruises or cuts from training, female fighters might have looked like any other middle-class lady on the streets.

Unlike Stewart and Leslie, who maintained some semblance of culturally normative femininity, Gussie Freeman was known for her masculine ways, as she swaggered amongst men, smoking a pipe, drinking whiskey, and swearing like a sailor. Despite her shockingly unfeminine practices, Freeman was not a low-born lady, but the product of a "Long Island family of excellent reputation."[64] Like Babe Didrikson, the famous female golfer, she was an inveterate athlete, playing numerous sports and even besting professional baseball player Jack Cassidy by throwing farther than he did one day. Freeman's mother was reportedly brokenhearted by this anomaly of a daughter, who defied her mother's instruction and acted more like a boy than the lady-like child of a Long Island matron. Nonetheless, although Freeman was no elegant lady, she did nothing to blacken her name morally. She was "simply a tough girl,"[65] but not an amoral one (except for the swearing, I imagine).

Freeman's boxing skills were praised by publications throughout the country.[66] Like many boxers of the period, she would appear at a venue for a specified number of days, taking on all challengers as an exhibition of her skill. She challenged Hattie Stewart to a bout in February 1893, for a purse worth at least $1,000. At the time of her challenge, Freeman weighed 220 pounds, but her manager asserted that she could cut to 180 for the fight and still be strong. She apparently had a financial backer who would provide a purse of any price as long as the women were able to fight uninterrupted by the police.

In 1893, boxing matches were allowed to continue as long as the contestants wore four-ounce gloves, the same size and weight as the glove used in modern MMA. Interestingly, Freeman's manager was named John Leslie, the widower of boxing legend and recently deceased Hattie Leslie Hattie and Gussie purportedly met for a match at some point before the former's death. In 1941, an editor for the *Brooklyn Daily Eagle* recalled Gussie "giving a good account of herself until her hair came down in her face and she lost temper. The crowd went wild with excitement, and I thought there would be a riot." John Leslie coached Gussie in the aftermath of his wife's death, perhaps feeling sympathy for the woman who lost to the undefeated championess. [67]

Freeman entered the world of business in her typical unladylike fashion by opening up a saloon in Brooklyn, but she continued to train and fight as well. In April 1894, she appeared at the Howard Athenaeum in Boston, Massachusetts, and fought alongside the delightfully named Fatty Langtry, a famous male boxer of the period.[68] Langtry and Freeman trained together in preparation for their matches, evidence that some male and female boxers worked as training partners during this time. Freeman used her sparring experience with Langtry in 1895, when she pummeled one George Schmitzer, an iceman who had insulted her and denied the supply of ice he typically provided for her saloon. At this point, her weight had crept up to a ponderous 250 pounds, and at nearly six feet tall, she was solidly built and technically sound as a pugilist. After confirming that Schmitzer, a diminutive man of only 120 pounds, did indeed slander her, Freeman demanded that he face her in the typical stance. She then roundly thrashed him, despite his efforts at a defense, and left him knocked out in front of a crowd of hundreds. Her legacy remains one of a joyfully unique woman who lived as she wished to live without adhering to the social standards of the day. And like all of the female pugilists explored in this chapter, she courageously delighted in her craft, despite criticism or social obligations to do otherwise.

NINETEENTH-CENTURY FIGHT PROMOTION

Historically, fights were organized by venue promoters, for example, the *National Police Gazette*'s Richard Fox, or via the press through a series of challenges. This aspect of fighting sports continues, of course, with Ronda Rousey famously calling out Miesha Tate in 2011 (see chapter 5). In the pre-Internet days, challenges were made through newspaper advertisements and interviews à la the British championess Elizabeth Wilkinson Stokes. The language of these self-aggrandizing challenges has remained consistent throughout time: The fighter declares herself to be the best at her sport. Then the fighter puts forth her requirements, for instance, a weight limit, although she typically asserts to be willing to meet all comers. Finally, the challenge ends with a taunt, wherein the fighter declares that any person who meets her will only fall, because she is, in fact, the championess of the world.[69] Champion fighters might appear at a venue and wait for an opponent or two to appear. Cora Livingstone, an early twentieth-century wrestler (see chapter 3), fought whomever showed up to take her up on her challenge, which sometimes meant two or three bouts each night. But many fights were set up following a newspaper challenge through the venue hall or coach of the primary fighter.

Nevertheless, plenty of boxing matches still occurred, not just for sport, but to settle personal vendettas between fighters. In 1894, Elizabeth Jones and Florence Zip of Indiana battled over a lover, but the fight was surprisingly by the book.[70] The women agreed to the Queensbury rules and fought to the finish, which was a brutal one. Jones knocked Zip out in the first round, and the latter broke her arm during the fall.

Fighting sports continued to operate within the margins of society, outside of the normal practices of "real ladies" whose primary objective in life was to nab a husband, start a family, and maintain her home. Yet, as the last decade of the nineteenth century progressed, the desire for female fragility diminished, as doctors and social thinkers advocated for women's health and well-being. One function of creating a new generation of healthy girls far removed from their pale and fragile mothers and grandmothers who sought to look anemic was an increase in promoting women's sports.

WOMEN IN SPORTS

In the final few years of the century, women's participation in sports grew and became more widely accepted in the United States. An 1893 article in the *Atchison Daily Globe* declares that women had attempted almost every type of popular sport and were much the better off for it: "During the past few years, woman has been doing well so many things that were considered exclusively within the province of man that the term *weaker sex* has been losing strength almost as rapidly as woman has been gaining it."[71] The paper recognizes certain women who were unusually skilled, including female sharpshooters like Annie Oakley, female swimmers, billiards players, horseback riders, and weight lifters. As for female pugilists, it claims that except for a handful of skilled women, the "less said about [the rest of them] the better." While the paper praises the efforts of women in other sporting practices, it denounces pugilistic efforts amongst women, stating, "The late Hattie Leslie was the best-known woman boxer, but happily her handful of successors have been so little encouraged that they are rarely heard of." The article concludes by claiming that fighting women have no place in the United States, although saying that they "may be all right in Dahomey," an African nation.[72] Thus, female fighters became associated with the Other, the savage, the exotic, the freak.

It is certainly this "otherness" that made female fighters a regular part of the sensational style of journalism found in the *National Police Gazette*. In 1892, the *Police Gazette* published a compendium on women in the prize ring, which, although entertaining, was not necessarily historically accurate. The paper praises a woman named Lib Kelly, a "tall, athletic-looking girl" who possessed a "long reach and understood how to hit, stop, and counter to perfection."[73] Kelly fought in the late 1870s and was always victorious. She went on to inspire numerous female pugilists in the United States, including Hattie Stewart, who the paper describes as a "beautiful specimen of physical development," and that when she was "stripped," "she looked a perfect amazon." Fellow champion Hattie Leslie is also deemed a "famous Amazon" and "powerful specimen of humanity."[74] The *Police Gazette* treats all three women as legitimate athletes, even while they sensationalize their fights in other articles. But unlike many other newspapers that criticized and condemned female pugilists, the *Police Gazette* celebrated the women who entered the ring and made Richard Fox a great deal of money through tournaments sponsored by the newspaperman.

In November 1894, the *Los Angeles Times* reported rather acidly that "women [were] certainly driving men from many fields," including the sport of wrestling.[75] A small town in Austria hosted a women-only wrestling tournament, during which six women competed in a wrestling match in front of four hundred lively spectators. The American newspaper declared it a "disgusting exhibition," but the Austrian crowd was delighted. Even so, the women were not well-versed in the science of wrestling, and participants quickly resorted to hair pulling.[76] The spectacle obviously generated enough interest in Austria to create an international story. Several different newspapers covered this and other female wrestling events in the late nineteenth century.

Whether the women were praised for their skill or ridiculed for their lack thereof, newspapers treated female wrestling events as performances, rather than displays of sport. Female fighters became even more associated with the idea of spectacle when a Parisian music hall featured female wrestlers alongside typical venue performances.[77] The women were large and strong, but somewhat disconcertingly, were given typically feminine stage names, for example, Fleurette and Mimi. The bouts consisted of intense throws and slams, as well as pins. Parisian citizens appeared to have enjoyed the shows, but reports in the United States, the land of the Puritans, deemed them unpleasant.[78]

Yet, in 1897, the *Washington Post*, a more imposing and critical publication than the *Atchison Daily Globe*, published an article praising the new female pugilist, at least to a certain extent. Even though women were already practicing boxing, the *Post* declares that while women had made strides in other sporting activities, the "boxing woman . . . so far outranks all of the others so that they should not be mentioned in the same breath." Of course, the article explains that these women could not hurt themselves or anyone else because their gloves were so padded and their arms "not hard enough to land a blow sufficiently stiff" to cause injury. Furthermore, the purpose of the new gymnasiums designed to teach women the art of boxing focused on technique and exercise, not the art of fighting. Boxing was not only acceptable to the writers at the *Post* as a form of exercise; the fashionable society of New York flocked to the new, chic boxing gyms in droves.

The boxing master at the New York gym told plump upper-class matrons that boxing was the "speediest and most healthful method for the annihilation of superfluous flesh,"[79] but he was quick to explain to the *Post* that his students were not learning to box for self-defense, because he considered it highly unlikely that a woman would ever need to defend herself. Nor, he emphatically declared, did he think it reasonable for a woman to box competitively. He explained his position, commenting, "It is all nonsense about women boxing. A woman can't box because, if you hit her in the chest or the wind, you not only knock the breath out of her body, but you run the risk of starting some awful disease like cancer or something of that sort."[80]

It is unclear where the master got this idea of "starting cancer" via a blow to the chest, but it reinforces the concept that a woman's health, while benefitting from light exercise, is a fragile thing. The women at this particular gym learned the rudimentary skills and science of boxing, which were performed more like a dance than a brawl. According to the boxing master, women were better at precision than their male counterparts. Yet, this instructor asserted that women were decidedly less aggressive than men and needed to be urged to punch and use their usual posture of defense.[81] Ultimately, the purpose of this facility was to get women in shape, as svelte, light figures were preferable, much like they are today; however, some of the young women who trained in these posh gymnasiums were able to take their skills to the streets when necessary. A group of young women from Vassar soundly flattened a tramp going through the pockets of their unguarded coats while they were bathing at a local beauty spot.[82]

Boxing for exercise may have been approved to a certain extent for young women near the turn of the century, but fighting as a career remained on the margins of respectability. In California, a liberally inclined state even then, the *San Francisco Chronicle* published an article praising a young boxer, Miss Cecil Richards, as both a skillful and ladylike fighter.[83] The paper describes Richards as rivaling a Flaubert novel, portraying her healthy, slim figure and rosy complexion as the epitome of feminine beauty. The article primarily focuses on how lovely Richards was and suggests that boxing might become more socially acceptable if women like her would step into the ring—or at least it might not be as disgusting a spectacle if the fighters were attractive. Richards confessed to the paper that the reason she became a boxer was to make money, the same reason why anyone chooses a profession. Perhaps Californians were less judgmental about how young ladies spent their time than the social circles in New York and Boston. For Richards in 1897, boxing was as good a job as any, and spectators seemed to agree.

This article acts as a microcosm of the attitude toward female fighters at the turn of the century. The general public was fascinated, especially by shapely young girls performing in the ring; however, there remained the cultural stigma that boxing could be morally, socially, and physically corrupting. The divisive perspectives on female pugilists prevailed long into the twentieth century, but boxing, wrestling, and other fighting sports would only grow in popularity and practice, as we will see.

3

FIGHTING AS SPECTACLE

In 1904, the *New York Times* published a rather hilariously condescending article, "And Now It's the Boxing Girl," about the newest fad amongst young women. It assures readers that boxing would remain a man's sport and that women would never "invade the ringside. Heaven forbid!" Young women could practice the "science and skill" of boxing, "with all the brutality left out." And, of course, like many fitness articles assert today, the piece relates that boxing is great exercise—its ultimate appeal to the new "it girl," who apparently longed to squeeze into tight-waisted frocks.[1]

Most of the advice in the article is condescending and, at times, ludicrous, but the first set of instructions for young women, following a guide outlining proper boxing attire, explains the importance of wearing gloves. Six-ounce gloves were standard at the time, which was vastly different than the sixteen-ounce gloves now standardized by most boxing facilities. In fact, the six-ounce gloves are incredibly small and hard, since they are constructed from leather. Luckily, according to one boxing master interviewed for the piece, women were lousy at boxing because they were too excited and not calm or cool enough to fight. Thus, the new "boxing girl" boxed only for the thrill of the sport or the ability to boast to her friends; however, this boxing instructor believed that nervous women, whom, he says, are always thin, should not box, because it is too strenuous. Instead, boxing should be reserved for the "overweights, for the sluggish, phlegmatic women who take on pounds faster than they can let out the seams of their clothes."

The patronizing tone of the piece is obvious, but it happens to contain a few gems regarding the structure of some of these twentieth-century boxing gyms. The standard length of a round between men was three minutes, while women fought for two. In addition, men took one minute of rest between rounds, just like today, but women were given three minutes of rest between the two-minute rounds. This rest was ostensibly intended to revive the stout woman between rounds, although she was not allowed to go near an open window or the water cooler. As the author explains, this three minutes of rest would feel far shorter than the two minutes of hard work in the ring.

SPORTING WOMEN

The twentieth century could be considered the beginning of the modern sports craze. Women's activities expanded significantly in the early twentieth century, as sports and exercise became more socially acceptable, due in part to the support of several upper-class women. In 1894, Lady Greville published *Ladies in the Field*, a guide to women's sports that includes contributions from Lady Boynton and the Duchess of Newcastle.[2] The text discusses ten female-appropriate activities, including riding, hunting, cycling, and various types of shooting, including kangaroo and tiger hunting. Greville claims that sports can improve one's spirits, since ladies enjoy the bracing air of the refreshing outdoors just as much as gentlemen. She writes that riding, specifically, improves the appetite and makes "black shadows and morbid fancies disappear from the mental horizon," perhaps referencing the trend of hysteria amongst middle- and upper-class women.[3] Hysteria was a common medical diagnosis in the nineteenth century for women suffering from mental psychosis or women who wanted to live outside of the patriarchal structure.

Greville anticipated the type of criticism that would almost certainly accompany the promotion of sports amongst upper-class women by choosing sports that reinforced gendered norms and did not make a woman less feminine. Her position in the aristocracy situated her arguments within a specific and socially defined group because the upper echelons of society had different rules than the middle and, especially, lower classes. But her book normalized the desire for women to take part in physical activities, retrieving the female body from the fainting couches of the nineteenth century and releasing them to some semblance of freedom in the new century.

Of course, in England, aristocratic women were only encouraged to engage in activities befitting their social position, for instance, hunting and riding. Women in the middle classes were under less pressure to conform to certain social codes. At the turn of the century, doctors began encouraging young women to exercise to maintain their health and improve the strength of the American and British "races." Furthermore, this time period saw leisure and play as normal parts of modern life. Walking, hiking, and calisthenics became widely practiced by all classes (with the exception of the British aristocracy, to a certain extent).

HEALTH IS BEAUTY, UGLINESS IS A SIN

In 1902, Bernarr Macfadden, a well-known editor who published the type of magazine that we are familiar with today, produced a new periodical focusing on female beauty and health. The magazine, entitled *Woman's Health and Beauty*, promoted female strength and beauty through physical and mental development. The first edition includes articles on how to increase one's bust size through strength training; a lesson in fencing; tips on how to improve sleep; information on how to combat invalidism in young girls; as well as an advice column covering such topics as menstruation, drug addiction, and weight loss.

There is something quite modern about this magazine, which is now more than one hundred years old; it reads like an Edwardian-era *Self* magazine, although the second edition features a rather hilarious article about how to train a baby girl, which includes exercises for her to do, including a type of pull-up that seems incongruous with the type of child-rearing advice one would see in *Self* today. This British magazine may have been a bit overzealous in its columns about training children, but the publication offers good advice about certain topics. Women were encouraged to exercise more and get outside and prize strength rather than frailty. *Women's Health and Beauty* provides step-by-step instructions on how to properly fence, lift weights, do gymnastics, and stretch. While a majority of the British may have been willing to accept Macfadden's council of physical health, they were not disposed to treat female boxers as harmless eccentrics in the way that they had done one hundred years earlier.

In the late nineteenth century, American men and women began weight lifting using tools like the Indian clubs, which were weighted sticks, to perform movements that increased strength and flexibility. Roller-skating, tennis, and golf were wildly popular activities for women, all of which required specific gear and clothing, making these particular sports reserved for the middle and upper classes. But the most popular sport to arise in the early twentieth century was bicycling, although it initially created scandal amongst critics that women would be physically and morally corrupted. Women could not ride sidesaddle, so the implications of a young woman straddling a bicycle seat suggested that a woman's genitalia could be damaged or excited, both alarming prospects. Bicycle manufacturers eventually updated the design to accommodate women's skirts over the bar, which explains why women's bikes are dipped in the middle, while men's have a high bar.[4]

Cycling offered opportunities for young courting couples to spend time together, away from the prying eyes of overly protective guardians and meddling parents. Cycling races also became popular, but the bicycle was initially a mode of mobility and freedom, rather than a mode of competition. The first modern Olympic Games took place in Athens in 1896, and four years later, in 1900, in Paris, women joined in the competition. Cycling was one of many sports in the first modern Olympic Games, although women would not compete in cycling events until much later.

Wrestling was part of the first modern Olympic Games, and boxing became part of the Olympic program in 1904. Both sports maintained their popularity in American culture, even though matches still took place amongst the seedier stratas of society. For women, the early twentieth century was, surprisingly, a good time to compete in boxing and wrestling. It was not until both sports gained governing bodies that women were officially banned from competing.

During the early part of the twentieth century, boxing and wrestling matches primarily occurred on the traveling circuit, at circuses and carnivals. Unfortunately, the legacy of boxing as a sideshow would continue throughout the twentieth century, and even today, as fighting sports are sometimes referred to as "freak shows" by critics; however, with the dawning of the new century, performing in traveling circuses was considered a way to make a good living for some people, especially immigrants. And while some classes of society may look back at these carnivals as demeaning spectacle, plenty of performers have fond memories of that bygone era.

In the Depression-era United States and Europe, women wrestlers were a source of entertainment for many working-class people. These wrestlers were doubly marginalized because of their gender and economic position. In her impressive book *Sporting Females: Critical Issues in the History and Sociology of Women's Sports*, Jennifer Hargreaves recognizes that the women who participated in the "low-life" sports of wrestling and boxing were "ignored by the ideologues of female sports" because they did not conform to the bourgeoisie attitude regarding female athletes.[5] Ideally, female athletes were middle class to upper class, white, and conventionally pretty. These women only participated in sports like tennis, golf, and badminton, which were appropriate for their natural sex. Wrestling and boxing were not only too violent for women, they were considered damaging to the female physique. Yet, boxing proliferated in sports and popular culture at the turn of the century.

BOXING

Thomas Edison famously produced a short film in 1901, featuring two female boxers. It was a precursor of the forthcoming film industry and is still considered one of Edison's great productions. In this picture, currently available through the Library of Congress, sisters Bessie and Minnie Gordon touch gloves and engage in lively sparring sessions, while wearing thick, knee-length dresses with short sleeves. The sisters display fancy footwork, although their hands are a bit wilder than our current conception of the sweet science. The Gordon sisters are therefore well-documented in their pugilistic endeavors, but not all boxers from that time period can provide evidence of their prowess in the ring. And in an age where notoriety became synonymous with fame, some people claimed to have extensive careers in fighting, although no one can prove this to be true. In most cases, the truth probably lies somewhere in between.

POLLY BURNS: FEMALE BOXING CHAMPION?

The story of Polly Burns, also known as Polly Fairclough, circulated in the late 1990s, after the release of the documentary *My Grandmother Was a Boxer*, produced by Polly's great-granddaughter, Catherine Morley. Burns is often cited as one of the first female boxing champions, although as we have seen, that is not the case (see Elizabeth Wilkinson Stokes). In fact, much of the information we have regarding Burns and her boxing career is uncorroborated. This does not mean that she was not a boxer, but simply that she did not enter the records at the time. Many people argue that Burns's exclusion is due to shoddy record keeping and a lack of recognition for female practitioners in the art of boxing. Nonetheless, this book demonstrates that records of female boxers, even prior to the twentieth century, do indeed exist.

Much of the information about Burns's boxing career comes from her descendants, who point to articles that have either been permanently lost or perhaps exist in someone's personal collection, unavailable to academic databases and search engines. Most articles about the fighter use Morley's documentary as the primary source, which is currently unavailable for viewing. Those who have seen the film, which aired in 1999, on the Irish television network RTE, have admitted being disappointed by the lack of hard evidence of Burns's fighting days.[6] One of her grandsons, who was unaware that Morley was related to his grandmother, tried to contact the filmmaker but was unable to establish any connection to his supposed cousin or her production team. He believed this was because the filmmakers assumed he might try to discredit the documentary.[7] This family turmoil does not necessarily indicate that Burns was not a boxer. Indeed, her grandchildren grew up hearing about her boxing career. But it is difficult to believe that there would not have been any articles written about her exploits given the popularity of boxing at the time, the sensationalism of female fighters in the media, and the rumor of her most famous fight, which would have created a media storm.

In her documentary, Morley asserts that Burns once fought an exhibition match in Dublin against the world heavyweight champion, Jack Johnson. This feat, if nothing else, should have made headlines. In 1916, a match between Helen Hildreth and John Atkinson at a gymnasium received media attention, as well as police interference. The 103-pound Hildreth boxed the 105-pound Atkinson for two rounds. As the *Washing-*

ton Post delightfully describes, Hildreth threw a "succession of jabs, hooks, swings, uppercuts, and straight punches" that "materially changed the general ensemble of Mr. Atkinson's features before the first round ended."[8] The fight continued for another round, and Hildreth had Atkinson against the ropes when the police broke in and stopped the fight.

The bout took place at a gymnasium in front of a crowd and warranted a respectably detailed story in the newspaper. The idea that a fight between Burns and the famous Johnson would not have been featured in the news media seems unlikely. In fact, the only news story about Burns prior to the 1990s was her death notice in 1959.[9] The obituary is exceedingly colorful, with stories about her early life as a circus performer who at the ages of six and eight wrestled lions and sadly saw her trapeze artist mother fall to her death. Burns supposedly knocked her future husband out when she was sixteen years old and then went on to the infamous Johnson match. While the story is delightful and reads suspiciously like a fairy tale, Burns's life as a boxer, especially as one who sparred with Jack Johnson, remains unsubstantiated.

Burns was not the only elderly woman to assert that she had fought a famous male boxer in her youth. In 1989, the *Milwaukee Journal* published the story of a woman named Hessie Donahue, who claimed to have knocked out John L. Sullivan in 1892, during a boxing exhibition.[10] According to Donahue, during an exhibition match, Sullivan hit her a little too hard, and in anger, Hessie nailed him on the jaw with a strong right hand. Donahue claimed that Sullivan was out for almost a minute. The two remained friends after the event because they always believed that the knockout was an accident. While this story, like the one told by Polly Burns, has no documentation, it is a fun narrative, even if it may be amplified and a bit distorted by time.

As for Burns, even the documentary's producer, Adrian Lynch, admitted that the story is more legend than fact, but that does not make it any less interesting; however, there were numerous female fighters of the era whose experiences are substantiated through contemporary media coverage and who also deserve the attention afforded to the fascinating Polly Burns.

GIRLS BOXING GROWS

The late nineteenth-century trend of boxing schools for girls continued in the United States, and, in 1908, twelve-year-old Frances Moyer made headlines when she bested her female cohorts, along with four boys, in Bethlehem, Pennsylvania.[11] While boxing schools may have become respectable for chic young women in New York City seeking fun and diversion through exercise, this particular fight occurred in a vacant lot rather than a gymnasium. Moyer began her day by besting a thirteen-year-old girl, and she then fought four boys in a row, beating them before finishing the standard six rounds. Her last match, against Clarence Moser, was considered a draw, and it was the only bout that went the entire six rounds.

The following year, the *Boston Globe* featured the story of ten-year-old Ruth Townsend, a tough little girl who could defend herself when necessary.[12] Townsend learned to box from her father, who wanted her to be able to take care of herself. She was strong and able to lift more than two hundred pounds, and to the paper, she looked a "picture of health and beauty."[13] But she also had a tough side; after a neighborhood boy bigger than her stole her ball, Townsend knocked him out on her father's advice. Mr. Townsend told her never to seek out a fight, but that she should teach boys to mind their own business and leave her alone. There is no doubt that Ruth, a musician and budding scholar, prevented any further theft or teasing through her father's pugilistic instruction. News reports treat Moyer and Townsend with respect and a bit of admiration, not any type of disgust.

During this period, stories of plucky and adventurous women proliferated, especially in the days preceding the exploits of Amelia Earhart and other female progressives. By 1915, female boxers were so widely accepted that 1,400 women at Tulane Seminary gathered to watch a two-night female boxing event in New Orleans.[14] The first night featured a three-round boxing match between Miss McDonald of Mississippi and Miss Kline of Louisiana. The latter won by decision and earned honors for her home state. The following night included the bout for the 133-pound championship of Mississippi and Louisiana, between Miss Stevens of Louisiana and Miss Coleman of Mississippi. The only man allowed in the room of nearly 1,500 spectators was the referee, which was probably because the women boxed while wearing only bloomers. The location of the fights, a religious university, reveals the acceptance of female boxers in the early twentieth century. But the most shocking aspect of the event was the prevalence of betting; spectators bet candy and gloves on the fight results.[15]

Some society women sponsored boxing and wrestling events to raise money for charity, although these events always featured male fighters.[16] Although female fighters were excluded from the performances, the women behind the benefits fought in their own way. Prizefighting was still unlawful in many parts of the United States, so bouts were held on boats to avoid police interference. Boxing was met with disgust by many people well into the twentieth century. In the United States, Mrs. Victoria Booth Demarest, evangelist and writer of more than one hundred hymns, declared her disgust with the new female athlete, whom she described as "steel-muscled, flat-breasted women" and "channel-swimming, marathon-running Amazons."[17] Demarest may have believed that exercise would make women appear masculine, but that argument was beginning to lose credence as health specialists began advocating for women to exercise.

BRITAIN'S DISCOMFORT WITH FEMALE BOXING

Boxing in early twentieth-century Britain was not as widely accepted as it had been one hundred years prior. Perhaps the vestiges of Queen Victoria's prudish reign remained firmly embedded in the culture, or it may have been that the ravages of World War I left Britain and the continent disinterested in violence as sport. Boxing certainly did not disappear, but it did seem to lose the popularity it had gained during the late nineteenth century's "Cult of Manliness."

There are accounts of several proposed boxing matches between women in the 1920s, including one featuring Annie Newton, the niece of boxing "professor" Andrew Newton. In 1926, a championship match between Annie and Miss Madge Baker was cancelled one week before the fight was scheduled to take place due to extreme pressure from the general public and the home secretary.[18] Understandably, Newton and Baker were disappointed because they felt there was nothing shameful about the entertainment they intended to provide. The promoter of the event was also upset because he wanted to showcase Newton's skill and set up an exhibition for her to spar three male lightweights.[19]

The *Daily Mail* issued an editorial haranguing women's boxing and expressing gratitude that society had not fallen to the lowest level of decency by allowing the match between Newton and Baker to take place.[20] The editorial argues that women's sports were a sign of decadence in an amoral, post–World War I England that had lost all sense of decorum. The paper neglected to remember the more than two hundred years of female pugilistic history in England and instead claims that not only were women's bodies incapable of handling the rigors of boxing, but that they had no place in the sport. The *Daily Mail* continues on its soapbox and declares that the very soul of England was at stake in such a match. Nevertheless the paper graciously admits that women do have some place in sports, although only as spectators.

The Yorkshire Cricket Club considered revoking the right for women to watch cricket matches, and the *Daily Mail* congratulates them on continuing to allow women to occupy a seat, especially since the women were genuinely interested in the game. In addition, the paper notes that allowing women to purchase seats for cricket games greatly increased the revenue for the club, making the inclusion of women a profitable venture for the patriarchal establishment.

FIGHTING ON THE EUROPEAN CONTINENT

At the turn of the century, the French art of savate returned to popularity. Savate, dubbed "boxing with the feet" by the American news media, is French kickboxing. In the history of fighting sports, strict boxing, with hands only, was the primary striking style in the Western world; however, prior to the Queensbury rules, and even after their implementation in some less formal venues, boxing matches would often include strikes to the legs and feet, kicks of all types, and even throws and wrestling. The specific style of kickboxing, as it is known today, did not come into being until the 1970s. Prior to that, numerous cultures had fighting styles that featured punching and kicking, from Muay Thai to San Shou to savate, but kickboxing arguably did not truly gain recognition as a separate sport until Bruce Lee entered the popular lexicon in film in the 1970s.

The popularity of savate in the early twentieth century was rooted in nationalism, something that the French needed at the time. Parisians began to engage in exhibitions of savate at the turn of the century, including the infamous 1902 match between Britain's Jenny Pinkham and France's Mariette Augagneur, who defeated the former by a particularly vicious kick to the stomach, which left poor Pinkham spitting up blood.[21] The strict rules of boxing seemed to be no match for the kicks of savate. In the following years, more women made headlines in France. Twelve young women gave a demonstration of savate at a private club. Another French woman defeated several men using her savate techniques. Savate, however, remained a fringe fighting sport, located primarily in France, compared to the dominant art of boxing. But the more traditional sports of boxing and wrestling would see a number of changes and advances in the twentieth century, especially for women.

In 1926, the home secretary in Ireland denounced a proposed bout between two women, claiming that although he could not officially stop a sparring match (which was lawful because it did not include a prize), he hoped that the "influence of decent public opinion [would] prevent such an outrage from taking place."[22] By that time, boxing had become an international sensation amongst women, and not just because of the calorie-burning potential. Undoubtedly, nearly every country already had some form of fighting art taking place as a sport.

But the sport of boxing, as governed by the Queensbury rules and popularized by such fighters as John L. Sullivan, became increasingly practiced by women in countries like France, Ireland, and Mexico.[23] Mademoiselle Gouraud, niece of the famous French general, made headlines when she knocked out an opponent in 1918.[24] She was known for wearing trousers and reportedly having been the only woman to serve in the French army. Estonian Anette Busch wrestled in Russian troupes and even entered the seemingly impenetrable world of Japanese sumo wrestling in the 1920s.[25] Defeating her male opponents on a regular basis, Busch became a goddess in Japanese culture and was highly sought after in wrestling shows in Japan and throughout the world.

AMERICAN BOXING LEGENDS

Not all the women involved in boxing fought in the ring. Belle Martell was the first woman to act as a referee in the United States. In addition, Martell was also a boxing coach in Los Angeles and a radio sportscaster.[26] Radio brought sports into the home and helped increase awareness of the sport in the United States. Martell hosted a show on KLAC Hollywood three times a week, during which she promoted the sport of boxing and interviewed former and current champion fighters, including wrestlers. In 1929, she married a former boxer who opened his own gym, where she would eventually train and teach. Five years later, she acquired a license to promote boxing in California, and after a few years, she announced, kept time, and finally refereed in 1940. When Martell took the test to become an official boxing referee, she received a 97.5 percent score, two and a half percentage points higher than any male applicant that year.

In spite of this, not everyone in the boxing community supported her quest to become a referee. According to Martell, it was the male sports journalists who "ganged up" on her and convinced the state commission to change their regulatory practices, making it impossible for her to referee fights, even though the commission could not revoke her well-earned license. She circumvented this unfair treatment by refereeing events in her own boxing clubs. She also used her position as a local sportscasting celebrity to support the war efforts through the sale of war bonds, earning a Silver Medal from the U.S. Treasury Department. Martell regularly brought her boxing and wrestling champion friends with her to visit hospitals for paraplegics, presumably men injured in the war. Her charity, in addition to her status as the first female boxing referee, established her reputation as a champion of fighting sports during the twentieth century.

COUNTESS JEANNE LA MARR

Jeanne La Marr had an exciting and tumultuous life, during which she received two titles: countess and welterweight female boxing champion.[27] She claimed she married an Italian count in 1914, although there is no evidence of the union. A 1936 article identifies La Marr as a French woman who participated in a three-round exhibition match with Herbert

"Baby" Stribling. Per the news story, La Marr "swore her mission in life was to place the women of the world on a level with men—by proving her right to be known as the world's champion lady fighter."[28] The fight, however, was more comedic than a serious display of skill.

La Marr's second was a comedian named Michelena who goofed off in her corner by "accidently" catching his fingers in her hair and imitating her opponent's corner by rubbing her legs. La Marr kicked him in the teeth and later bashed him over the head with a stool when he attempted to douse her with water and wipe off her chest with a towel—a standard practice for male fighters but insulting for this lady boxer. The "Countess" may have indeed been successful against female fighters, but in this instance, she apparently tried to have her opponent arrested for striking a woman when he tapped her on the nose with his glove.[29]

The newspaper indicates that La Marr's boxing career was a hoax, but a story in the *Evening Independent* claims that while her title of countess was fake, her boxing was real, although not necessarily in the ring. La Marr certainly knew how to defend herself: She once knocked out a bandit who tried to hold her up and scared off his cronies.[30]

La Marr asserted her own skill in the ring in 1925, when she declared to a judge (she was being arraigned for failing to keep a muzzle on her terrier) that she "knocked out twenty-five women and five men in Europe," but that no one would fight her in the United States.[31] She challenged Babe Didrikson to a match in 1933.[32] Didrikson, considered the greatest female athlete in the United States at the time, was training to fight the other famous Babe, the great Bambino, Babe Ruth himself.[33] She trained at Artie McGovern's famous gymnasium in January 1933, where she did an extensive and exhaustive workout, including a turn on the rowing machine, a routine on an exercise bike, and a few rounds on the heavy bag. Nineteen-year-old Didrikson excelled at numerous sports, although the press accused her of being naïve because she said whatever she thought. She expressed a desire to box with the other Babe, whom she had never met, but Mr. Ruth never showed up to the gym during her visit. The female Babe boxed another man instead, but she never entered the ring with the demanding Jeanne La Marr. It seemed that La Marr would never find the championship bout she desired.

Surprisingly, La Marr's fighting career was not the most scandalous part of her life. In 1938, a skeleton was found in a gully near her ranch home in San Bernardino, California, belonging to her nephew, Gustave van Herren.[34] Young Gustave had gone missing a year earlier, shortly after being released from the state hospital. The skeleton, with a rifle by its side, was found by one of La Marr's employees on a Thursday, although the young man did not report the bizarre finding until the next day. Van Herren's death was ruled a suicide, but that did not stop La Marr's name from being smeared during the investigation.

Papers often pointed out that the title of countess was probably false and constantly reiterated that fact by referring to her as "countess," with quotation marks.[35] Her recent legal trouble was also revealed; she was arrested for drunk driving the day her nephew's body was found. But most damningly, although La Marr denied that her nephew was dead, she had long been receiving mail addressed to him, some of which contained money. Several papers claimed that she was already under investigation by the district attorney for having some type of relationship with the young men working at a nearby Civilian Conservation Corps (CCC) camp. The CCC was a public relief camp, so the insinuation was that the thirty-eight-year-old La Marr had some inappropriate contact with the young men, most of them between the ages of eighteen and twenty-five. La Marr's name does not appear in any public record after this time, and, sadly, her legacy is one of sensationalism and scandal.

WRESTLING

While boxing dominated as the most popular fighting sport in the United States and Europe in the nineteenth century, wrestling had its own period of prominence. It remained a popular, albeit agrarian, sport in Britain and on the European continent in the following centuries and took many forms. With no set rules like the Queensbury style, various types of wrestling emerged in different areas throughout time.

In almost any culture, there exists a type of wrestling specific to that group of people. There are a number of texts that investigate the various types of folk wrestling, which are often organized around the landscape (whether wrestlers wrestle standing up to avoid mud or on the ground in grassy areas) and social structure (which determines whom can wrestle whom). While wrestling has been practiced in cities and courts, the practitioners of wrestling, despite its royal antecedents, primarily lived in rural areas. The country often provided spaces for women to participate in

Figure 3.1. The Bennett Sisters. Courtesy of the Library of Congress.

activities that would have been frowned upon in a more cosmopolitan setting. But in England at the turn of the century, as women pushed for equal civil rights, another form of grappling, Japanese jiu-jitsu, helped them join the fray.

JAPANESE JIU-JITSU ENTERS THE WEST

In the early twentieth century, Japanese jiu-jitsu became the rage for men and women in England and the United States. Prompted by the publication of H. Irving Hancock's *Japanese Physical Training*, Japanese culture was praised for the overall health and physicality of its populace, as well as the discipline and strength of its women. Hancock proposed to publish a subsequent text, *Physical Training of Women by Japanese Methods*, but there is no evidence that such a book ever made it into production. Instead, in 1906, Mrs. Emily Diana Watts published *The Fine Art of Jujutsu*, which extols the close-quarter fighting style as being ideal for both men and women.[36] The book is filled with fantastic action photography featuring the author and her female training partner demonstrating various throws. The purpose of the volume is not to convince the reader to practice jiu-jitsu; rather, it is intended for someone already practicing the art. In other words, Watts wrote the book for an already indoctrinated audience that believed in jiu-jitsu as much as she did. Her quest was not to convince, but to inform. The work is fantastically detailed, with step-by-step instructions for numerous types of throws and maneuvers. A female expert in jiu-jitsu, let alone one who published an authoritative text on the martial art, was a rare find in the early 1900s. The most famous female practitioner of the art was not only a jiu-jitsu teacher, but also an activist, feminist, and fighter.

The craze for Japanese jiu-jitsu flourished, primarily due to its most famous female practitioner in Britain, Mrs. Edith Garrud. Garrud taught jiu-jitsu to the suffragettes in London who were fighting for women's rights. She demonstrated her skill in front of a large crowd by throwing a 220-pound London policeman. The policeman was apparently delighted by Garrud's ability to toss him, as were the many newspapers who covered the demonstration, but the purpose of Garrud's jiu-jitsu practice was to help protect the female suffragettes, some of whom had been bothered by "male rowdies."[37] Garrud also published several articles in *Health and Strength* that explain how women can use the art of jiu-jitsu to protect themselves and performed a series of maneuvers in a play entitled *Ju-Jutsu as a Husband-Tamer*. The story revolves around Liz, played by Garrud, who uses the techniques she learned from Garrud herself to beat her husband into submission.[38]

Garrud remains a legend in self-defense history, but jiu-jitsu did not function as a fighting sport at the time. It was, instead, a physical embodiment of the cause of women's rights. In the early twentieth century, women in England fought for the vote and equal rights, but in a time of strike-breakers and aggressive male opponents, they also had to fight physically for their well-being.

CIRCUS LIFE AND THE SPECTACLE OF WRESTLING

There are numerous examples of women who wrestled hundreds of years ago. In 1799, a Welshwoman named Margaret Evans was such a terrific wrestler that "few young men dared to try a fall with her," even at the ripe age of seventy.[39] Wrestling was typically practiced in rural environments, but by the twentieth century, it had become part of traveling circuses and other types of sensationalized venues. The history of wrestling is interesting, because in the twentieth century, the sport became bifurcated into "professional" wrestling, exemplified today by the WWE (World Wrestling Entertainment) enterprise, and the actual sport of wrestling, primarily seen in the Olympics and in high school and collegiate sports programs. During the early part of the twentieth century, these two typologies, entertainment and sport, were indistinguishable, because the sport was presented as a spectacle amongst other forms of popular entertainment. Wrestling, as explained in the introduction of this book, is a grappling art. Other grappling arts, for instance, Japanese jiu-jitsu, judo, and Brazilian jiu-jitsu, would also emerge in the twentieth century in Japan and Brazil, but this section on the formation of wrestling as a sport of spectacle and skill focuses on the United States and Britain.

As traveling circuses and carnivals became popular in the early twentieth century, fights often took place alongside the strongman, bearded lady, and Siamese twins. In 1895, the *Salt Lake Herald* recounted the delightful affair of the Wallace circus, which featured exotic animals, contortionists, jugglers, and aerial performances. Moreover, there was a woman who performed as a boxer, although it is difficult to tell from the language of the article whether it was a theatrical performance or a legitimate fight.[40] But this was not unusual for boxing or wrestling at the time. There was no compulsion for promoters to reveal to the audience whether a fight was choreographed. The claims from actors and actresses performing as fighters were almost exactly the same as the claims of legitimate prizefighters. By the middle of the twentieth century, both boxing and wrestling had been institutionalized by governing bodies that regulated matches, which, for the most part, put an end to speculation as to whether a fight was real or a performance. But in the early days of the carnival and dance hall wrestling matches, the line between performance and sport was sometimes unclear.

The early twentieth century marked the shift into the two distinct camps of "professional" wrestling and sport wrestling, exemplified by wrestling reentering the Olympic Games after a 1,500-year hiatus. Freestyle wrestling became an Olympic sport in 1904, with Greco-Roman following in 1912. Wrestling continued to be part of the touring entertainment culture in the twentieth century. Wrestlers, boxers, strongmen, and women toured with troupes throughout the United States and England, performing their athletic feats alongside jugglers and acrobats. Traveling athletes were part of the cultural climate, and certain styles, for example, catch-as-catch-can wrestling, flourished. Before the ubiquity of the television in the home, and even before the cinema, circuses and traveling shows were primary forms of entertainment.

Not all wrestling events occurred through the moderately regulated form of the traveling show match. In 1900, in Cumberland, Maryland, a wrestling match occurred between Miss Ada Taylor and a Miss Grass at the hotel where Taylor worked.[41] Taylor boasted that she was the strongest woman in the room, which was immediately denied by other women at the hotel. She challenged all of them to a wrestling match, and Grass took up the charge. Rather graciously, the many spectators in the hotel prepared the room, pushing back the furniture and setting up an appropriate arena for the bout. The women were evenly matched and fought vigorously for some time before Taylor slipped and hit her head on the edge of a large table. She was unconscious for several hours, but despite her injury, the fight was considered a draw. The women tenderly cared for Taylor and resumed being friends again in the aftermath of the fight.

In the United States, the beginning of the twentieth century saw increased interest in the "new girl," a flapper prototype who boxed or wrestled as part of a physical fitness program; however, the sport of wrestling became increasingly popular, in part due to the prominence of the traveling circus, but also because of the rise of a few exciting female wrestlers.

CORA LIVINGSTONE: WRESTLING CHAMPIONESS

Cora Livingstone is considered America's first great female wrestler. She had an extensive career and, in the early twentieth century, was recognized as the world champion female wrestler. Numerous women took up the challenge to face Livingstone in battle, some of whom simply fought to withstand her throws, while others competed with her in the typical Greco-Roman style.

At the time that Livingstone earned the right to declare herself the female champion wrestler of the world, the American press was displeased with female wrestlers because, up until the early 1900s, there had never been a particularly skilled one. This was perhaps because most of the women billed as wrestlers were either actresses pretending to be competent fighters or untrained women looking to fill a particular niche. Livingstone may have been one of the first well-trained wrestlers of the day, which undoubtedly stemmed from her marriage, although it remains unclear to whom she was married. Several sources claim that she was married to lightweight wrestler Carl Livingstone; however, she is also listed as the wife of Mr. Paul Bowser, another wrestler who became a promoter.[42] Most likely, Cora was married to Carl Livingstone, and either by death or divorce, later married the prominent Paul Bowser. The Livingstones were often listed as performers in the same event, so their relationship was unquestionably grounded in the sport of wrestling.

In 1908, Cora shared the headlines with male wrestling champion Ernest Fenby when she entered a week-long engagement at the Avenue Theater in Detroit.[43] Livingstone was billed as the championess wrestler of the world, willing to take on all female comers. Somewhat surprisingly in 1908, young women lined up to meet the champion. The previous week, Livingstone had issued a similar challenge in Cleveland and managed to defeat her opponents.

After the first two nights, the *Detroit Free Press* published an article praising the skill of both Livingstone and Fenby. Livingstone's easy defeat of Florence Hilton was approached with the same simple reverence as her male counterpart. This was a clear departure, as we have seen, from many of the previous approaches the media took with regard to female wrestlers. Livingstone was respected as a fighter and woman. The *Free Press* wrote an extensive article on the lady, complete with a photo of her in a dashing, if rather massive, hat. Livingstone anticipated all critiques of her sport as unwomanly, arguing that plenty of women in 1908 played basketball or bowled, but that wrestling was the best exercise of all. She insisted that she would "keep on wrestling," adding, "I won't be satisfied until I have beaten everybody who has a chance to dispute my title." Much like Elizabeth Wilkinson Stokes, Livingstone's fame grew from her self-aggrandizing challenges in the media, along with regular demonstrations of her skill and prowess on the mat.

Two days before, during the event at which she coheadlined with Fenby, Livingstone had wrestled two women. The rules dictated that she needed to "dispose of them in the allotted time or forfeit $25."[44] It is uncertain whether her opponents were fighting under the same conditions; if not, the agreement obviously recognized Livingstone's superior skill. Her first bout against Bertha Stark was over in a mere three minutes. The *Free Press* suggests that Livingstone went easy on Stark and laid her down gently on the mat rather than the usual hard toss or throw. The fight against Florence Hilton was supposedly more difficult, since Hilton was somewhat knowledgeable about wrestling; however, Livingstone managed to defeat her adversary in a swift five minutes.

The paper also announced that Livingstone was to go up against an unknown lady who had previously managed to avoid her takedowns in the allotted time and thus won the $25 forfeit. The format of these bouts demonstrates that Livingstone was the true athlete. Even though the "unknown lady" managed to avoid her throws in three fifteen-minute matches, the woman never threw Livingstone herself. A wrestler is more vulnerable when she attempts a takedown. Thus, if the "unknown lady" tried a takedown, Livingstone may have been able to achieve a throw.

The purpose of these fights, then, was not to pit two equally skilled fighters against one another, but, rather, to test the effectiveness of Livingstone's offense. Later that same year, however, Livingstone fought a real wrestling match against Miss A. Smith. After fourteen minutes of a reportedly brutal battle, Livingstone was disqualified due to "foul tactics."[45] The *Cincinnati Enquirer* writes that Livingstone was "cautioned by the referee for using 'Maud' tactics and lost through using the strangle hold after being warned."[46] Although it is unclear what the paper means by "Maud tactics," this was Livingstone's first defeat in a legitimate wrestling engagement.

In an article entitled "Cora Livingstone Is Deep in Love with Wrestling Game," the female wrestling champion explains how she became involved in wrestling and why she chose it over other types of sports.[47] A native of Montreal, she is described as a "woman of remarkable beauty, both of face and physique, added to which she takes herself and her work with a quiet seriousness and dignity."[48] Livingstone explains that she always enjoyed exercise like gymnastics. At the age of sixteen, she joined the circus and began her career as a wrestler. She worked diligently for the first three years to learn the art of wrestling and continued to carefully train her body. She claims that "bathing is weakening" to the body, so she turned to Turkish baths instead, although she only relied on this method once a week. Livingstone also followed a strict diet, eating light meals and consuming meat only at noon. While she may have been a little on the smelly side, athletic clubs throughout the country appealed to her to teach athletics at their facilities, but she was not ready to quit wrestling at that point. Instead, she traveled the United States, challenging any woman to take her on in wrestling, whether as an equal opponent or a mere defendant.

In 1910, Livingstone and her opponent, Miss Lou Harris, were fighting at the Empire Theater in Chicago in front of at least 1,200 spectators when they were interrupted by the police.[49] Harris was in the process of trying to gouge out Livingstone's left eye when the champion administered her "famous strangle hold." The crowd, which consisted of more than a dozen women and one thousand men, cheered excitedly, while the referee urged the women to abandon the illegal maneuvers and be "more ladylike." At this point, according to the newspaper report, three detectives were viewing the fight from a theater box, and when Detective Charles O'Donnell, who was acting as official censor for the police department, decided the bout had reached his threshold of decency, the two women were arrested. Livingstone, Harris, and another female wrestler, Miss Daisy Johnston, were charged with disorderly conduct.

The *Chicago Tribune* declares the fight between Livingstone and Harris the "most disgraceful thing of the kind ever seen in Chicago." As always, the costuming of the women was part of the critique: They wore tights showing off their legs to a shocking degree. Furthermore, the *Tribune* was disturbed by the animosity between the ladies; their obviously strained relationship was not drama for the sake of entertainment. Yet, again, Livingstone's challenge was to throw Harris within ten minutes or forfeit the $25 prize. Says the report, Harris was the crowd favorite because Livingstone displayed some rather unsportsmanlike conduct, including biting, clawing, and eye-gouging.[50] O'Donnell explains that the "show was offensive and that the women, especially Miss Livingstone, roughed it considerably."[51] The police stepped in, and the fight was effectively over. Both women were charged with disorderly conduct, which, in this case, it sounds like the feisty Livingstone deserved.

Livingstone had a long and busy career as a wrestler, fighting for more than fifteen years in venues throughout the United States. The *Richmond Times-Dispatch* notes that in 1919, she wrestled Miss May Wilson in an unprecedented bout for the city, which had never seen two women meet in combat before. The paper pours complements on the two women,

declaring that "both women have been in the wrestling game for a number of years and have just as good a knowledge of the game as the
men."[52] The women came back to Richmond for a highly anticipated
rematch in 1920. The *Times-Dispatch* explains that while many wrestling
fans believed that women did not understand the game, these particular
ladies were as "handy in the art of catch-as-catch-can as any of the masculine mat artists ever seen in action in [the] city."[53] The article promises
that "their match will be one of the most hard-fought contests ever witnessed and will be full of pep from the tap of the gong."[54]

At the last minute, however, Wilson dropped out, and Livingstone met
Grace Brady on the mat instead. The two had fought at a previous event,
in which Brady almost took the championship belt from the championess.
Brady spoke with the *Charlotte Observer*, saying, "The last time we
wrestled here I came within a hair's breadth of beating Miss Livingstone,
and this time I mean to finish the job."[55]

Livingstone dominated the mat during the bout, although her challenger apparently gave her some trouble. Livingstone started off the first
round by throwing Brady to the mat so hard that it took the woman
several minutes to get off the floor. When she returned to standing, Brady
was shaky, but she managed to get at least one fall using a "crotch hold
and deadlock." Livingstone, however, still came off with a decisive victory using several hard throws and pins. Two years later, she was still
considered the champion. Several papers ran the following line about her
in 1922: "Notwithstanding many strenuous years spent in the wrestling
game, Cora Livingstone is still the cleverest of female grapplers."[56]

One of the most interesting aspects of researching Livingstone and
other female wrestlers of the early twentieth century was the divergent
attitudes toward female fighters throughout the country during that time.
The *Chicago Tribune* spat vitriol on the women in 1910, but by 1920, the
Richmond Times-Dispatch, a southern newspaper, was praising them as
skilled fighters. Newspapers are, of course, the product of publishers, as
well as the location and moment in time in which they are published, but
the varying feelings toward female grapplers, especially the popularity of
the sport in the conservative South, demonstrate the growing acceptance
of women in fighting sports in the 1920s.

Cora Livingstone passed away in 1957, but not before imparting much
of her wrestling knowledge to future generations of female fighters. The
famous Mildred Burke called Livingstone her mentor. There is a charm-

ing photo of the two women, with Livingstone looking like a prosperous matron and Burke in her usual costume and wearing her championship belt in 1955. Burke is clutching Livingstone's arm, looking delighted at the sight of her mentor's diamond bracelet, while the older woman, dressed in furs and a smart hat, is staring off to the side. Some wrestling histories claim that Livingstone retired from the sport with an undefeated record, but the actual source material seems to reject that idea. Her wrestling career was certainly long and worthy of celebration, but it is unclear exactly how many bouts she won, especially since two papers oftentimes claim a different outcome for the same fight. Regardless, Livingstone forged a path in the early twentieth century for wrestling as not just a form of entertainment and spectacle, but as a legitimate sport.

CULTURAL HISTORY BETWEEN THE WARS

During both World War I and World War II, women helped on the home front through various types of work. In the early days of World War I, men left in droves to sign up for battle, and their places on farms and in factories and businesses were filled by those left behind. Many of these positions became occupied by young women who were both eager to help in the war effort and ready for some semblance of financial independence. Although the United States did not use its female population to the same extent as Britain, many young women entered the workforce. The women who moved to large cities certainly helped the country during a time of war, but they also gained a type of financial and social independence that seemed unattainable on family farms or in small, close-knit towns.

When the war ended, many of these women did not return to their small-town homes and instead opted to remain in the cities, where they were more socially mobile and self-sufficient; however, at the war's end, many women in the United States and Britain felt discouraged that their governments still did not feel the need to grant them the right to vote. In 1918, British women thirty years and older were granted voting rights. Years later, women twenty-one and older received the ability to cast their vote. In the United States, women of all ages were granted the right to vote in 1920, a sign that the times had indeed changed and that women were gaining unprecedented freedoms.

The period between World War I and World War II is often described as a time of explosive growth of consumerism. The Victorians certainly had their own brand of consumerism, which manifested in home decor and intricate clothing, but after World War I, goods became more readily available to all classes of women in the United States and Britain. It may seem odd to discuss conspicuous consumption in a book about fighting sports, but the underlying ideologies that supported or criticized this interwar consumerism reveal a great deal about gender expectations and the simultaneous restriction and release of gendered social norms, especially those surrounding female sexuality.

In Europe and, more specifically, England, World War I devastated the landscape, as well as the rigid social order established most recently by the Victorians and Edwardians. The structures that divided the aristocracy, gentry, and working class started to crumble, although older generations grasped at those social delineations with wizened hands. The most prominent character to emerge from this period was the "modern girl," a sort of prototype flapper who exemplified everything that was new in this postwar era. With short hair and a boyish figure, this girl was skilled in typically upper-class masculine pursuits, for example, race-car driving, dancing, golfing, and drinking American cocktails. The new girl featured in advertisements was the epitome of leisure who was pictured as being removed from rank and social hierarchy, although that was almost certainly not the case.

The marketing of the new girl made it appear that anyone, regardless of social position, could live this luxurious and leisurely lifestyle, but these advertisements were promoting a lifestyle unattainable by most. The type of youth, male or female, who had the time to pursue sports, travel, dancing, and drinking was almost exclusively part of the aristocracy. And while the young British lords and ladies or American blue bloods might have made pretentious and feigned attempts to create distance from their titled and moneyed families, these social codes remained in place. Conspicuous consumption, mass production, and the mythology of the American dream created the narrative that social freedom was available to everyone; however, not everyone could afford to travel to the Riviera, gamble in exclusive clubs, purchase designer frocks, and drink expensive champagne. But the pursuit of sporting activities was one of the few elements of the upper-class lifestyle that became part of nearly every social stratum. One might not have been able to purchase a yacht, but he or she could certainly spend their leisure time playing baseball.

SPORT, LEISURE, AND FASHION

Women's involvement with sports became even more widely accepted in the post–World War I era, since physical activity was linked, through advertising, to health and, more importantly, beauty. But young women of any social standing were only supposed to play sports appropriate to their class and gender. Golf and tennis were the most popular sports for young middle- and upper-class women, in part because they were activities that involved social interaction with young men. Gone were the critiques claiming that women who played sports would gain absurd amounts of muscle, lose their breasts, and grow mustaches, at least within the confines of these socially acceptable activities. Field hockey, football, and rugby were still considered male sports, and the women who chose to participate in these activities did so with the knowledge that their actions placed them outside of the status quo. Fighting sports remained sordid activities practiced by lower-class and presumably amoral women.

The new woman was a figure of independence (of a sort) and leisure, but she was also quite literally a figure of fashion. The interwar period introduced sartorial changes that shocked and scandalized grandmothers in drawing rooms throughout England and the United States. Female attire for the middle and upper classes typically confined women from activity, whether through the use of delicate fabrics, voluminous skirts, restrictive corsets, or precarious high-heeled shoes. Unwieldy fashions that bordered on the absurd and effectively hobbled women were popular prior to the war, but afterward, apparel reflected serious social change and the independence of the new woman. Silhouettes were clean and simple, with shorter hemlines and sleeves. These designs not only used less fabric than those popular during the Edwardian period, they allowed more movement and created the concept of women's sportswear, a new subset of the fashion industry that consisted of sleek suits rather than the stretchy pants commonly associated with sportswear today.

But there was a need for actual sportswear as well, and fashion changed rapidly during this time. The image of the sports woman, dressed in white with short hair and a lean physique, was often used to sell sports products, of course, but also items that had nothing to do with athletics, for instance, chocolates. Since the new woman was the symbol of modernity, her image proliferated in advertising for products that wished to demonstrate their adherence to this new period of innovation and creativity. Advertisements for cars, beauty products, household products, and cigarettes often included the modern girl as a sexualized figure, desperate to distance herself from the restrictive past and naïve about what that type of independence truly meant.

Trends were similar in the United States, where certain frivolities of the prewar period ended, even in a landscape relatively unscathed by the horrors of World War I. Nonetheless, the end of the war gave way to new forms of frivolity. The 1920s are remembered as a time of hedonistic celebration that seems almost fey considering the decimation of the stock market in 1929. Scholar Marilyn Morgan describes the two images of the modern woman proclaimed by magazines and featured in newspapers and popular fiction: the flapper and the athletic girl.[57] While the flapper rebelled against social mores by drinking, smoking, dancing, and bobbing her hair, she did not really threaten traditional masculine authority because the type of girls who tried to follow this lifestyle needed financial independence. Upper-class girls already had the means to live as hardpartying flappers, as exemplified in F. Scott Fitzgerald's *The Great Gatsby*, but most women relied on wealthy men to follow this new, rather hedonistic lifestyle. That did not necessarily mean that flappers living off rich men had no self-authorizing power. Instead, it indicates that the life of the flapper was contingent on economic status above all else.

Female athletes, meanwhile, forever linked athleticism and strength to beauty, an innovative idea given the preference for weak, pale women in the nineteenth century. Women's magazines encouraged readers to exercise and play sports to eliminate fat or increase curves. Magazines also incorporated advertisements for the proper clothing to wear in this new sporting environment. The new athletic attire, from short tennis skirts to bathing costumes, was designed to fit snuggly (and protect the swimmer, since previous swimming costumes made of heavy wool could easily cause drowning). Female swimmers featured heavily in ads because of their bathing costumes and physical ideal of womanly beauty. In addition, because of her athletic attire, which was much more form-fitting compared to any vestments previously worn, the athletic woman was also sexualized.

The new female athlete was strong and robust, a sign of the health of the English and American populace. This growing interest in female athleticism occurred in other countries as well and was frequently tied to images of nationalism. A strong female body symbolized a nation's health and ability to produce strong future generations. The interwar years emphasized the idea that citizens, both men and women, should be physically fit enough to serve their country, in whatever capacity. Physical education became standard in schools, and young children were introduced to certain sports, alongside reading and arithmetic. Children living in poorer urban environments made do with insufficient space and equipment to play yard games. Young girls without the new, "proper" exercise attire tucked their skirts into their knickers.[58] Middle-class schools included sports like swimming, tennis, hockey, and gymnastics, the latter an especially popular activity in the 1920s and 1930s.

This era also marked the beginning of the institutionalization of sports. Governing bodies, almost invariably consisting of men, ruled every aspect of sports, including who could participate. With these new administrations in place to establish rules and regulations, women were routinely excluded from certain sports or from playing at clubs and fields. While great strides were made toward equality in sports for women, criticism and opposition from these official governing bodies continued to thwart many efforts to fully integrate the sporting world.

FIGHTING DURING WORLD WAR II

Pugilistic fighting became subsumed by actual fighting during World War II. Many sporting events took place during the war, but they were diluted by the absence of most young men, who were serving their countries. The all-women baseball league in the United States famously competed with regular professional baseball. During the war, many American women took over jobs that had once been held by men to perpetuate America's industry and economy. Women entered the workplace in unprecedented numbers. While individual men may have scorned the idea of dealing with women in the workplace, the government's support of the female laborers trounced any hostilities. Women were fully integrated into the war effort and, because of their new position outside of the home, gained an extraordinary amount of freedom.

There were many milestones for women in fighting sports during the years of American involvement in World War II. In 1942, Miss Angela Wall became one of the first female reporters to cover boxing news in the United States.[59] A charming photo shows her sitting between her father and Louis "Kid" Kaplan, the former featherweight world champion. Wall is wearing a large, ruffled hat reminiscent of a bonnet and red lipstick. But the funniest part of this story is the picture of a woman to her father's left who is screaming with abandon at the fight. There is no indication of who this woman is, but as more women began to attend boxing matches, the knowledge and zest of the fan base grew considerably. The following year, still in the midst of the horrors of war, the C.Y.O. gymnasium, a famous amateur boxing gym, opened its doors to young women.[60] The Chicago gym provided training for girls at a time when physical fitness was an important part of the war effort. The athletic director specifically invited women working downtown and women who did war work to take advantage of the gym's facilities. Women not only took part in men's work, they were now taking part in men's athletics.

THE END OF THE WAR

When the war ended, most women were expected to give up their factory and industry jobs to allow returning soldiers a place to work. During this decade, there was an insistence in popular culture to remind women of their roles as homemakers and wives. While the 1940s saw a historical shift in women's roles outside the home, the 1950s bore the brunt of the reaction to those shifts. Prior to World War II, the home remained the woman's sphere, while during the war, the factory became the woman's new home. After the war was over and women were encouraged, if not forced, to return to their homes, the following decade in America's popular culture sought to perpetuate the domestic fantasy of the good, stay-at-home wife who was passive and feminine.

Clothing has often been used to regulate the female body; women's clothing of the post–World War II era restricted movement, signifying the return of women to the home and retreat from the workplace, where clothing had been forgiving to allow for work. Christian Dior's new look, while incredibly beautiful, is remembered as the return of the constricting corset and hobble skirts. Postwar fashion reminded women of their duties to their homes and husbands as mothers and wives.

Nevertheless, the end of the war did not completely diminish the gains made by women during the war years. In 1948, twenty-six women joined the police force in New York City.[61] At the Randall's Island stadium, the women demonstrated their skills in boxing and jiu-jitsu to an impressed audience. Lieutenant Julius Brilla, who was in change of the physical training of new police recruits, claimed that this class of women was the "best one he had ever had."[62] Nearly all of the women had worked for the military during the war, several as officers in the marines and air force. During the demonstration, many of them displayed extraordinary skill in the fighting arts. Twenty-four-year-old Lorette Ingram easily threw Brilla to the mats, despite his nearly fifty-pound advantage. The *New York Times* praises the women and their skill and does so without commenting on the novelty of their position in the police department.

In these last years of the 1940s, women's work became normalized, despite the many social pressures for them to return to the home. Married women left work for their expected roles as housewives and mothers, but young, single women continued to work before marriage. The desire for women to remain physically fit meant that all types of exercise, including fighting sports, became more regularly practiced. In 1949, twenty-five-year-old Gloria Thompson of Los Angeles was touted as the female boxing champion of the world.[63] Training under Joe Louis at the Chris J. Perry Elks Gym, Thompson fought professionally for several years and had a 9–0 record, but only one of her opponents was a woman. Only twenty years later, women throughout the United States would be denied the right to box professionally, but in 1949, female boxing grew in practice and popularity.

POSTWAR FIGHTING

Barbara Buttrick and the Boxing Greats of the 1950s

In 1948, an eighteen-year-old British girl, Barbara Buttrick, known as "Battling Butt," was a tiny and scrappy fighter, standing at only four feet, eleven inches tall and weighing a little less than one hundred pounds. A typist by day, Buttrick issued her first public challenge that same year to any 98- to 112-pound girl who would face her in the ring. Three young women immediately responded.[64] Buttrick's mother was nonplussed because she had hoped that her daughter would only box as a hobby and not in public.[65] But Barbara faced other difficulties in her boxing career aside from her mother's consternation. First, given her small frame, she had difficulty in finding an opponent of appropriate size.[66] She entered the headlines before her career truly began, not only by calling out women in 1948, but by agreeing to participate in an exhibition fight against a man.[67] The fight was called off, but by the following year, Buttrick had fought professional boxer Bert Saunders in a three-round exhibition match.[68] Unfortunately, exhibition sparring was Buttrick's only real fighting option in Britain at the time, which meant that her venues were primarily theaters and performance spaces rather than boxing arenas.

The British Boxing Board of Control refused to give Buttrick a license to officially fight, despite her promise to represent her country as the greatest female boxing champion ever known.[69] And the Boxing Board was not the only institution that took a stance against her. The Variety Artists' Federation, a trade union formed to protect the rights of various types of performers, spoke out against female boxing, claiming that it was "degrading to the best interests of variety public entertainment, the boxing profession, and womanhood."[70] The federation's claim that the event would be degrading to women was ridiculed by Nat Tennens, the promoter of Buttrick's first intended fight, who noted that the organization supported stripteases and other nude performances, which were much more degrading to women than female boxing.

Despite the many critics who denounced Buttrick, the petite fighter continued her quest for boxing glory. During her nearly fifteen-year career, she scored twelve knockouts and lost only once, to JoAnn Hagen, who was thirty-three pounds heavier.[71] After working her job as a typist during the day, Buttrick spent her evenings training at the YMCA under the tutelage of her coach, Leonard Smith, whom she would eventually marry. She was known for having a stiff jab, which she used to break her husband's nose and floor an impertinent reporter who "suggested that women were better off inside sweaters than in a ring."[72]

The restrictive British antifemale boxing campaign waged against Buttrick eventually led to her relocating to the United States to further her career. A story in the *Dallas Morning News* finally gave her the respect she had certainly earned, as it details a sparring session between her and a

Figure 3.2.   Barbara Buttrick. Courtesy of Mary Ann Owen.

140-pound "porky" veteran fighter named Jose Andres. Buttrick had Andres up against the ropes, and after the second round, he told the reporter,

"She's good. Punches hard as a man. Boxes like a professional. I've been fighting fourteen years, and I've fought some pros that were worse."[73] At the age of twenty-six, Buttrick finally received her opportunity to fight for the world title, but the event was not without criticism. One particularly rude announcement in the *Seattle Daily Times* from 1957 introduces Buttrick and her opponent, Phyllis Kugler, but then goes on to state, "[you can] forget them as soon as you learn they are scheduled to box 'for the championship of the world.'"[74]

Kugler grew up in South Bend, Indiana, and became internationally recognized in the boxing community in the 1950s. According to an interview with Kugler in the *South Bend Tribune* in 2005, she retired with an impressive record, at fifty-five victories with only one loss.[75] She recalls that half of the battle was being allowed in the ring in the first place. Events were often cancelled because two women appeared on the fight card. Kugler flew under the radar for a little while, because she was often called Phil instead of her full, feminine name, Phyllis. And Kugler was known for her femininity, in addition to her prowess in the ring. In 1957, the Fraternal Order of Police chose her as "woman boxer and beauty queen of the year."[76] When she was not fighting, Kugler wore dresses at the behest of her trainer, who must have assumed that this practice of normative femininity would help the fighter gain acceptance outside of the ring.

Buttrick beat Kugler in that historic battle, unanimously winning each of the six rounds and claiming the title of female boxing champion. Three years later, and four months pregnant with her first daughter, Buttrick retired from the ring, but not from the world of boxing. She founded the Women's International Boxing Federation and was elected to the International Boxing and Wrestling Hall of Fame in 1990. She also served as president of the Veteran Boxers Association from 1988 through 1990.

JoAnn Hagen, the boxer who provided Buttrick with her only loss, was another celebrated fighter of the era. Most of the information regarding fighting sports in the 1940s and 1950s comes from interviews with the people involved several decades after the fact. JoAnn's younger brother recalled watching his sister spar at the gym and being teased by classmates that his sister could beat him up.[77] Her parents were not thrilled when they learned about their daughter's career, but one of her brothers claimed that once their father saw her fight, he said, "Well, it looks like you can take care of yourself."[78] Hagen defeated the famous

Figure 3.3.   Barbara Buttrick as president of the Veteran Boxers Association.
Courtesy of Mary Ann Owen.

Buttrick in 1956. That same year, Hagen was defeated by Kugler, making this triad of female champions inextricably connected in a small fighting community. Kugler and Hagen both made appearances on the popular televisions shows *The Steven Allen Show*, *What's My Line*, and *I've Got a Secret*. Hagen rarely spoke openly about her boxing career, although her siblings note that she often said it was fun. When she passed away in 2004, her family donated her gear and newspaper clippings to a local museum for an exhibit so that her legacy would live on.

Another female fighter who made headlines in the 1950s was Australia's bantamweight champion, Cath Thomas, who won fourteen of her eighteen bouts and reportedly knocked out five male opponents.[79] After a devastating automobile accident, she gave up boxing, but her competitive nature inspired her to enter the world of ballroom dancing. Reporters lined up to watch her tango, and while wearing an elegant pink evening dress and looking every bit the ballroom dancer, she explained that her boxing footwork aided her dancing skills. She won a gold medal in a Sydney dancing competition and regularly practiced with her two young daughters, both of whom enjoyed dancing and boxing.

Thomas, Hagen, Kugler, and Buttrick competed in boxing despite the harsh criticism leveled against them. Women who did not adhere to the requirements of the 1950s cult of domesticity were often censured in such women's magazines as *Good Housekeeping* and *Ladies Home Journal*, and unlike many of their predecessors, who boxed during a time when matches were arranged and fought through individual promoters and businesses, these women were limited by the various governing bodies, who deemed them unfit to represent boxing. Yet, all four women remembered their time in the ring with fondness, and the women who fought in the following decades remembered them as pioneers.

4

THE FIGHT TO FIGHT

The state of women's rights improved immensely in the twentieth century, and women's involvement in sports increased correspondingly. In the nineteenth century, doctors had claimed that young women playing vigorous sports might disrupt their delicate uterine ecosystem and make it difficult for them to give birth. In the early days of the twentieth century, women were still restricted from playing sports for "health" and moral reasons, but by the middle of the twentieth century, the medical community had recognized that exercise benefits women more than it harms them, although certain sports, especially contact sports, were still considered detrimental to female health.

SPORTS IN THE TWENTIETH CENTURY

Sports also united men and women in activities that were a far cry from sitting in parlors and walking through the countryside. The suggestive nature of certain sports frightened some spinsters, but by the 1920s, golf and tennis were encouraged activities. The Olympic Games, which had long been reserved for men, allowed women to participate in the bizarre 1900 Paris Olympics, the games that famously lasted six months and became confusingly mixed up with the simultaneously occurring World's Fair. The disorganized structure of the Paris Games allowed women to compete in tennis and golf, with the first American woman, Margaret Abbott, winning the nine-hole golf tournament.[1] Golf has not been played at the Olympics since then, but the chaotic Paris games marked a seminal moment in women's sports history. Nonetheless, it would not be until the twenty-first century that women could compete in boxing and wrestling at the Olympic Games. Women, while rather grudgingly accepted in certain sports, were still outside of the new governing bodies of fighting sports.

Physical education was standard practice in most schools in the United States, but the types of athletics offered were dependent on each school's financing, as well as regional location. Students in the colder regions of the country were more likely to play hockey, while children in the South might practice tennis, track and field, swimming, and other outdoor sports. Sadly, the growing presence of girls in sports did not necessarily mean that they were treated respectfully at all times. In the 1950s, numerous newspapers published stories about young men wearing boxing gloves while playing basketball against girls to diminish their clear advantage.[2] Accounts of these games were printed with an obvious delight; news stories explaining the ridiculous measures taken to create equality between the sexes were coupled with pictures of young men in boxing gloves towering over small and seemingly inept female players.

That the twentieth-century woman would play sports was a surety, but there were still significant problems facing female athletes. Many institutions, from high schools to professional organizations like state boxing commissions, restricted women from participating in sports. No amount of cajoling or changing social views could sway many of these institutions' staunch positions against female athletes. Instead, it would take the courts and a number of plucky and determined female athletes to push for equal rights in the sports realm.

WOMEN ARE BANNED

Historically, we have seen that most fights between women were stopped for two primary reasons: illegal prizefighting and social pressure. There were cases, as discussed in chapter 3, where events were discouraged, even by government officials; however, they were allowed to go on because there was no law in place to stop such practices. Fights were sometimes cancelled because the promoter or owner of a venue fell to the socially conservative pressures of the community. Other times, bouts were stopped in medias res by police officers enforcing laws against prizefighting. Nevertheless, plenty of women competed in fighting events through the guise of exhibition fights. Official sanctioning is not required for an exhibition fight, and many fighters worked in traveling circuses or carnivals to compete. Wrestling still occupied that strange line between sport and theater in the 1950s, when several women ruled the mat and the headlines.

Wrestling may have functioned as entertainment in the 1940s and 1950s, but the action was typically nonscripted and still required skill and athleticism. The famed female wrestlers of the mid-century were also beautiful and sexy, as exemplified by the Amazing Mae Young and the "Fabulous Moolah," also known as Lillian Ellison. Young, a statuesque blonde beauty à la Marilyn Monroe, began her professional wrestling career in 1939, but her athletic talents manifested in high school, where she regularly bested boys on the wrestling team and kicked field goals for the high school football team.[3] Young trained Lillian Ellison, who earned the nickname the "Fabulous Moolah" after explaining that she wrestled "for the money . . . for the moolah."[4] The girls worked with a troupe of female wrestlers, including Ellison's adopted daughter, Katie Glass, aka Diamond Lil, a little person who also wrestled professionally.

They eventually teamed up with Vince McMahon Sr., the scion of the McMahon professional wrestling empire. At that point in time, wrestling was still transitioning into the theatrical and scripted professional wrestling that the McMahon family still runs today as the WWE (World Wrestling Entertainment). The women wore what was essentially a one-piece bathing suit, sometimes fabulously decorated with sequins or rhinestones, although the costumes were often simple and revealing. While their performances were more theatrical than sport, they still had to contend with gender biases to become accepted in the wrestling community. But Young and Ellison were respected for their strength and skill, and before their deaths, both women were inducted into the World Wrestling Entertainment Hall of Fame.

While these highly sexual and theatrical wrestlers became popular in the 1950s, appearing in pinup-style trading cards, women who wished to wrestle in a sanctioned event were restricted from competing. In 1955, the state of Oregon prosecuted Jerry Hunter, whom they describe as a "person of the feminine sex," with the crime of "participating in wrestling competition and exhibition."[5] Hunter appealed her conviction, claiming that the court had no jurisdiction because it violated the Fourteenth Amendment of the constitution, which guarantees equal protection under the law to all citizens; however, in Oregon, women were prohibited from receiving licenses for wrestling and boxing to promote "general welfare and good morals" to Oregon citizens.[6]

The case against Hunter was upheld because, according to the Oregon Supreme Court, wrestling and boxing were not civil rights, but the domain of the governing bodies of those sports. In addition, the Supreme Court, which consisted entirely of men, decided that it needed to uphold laws protecting public health and morality, as well as the rights of men to stop the "ever-increasing feminine encroachment upon what for ages had been considered strictly as manly arts and privileges."[7] Women infiltrated every aspect of American culture, but Oregon's high court refused Hunter, and all other women in the state, the right to fight in these most masculine sports of wrestling and boxing.

Not all states banned women from competing in boxing and wrestling. Barbara Buttrick famously fought in Florida, and, in 1952, four women entered the ring at the City Auditorium in Atlanta, Georgia, under the sanctioning force of the National Elks Athletic Committee, for a one-hour tag-team wrestling match.[8] Hailing from Australia, Babs Wigo and Betty White teamed up against Ethel Johnson and Kathleen Wimberly for what was predicted to be an "action-packed" grappling match.[9] These women headlined the event, which also featured male boxing, and the *Atlanta Daily World* excitedly promoted the event without any condemnation or suspicion of the female wrestlers.

Other countries also banned women from participating in contact sports. The Canadian Boxing and Wrestling Commission refused to provide wrestling licenses to women, saying, "Ladies wrestling will add nothing to the general benefit or enjoyment of the citizens at large."[10] Yet, at the same time that these institutions banned women from obtaining licenses to fight, Mrs. James D. Waldron was named head of the Louisiana State Athletic Commission.[11] Governor Earl K. Long appointed Waldron head of the boxing board after the death of her husband and announced, "Why not a woman? We have women in a lot of sports now—even wrestling."[12] Governor Long's pronouncement was significant in a state that still refused to sanction fights between men of different races. Meanwhile, Mrs. Margareta Sjoelin, an attractive twenty-five-year-old mother of three, became the first female boxing referee in Sweden in

1958.[13] Sjoelin was initially denied a referee's license because boxing officials believed it would cause Sweden to "lose face" in the international boxing community. Instead, she refereed smaller amateur fights through the provincial Smaaland boxing section, which found her ready and more than able to perform the duties required of a boxing referee. Margareta's husband Stig was a former boxer and part-time coach for the Swedish Amateur Boxing Federation.

SPORTS AND TELEVISION

Sports became more deeply entrenched in popular culture once the television became a mainstay in homes in the 1940s and 1950s. Boxing commentator Russ Hodges explained in an interview with the *Los Angeles Times* that women were tuning in to watch boxing matches in increasing numbers, and he was delighted.[14] Hodges revealed that when boxing was initially offered in a primetime slot on Wednesday evenings, many naysayers claimed that women would never watch with their husbands, which would cause strife at home, but instead, women embraced the sport, recognizing that boxing was, according to Hodges, a "dramatic spectacle—that the combination of skill, grace, physical fitness, courage, and competitive spirit has no substitute as a spectator sport."[15] Since women were used to sitting at home, where both the article and Hodges suggest they belong, they might as well watch boxing, since female admiration only heightened the sense of male superiority in the sport of boxing.

Women admired fighters in the same way they admired any masculine man on television, Hodges says, because they viewed boxing the same way they viewed any other form of entertainment on television, and that was not a bad thing for boxing, television ratings, Russ Hodges, or twenty-eight-year-old Joyce Brothers, who won the top prize on *The $64,000 Question* in 1955, by correctly answering a series of questions on boxing.[16] Brothers studied psychology at Cornell and Columbia universities, and the art of boxing watching bouts on television alongside her husband and their infant daughter. Televised boxing matches not only provided the American public with entertainment and athletic skill, they provided Dr. Joyce Brothers and her family with $64,000.

THE SOCIAL MOVEMENT IN THE 1960S

The 1960s began with a bang in the world of women's boxing. Mr. William Smeeth, a cinema manager from the English midland county of Derbyshire, created a scandal when he attempted to organize a fight for a Parisian female boxer. He had previously staged a boxing match between two eleven-year-old girls, with some success.[17] Although the owners of the cinema seemed to accept the fight between the two young girls, Smeeth's idea to bring the twenty-two-year-old Parisian boxing champion, Mademoiselle Odette Thierry, to box two English girls was not welcome. It seems odd by our modern-day standards to allow children to box rather than women, but the Derbyshire incident was not the only example of young girls boxing.

In the United States in 1969, the career of twelve-year-old Laura Bloomberg ended when state officials, including the district attorney, decided that she could no longer compete in boxing competitions in Massachusetts.[18] The young boys she trained with at the local boxing club were allowed to compete at a local benefit show, but Bloomberg was banned from fighting. She retired undefeated, a fantastic feat for any fighter, let alone a twelve-year-old girl, and was honored during the event by a local heavyweight titleholder. Although the state condemned the idea of young girls boxing, the local community rallied around Bloomberg and celebrated her success in the ring, even as it was short-lived.

In 1967, sports journalist Dick Beddoes published an article on the history of women acting as promoters or coaches for male fighters. In an interview with Beddoes, Jack Hurley, the famous boxing promoter and trainer, explains his perspective on women in the ring, commenting, "Ha! Dames in boxing are all batty as bedbugs! Look it up."[19] Beddoes did some research and found exactly what Hurley wanted him to see: evidence of women meddling in the sport of boxing to no good end. In the majority of these cases, the women were not fighters, but promoters and coaches who had led men astray, leading to the conclusion that a female in a man's corner was a pugilistic succubus. One example is Mrs. Cal Eaton, a fight promoter who was unable to raise the $75,000 needed to rent an event center for a fight between Cassius Clay and Floyd Patterson. Beddoes admits that Eaton's failure to raise the money "suggests she [was] not as adroit at money grubbing as the majority of her sex," but most of the examples in the article seem similar to claims that famous musicians are ruined by women.[20] Beddoes hunted for instances of female mismanagement of male fighters and found what he needed for his piece.

These types of denouncements of women were common in certain arenas of the 1960s, where women's rights movements were treated with disdain and disgust by men who felt that their patriarchal power was being threatened. People often misremember the past in ways that suit their own ideology, and many people in the mid-twentieth century believed (and people continue to think this way today) boxing and wrestling had always been exclusively male territory. Not only was this type of thinking incorrect, as demonstrated in the previous chapter, people managed to forget the recent past.

Beddoes and Hurley believed that women infiltrating the boxing world was a result of the recent women's rights movements of the 1960s. While these movements did indeed open doors for women and call for equal rights and protections for women according to the law, fighting sports already included female fighters, referees, coaches, promoters, and writers far prior to the second wave of feminism. The consternation of Beddoes, Hurley, and other men in the hegemonic center of the boxing community blamed the feminist movement because it was easy, and, unfortunately, these men of power used their influence to attempt to block women at every turn.

Not all men agreed with Beddoes and Hurley's take on women in the boxing industry; there were numerous male advocates ready to back female pugilists, trainers, and promoters. According to a 1965 *Washington Post* article, a British woman applied to be a trainer at the British Boxing Board of Control's new gymnasium. The woman, whose name is not provided, regularly practiced with her husband, and she taught her son to box.[21] It is unclear if she obtained the position, but it is evident that, like many female boxers throughout history, she was supported by her husband. England has perhaps the longest history of organized boxing as a sport, so it makes sense that fighters would emerge from that country, along with the United States, in large numbers. But boxing greatly increased its international presence in the twentieth century. In 1966, Trinidad introduced competitive women's boxing, with Barbados-born Eatrice Clarke, a former cycling champion, challenging all comers. Boxing promoter H. A. Clarke defended his decision to put on the bouts by reasoning that "women are taking part in almost every other sport, so why not boxing, too?"[22]

In 1969, Abigail Van Buren, the author of the famous and nationally syndicated "Dear Abby" advice column, received a letter about women in fighting sports. The article is beyond delightful to a fighting historian who is also a fan of etiquette guides of all kinds. This installment of "Dear Abby" includes advice on fighting, as well as how to deal with rude dinner guests (the woman ate out of the serving dish . . . with her fingers!), apathetic parents (don't complain if you do not attend PTA meetings), and child safety (kids should not put plastic bags over their heads when playing robot). The question, signed Milwaukee, is supposedly written by a group of women:

> DEAR ABBY: Our group is comprised of women who are interested in learning to wrestle and box for fun and amusement. We are not advocating bouts between men and women, but we wouldn't refuse such encounters if they were to arise. The girls wear bathing suits and work out on the mats in the health studio. We want to know if there is any danger factor in this kind of sport for women? This is not a put-on. We are sincerely interested in a serious reply.

Van Buren answers the question intelligently and briefly, somehow skipping the more interesting fact that the women work out in bathing suits, to advise them:

> DEAR MILWAUKEE: My medical authorities agree that repeated blows in the area of the breasts can be dangerous to women, so unless some kind of protective covering is worn, you'd better skip the boxing. As for wrestling, you can bend each other into pretzels if you like, but coed bouts are not recommended.[23]

Abby's response is surprisingly open-minded, considering her position as champion of polite society. Granted, Van Buren is famous for being unexpectedly liberal in the cause of gay rights, so why would she deny women the right to train? Her advice that women should practice boxing while wearing chest protection is standard in many fighting communities today, and her belief that coed bouts should not happen is shared by most people; however, it was still a delightful surprise to find a "Dear Abby" column supporting female fighters in 1969.

TITLE IX: OFFICIAL RECOGNITION BEGINS

In 1972, Title IX, the largest piece of gender equality legislation to date, was passed by Congress. The bill, which was part of the educational amendments to the Civil Rights Act of 1964, protected students and employees from legal discrimination based on gender. The official document begins by stating, "No person in the United States shall, on the basis of sex, be excluded from participation in, be denied the benefits of, or be subject to discrimination under any educational programs or activity receiving federal financial assistance."[24]

Many people point to Title IX as the reason female athletes are able to excel in sports today. Nevertheless, Professor Sarah Fields points out that it was not Title IX, but the Fourteenth Amendment, ratified in 1868, that is often invoked when discussing equality for women in sports. The Fourteenth Amendment gave the newly freed male slave certain rights, although the practice of equality was limited. Fields explains that Title IX primarily addressed increasing the amount of sports opportunities for girls and decreasing the difference in funding between boys' and girls' sports. For certain sports, especially contact sports, to be available to girls, it was the Fourteenth Amendment, not Title IX, that was invoked in court cases.[25]

The Department of Health, Education, and Welfare enforced the regulations of Title IX but also amended it by adding its own language, which essentially restricted gender equality in contact sports. Boxing and wrestling were obvious contact sports, but activities like soccer, basketball, football, and hockey, popular American sports, also excluded girls. Thus, while Title IX seemed to end sexual discrimination in schools, it still limited the sports that women could play. Instead, Title IX provided a language for court cases brought against schools and institutions regarding funding, but it did not name the sports that girls should be allowed access to play. Fields explains that the general public perceived Title IX as the end to gender discrimination,[26] but, in fact, it was the beginning of numerous lawsuits and cases for the women who sought to participate not just in sports in general, but in contact sports specifically.

There were several boxing and wrestling programs created in the 1970s for young girls wishing to compete. One fifteen-year-old girl, Brenda Ducksworth, of Dallas, Texas, made headlines in 1973, as a champion boxer fighting against both male and female opponents. Her mother declared, "She ain't much at keeping house, but she sure can box."[27] The article points out that while some states banned little girls from playing baseball, in the great state of Texas, Ducksworth lost only two of her sometimes coed fights. She boxed at Missy, Inc, a program created by Doyle Weaver, who felt that it was not fair that girls were forced into such stereotypical sports as baton twirling. The program included regular boxing tournaments where the girls were treated the same as the boys. There was no extra padding, no special rules, and no differences between the competition and training. In fact, the boys and girls sparred together, making this program significantly different than many other boxing and wrestling clubs at the time. Weaver explains, "We want to disprove the myth that girls can't compete against boys."[28] As the title of the article succinctly puts it, "Kid Gloves Are Off for Girls in Dallas." But not everyone was as forward thinking as the genial Doyle Weaver.

In 1973, two high school girls denied the right to compete with boys in noncontact sports sued their principals in federal court.[29] The girls argued that they should be able to compete against boys in swimming and running. The lawsuit argued that swimming and running were noncontact sports, which meant that the girls should be able to compete alongside their male schoolmates. This argument unfortunately set the precedent that girls could compete against boys, as long as there was no contact. The lawsuit specifically cited wrestling and football as inappropriate for coed play. The language of the case suggested that girls were capable of competing in running and swimming but did not belong in contact sports.

When school boards and educational leaders denied girls the opportunity to box and wrestle in middle and high schools, people like Doyle Weaver stepped forward to provide training for all kids, no matter the sex. In Atlanta, in 1975, Thunderbolt Patterson, the "King of Wrestling," created a school of wrestling for young boys and girls.[30] He was joined in his endeavor by none other than a nun, Sister Louise Reese, who was mother of professional wrestler Jerry Reese. Patterson set up his school as a nonprofit designed to keep at-risk children off the streets. The program also provided a space where young boys and girls could learn the art of wrestling from a famous athlete and, presumably, a nun.

The passing of Title IX opened up a dialogue about what types of sports are appropriate for kids. It did not immediately fix the many problems that faced children in schools who wanted to play sports, but it did force schools to provide equal amounts of funding for sports programs for boys and girls. And that was the primary purpose of Title IX: to stop schools from underfunding girls' sports. In 1974, in the wake of the legislation, the environment was ripe to start a larger conversation about why women were restricted from certain sports, not just in schools, but on the professional level as well.

THE FIGHT AGAINST THE BOXING COMMISSION

In October 1974, at the New York State Athletic Commission, Marian "Tyger" Trimiar and Jackie Tonawanda applied for professional boxing licenses.[31] The women were reportedly met with snickers as they went through the routine application process. Despite the sarcastic comments made by some men, Trimiar and Tonawanda were excited, as was the young woman accepting their applications, who eloquently said, "This is where it will start."[32] But it would not be an easy road for Trimiar, Tonawanda, and the many other female fighters looking to go pro in the 1970s. The athletic commission unanimously denied the request for licenses, citing Rule 205.15, which stated that, "No woman may be licensed as a boxer or second or licensed to compete in any wrestling exhibition with men."[33] The chairman of the commission, Edwin Dooley, admitted that he believed licensing female boxers would "erode the sport's image as the 'manly art of self-defense.'"[34]

But the fight was not over. Tonawanda filed an appeal with the Human Rights Commission in New York, complaining that by not licensing her as a professional fighter, the board revoked her ability to make a living.[35] Dooley's words were part of the lawsuit she brought to court, hoping they would help her cause. Dooley claimed that, "Licensing of women as professional boxers would at once destroy the image that attracts serious boxing fans and bring professional boxing into disrepute."[36] He also argued that the commission had a responsibility to protect fighters and the available equipment for female boxers would be "insufficient to protect them."[37] Hiding behind this argument of safety and benevolence for the well-being of female fighters, the commission continued its refusal to license professional female fighters and remained in litigation with Tonawanda for the next several years.

Tonawanda and the other women who fought for equality in the boxing world were aided in their quest by a number of male trainers, coaches, promoters, and fellow boxers who supported the idea of professional female boxing. Paul Mitrano, the famous Boston boxing promoter who gave Rocky Marciano his start, said in 1976, at the ripe age of seventy, that when he first heard of female boxing, he "thought it was a gimmick."[38] But Mitrano soon changed his mind, explaining that once he saw female boxers working in the gym, he realized they were skilled and deserved to be professional. He managed Jackie Tonawanda, as well as Gwen Gemini and Tyger Trimiar, who were granted professional boxing licenses in Connecticut, one of the few states in 1976 willing to allow women to box professionally. Interestingly, the commissioner of consumer protection for Connecticut was Mrs. Mary Heslin, who admitted that she personally did not approve of women in the ring; however, Heslin understood that her personal beliefs could not impinge on the constitutional rights of female boxers, so she granted licenses to women as long as they wore chest protection in the ring.

Other female skeptics, including Mitrano's wife Edna, went from doubting women to supporting them after watching Trimiar, Gemini, and Tonawanda practice, and Paul, who spent nearly $50,000 per year housing, feeding, and training his stable of fighters, male and female, believed that women could reinvigorate the sport of boxing. Taking a cue from the wrestling world, which still walked the line between entertainment and sport and included female fighters, Mitrano felt that the presence of women could increase viewership and interest in the sweet science of boxing. Nonetheless, not everyone agreed with him.

In the wake of the popularity of Tyger Trimiar and other female fighters, two approaches to women's boxing emerged. One delighted in the new opportunities for women, while the other decried female pugilists who infiltrated the last "men-only" space. The women's liberation movement was blamed for women's boxing, and numerous male journalists made it a point to emphasize their disgust for feminists and female pugilists. In 1978, Nick Thimmesch wrote in the *Chicago Tribune* that he felt women's boxing was "awful" and a product of the same feminist movement that promoted gay rights and abortions. He describes people of both sexes who attended boxing matches between women as either "fools" or into some sort of kink.[39]

The women who were seeking boxing licenses would stop at nothing for the right to box. Although Maine, Connecticut, and several other states licensed professional female boxers, New York remained firmly opposed. By 1977, thirteen states allowed women to box, although California and Nevada did so with strict restrictions: Women's bouts were limited to four 2-minute rounds, the fighters had to go through rigorous physical evaluations, and both women had to sign affidavits confirming that they were neither pregnant nor menstruating at the time of the fight.[40] After Tyger Trimiar, Claire Piniazik, and Jackie Tonawanda were refused licenses in New York, fighter Cathy "Cat" Davis put forth her concerted efforts to have the ban on female fighters lifted, but not without creating controversy of her own.

CAT DAVIS

Cat Davis was a twenty-five-year-old lightweight fighter with fourteen wins and only one loss. She lived with her manager, Sal Algieri, a former fighter with a murky reputation, and the two struck out to create a women's boxing federation in 1977. Although the federation did not take off, Davis's career certainly did. She was featured on the cover of *Ring* magazine in August 1978, beneath the headline, "Is Women's Boxing Here to Stay?" Davis was the first and only female boxer to appear on the cover of a major athletic magazine until Christy Martin appeared on a 1996 *Sports Illustrated* cover. She was praised for her beauty, diligent training, and diet. She advised fighters to eat plenty of vegetables and, for breakfast, a raw egg with tomato sauce.[41]

Apparently her diet and her media appearances paid off, because in March 1978, Davis signed a contract to fight twenty-one-year-old Chicago fighter Jo Jo Thomas in Fayetteville, North Carolina, for an astounding $20,000.[42] Whether Thomas received the same payment remains unknown, but $20,000 was a record amount for women's boxing. Only months after fighting Thomas, the *Chicago Tribune* published an article that revealed several suspicious circumstances that placed Davis in a difficult position. According to the article, several people were claiming that Davis and Algieri were guilty of fixing fights.[43] The two argued that any accusations of corruption were caused by jealous rivals because Davis was pretty, well-educated, and white.

Although she may have felt unfairly criticized for her white privilege, Davis was able to back up her accolades in 1979, when she defeated German boxer Uschi Doering for the women's world lightweight title.[44]

The fight ended in the sixth round, when Davis drove Doering against the ropes and scored a technical knockout through a series of jabs. The German fighter felt that the bout had been called too soon, complaining that she "was not hurt at all" and that "they never would have stopped that fight in Germany."[45] The crowd apparently agreed with her, because the referee was booed and catcalled when he stopped the contest.

Davis continued to rouse interest in the nonboxing-related news media. In 1978, *People* magazine published an article in which she explains that she disrupted the stereotype of the female boxer because she did not have a pug nose or cauliflower ear and was not a 180-pound Amazon.[46] The magazine praises her girl-next-door good looks and skills in the ring.

As before, women's boxing uniforms reflected the fashion trends at large. In the 1970s and 1980s, women wore rather short shorts, revealing a great deal of thigh, just as miniskirts were worn ubiquitously in the United States and Europe. Most women wore chest protectors, as dictated by their state's boxing commission, which often meant that they wore short-sleeved tops. But for the most part, women's boxing uniforms were similar to those sported by their male counterparts, although they were altered to fit the female physique. It was not until later in the twentieth century that uniforms became standard for female athletes.

NEW YORK RELENTS

In 1978, after numerous lawsuits, the athletic commission finally agreed to license professional female boxers, but the historic moment was overshadowed when Tyger Trimiar challenged Cat Davis to a fight at the athletic commission office. When the commission handed out the first female professional boxing license, it was Cat Davis who received it, not Tyger Trimiar or Jackie Tonawanda, who had been fighting for licenses years before Davis came onto the scene.[47] This was a source of animosity between the women, especially Trimiar, who challenged Davis to a fight at the commission the day the licenses were finally granted. Davis retorted, "You'll have to learn to box first," and the two were in one another's faces within minutes.[48] Although some felt that this spat was theatrical and in the style of Muhammad Ali, promoters for both fighters swore that the animosity was long-standing.

It is easy to see the case for enmity between Davis and Trimiar, both of whom had names of the feline variety. Davis was often described as graceful and beautiful in news stories, while Trimiar and Tonawanda were typically referred to as Amazons. In one story, writer Prentis Rogers asks if Davis is the "Great White Hope" and again compares her to the Amazonian and nonwhite Trimiar.[49] Rogers argues that in the era of the unbeatable Muhammad Ali, the only chance for a white boxer to rise above the domination of the black race was, perhaps, in the female division. Rogers also praises Cat's looks, commenting, "In thinking of a woman pro boxer, images of hard-toned, muscle-bound Amazon-like women come screaming into mind. But Davis belies that. She looks more like a ballet dancer than a lady whose right hand has cut the lights out on fifteen foes."[50]

Race was, of course, still a major issue in American sports in 1978. The Civil Rights Movement of the 1950s and 1960s, undeniably the largest social movement in twentieth-century America, was articulated in the fighting world through various channels. Many states still banned bouts between white and black fighters, although other ethnicities did not seem to come into any such strictures. Because of these separations, some boxing and wrestling events featured fight cards of entirely African American or Mexican fighters. In 1962, in Cleveland, Ohio, one wrestling show included "four outstanding Negro girl wrestlers."[51] Champion fighter Muhammad Ali used his boxing fame to aid the Civil Rights Movement in the United States. Whether Cat Davis received the first professional boxing license in New York because she was white is unclear, but for Tyger Trimiar, race was only one of the components that she would have to overcome to attain her dream of becoming the first lady of boxing.

"LADY" TYGER TRIMIAR

Cat Davis and Jackie Tonawanda received a great deal of media attention during and after their fighting careers. Their colleague, Tyger Trimiar, also had an interesting career, filled with the drama of calling out Davis during their licensing, initiating a hunger strike against promoter Don King, and, of course, compiling her stellar boxing record. Trimiar was one of the more vocal advocates of women's boxing; in the 1970s, she recognized that boxing would be the next great sport for women and sought to create a supportive environment for current and future fighters. In addition, she was stunningly beautiful. She had a smooth, shaved head; ebony skin; chiseled cheekbones; and beautiful hands. Trimiar looked like she belonged on the pages of *Vogue* magazine rather than in a boxing ring, although Davis received more attention and praise, perhaps because she was white. The style section of the *Washington Post* dubbed her "Lady Tyger" for her delicate features and elegant attire but located women's boxing in the fringes of society, "somewhere between freak shows and the strange little tidepools of the demimonde."[52] This statement is, indubitably, hyperbolic, since women's boxing has never been confined solely to the realm of freak shows.

In March 1980, famed boxing promoter Don King wrote an editorial that appeared in the newly formed *WBB* magazine, the first publication focused solely on women's boxing.[53] In the piece, King explains that he supported women who wanted to compete in boxing because he believed in human rights and equality. He also claims that he would be willing to promote women's boxing, but, said Tyger Trimiar, he did nothing of the sort. In 1987, Trimiar went on a hunger strike to protest King's lack of initiative to help promote women's boxing; however, King did say publically that he supported women's boxing, and a few years later, he signed Christy Martin to appear in his professional boxing pay-per-view promotions. Nevertheless, the battle was still on to legalize all aspects of women's boxing in the United States.

USA BOXING LIFTS THEIR BAN ON FEMALE BOXERS

In 1988, Sweden became the first country to remove the ban on women's boxing, and the rest of the world soon followed. While New York's acquiescence to license professional female boxers was an important milestone in fighting history, the big move came in the 1990s, for it was not until 1993 that the USA Boxing Commission, the national organization that supported the U.S. Olympic boxing team, officially lifted the ban on female fighters. Prior to USA Boxing's decision, individual states could license women, but there could be no national competition and no federal regulation of rules and titles. It took a lawsuit brought by sixteen-year-old Dallas Malloy to force USA Boxing to rewrite their policy on women's boxing. In November 1993, only a month after the end of the ban, Malloy fought Heather Poyner in Lynwood, Washington, in the first official women's boxing match. That year, Malloy not only won the right to fight, she won her bout against Poyner. According to the new ruling, women could now register with USA Boxing and compete in sanctioned amateur bouts. Fifty-four women registered in the first year, and thus began the era of legalized female amateur boxing.[54]

But women's boxing in the 1990s was still marginalized in the sporting world. Female fighters were anomalies, and everyone wanted to try to diagnose why a woman, particularly a good-looking or petite one, would want to fight. In an article for *Playboy* magazine in 1997, Amy Handelsman shares her experience training and interacting with some of the best female fighters in Los Angeles. Handelsman offers several explanations for why women would want to box: because they can, because they are good at it, or because it makes them feel sexy.[55] Sex has always been inextricably linked with women's sports, from the bucolic farms with young country girls wrestling during their shifts, to the 1990s, when newly licensed female boxers wore makeup in the ring. The following chapter on mixed martial arts (MMA) discusses this topic in more detail, but in the 1990s, people criticized certain female boxers for looking glamorous in photos, while simultaneously praising them for having strength and beauty.

GOLDEN GLOVES

In 1995, more than thirty amateur female boxers competed in New York's Golden Gloves tournament. This was the first time women had entered the famous amateur boxing tournament, and it ended in a highly publicized showdown in Madison Square Garden. The 106-pound Jill Matthews defeated Dee Hamaguchi to become the first female champion. Hamaguchi famously applied to fight in the tournament as D. Hamaguchi, concealing her gender and allowing her to register for the event. Once Hamaguchi's sex was discovered, the Golden Gloves allowed other women to sign up, lifting the ban on female boxers. Prior to this breakthrough, the national Golden Gloves tournament had been reserved for male fighters, but that did not stop Hamaguchi and Matthews from making headlines as the first female fighters to participate. After the Golden

Gloves, Matthews began her professional career, but she also played guitar and sang in a punk rock band called "Times Square."[56] Hamaguchi also had an interesting career outside the boxing ring. A graduate of Yale University, she is a judo expert who teaches the art to women and school-children in Harlem.[57]

A 1995 article in *Vogue* magazine details the experiences of several of the Golden Gloves competitors. It is astonishing that the fashion publication would dedicate precious space to women's boxing, even if it is inaccurate in places. The article claims that women had never been properly schooled in boxing until the 1990s, which, of course, we know to be untrue; however, the piece does offer a fascinating picture of the state of women's boxing in 1995, noting that unlike the Hollywood portrayal of boxing as the great hope for working-class men to escape their lives of poverty and want, the women boxing in 1995 were often highly professional and well-educated individuals. The article points out that the stereotype of the "poor street thug"-turned-boxing champion was as much a myth as the idea that boxing was reserved for men. The reality of the underdog-turned-boxing champion is substantiated by history, as evidenced by various famous boxers, but Hollywood undoubtedly turned it into a trope. Furthermore, the *Vogue* article reveals the inverse of that mythology: that Hollywood always paints women as the victims when it comes to fighting. Many people at the time assumed that a woman would crumble when hit in the face, because that was the image propagated in film and television.[58] And while it is true that a woman who is assaulted should be seen as a victim, in this new period of televised women's boxing, women were not victims because they were recognized as athletes. They were empowered by their sport in much the same way that a woman felt empowered by her job as a physician or an executive in the corporate world.

The 1995 Golden Gloves in New York was a historic event, but it was not until 1997 that the first national tournament with female participants was held. In 1997, sixty-seven women competed in the first national Golden Gloves boxing tournament for the opportunity to win twelve titles. That same year, the International Female Boxing Association (IFBA) was founded. The first commissioner, Jackie Kallon, led the organization in holding its own fighting events and creating multiple weight classes. The IFBA continues to promote women's boxing in the international community, and, in 2009, with the help of other boxing institutions and committees, the International Olympic Committee (IOC) announced that women would, for the first time in history, compete in boxing in the 2012 Olympics.

Surprisingly, the official Golden Gloves website does not list a history of female winners, although male winners are detailed starting with the tournament's origins in 1928, but the addition of the women's divisions to the Golden Gloves venue provided amateur female boxers with a place to compete on local and national levels. Meanwhile, professional female fighters proliferated, none more prominently than Christy Martin, the new face of women's boxing.

CHRISTY MARTIN MAKES HEADLINES

Christy Martin stepped in between the ropes, removing her baby pink satin robe as the announcer called her name. She faced her opponent and, as the bell rang, erupted out of the corner, firing sharp combos as she drove her opponent into the ropes. When *Sports Illustrated* featured her on its cover in 1996, Martin's wavy, brown hair just touched her shoulders, and with gloved hands on her hips, she stuck her chin out defiantly. But in the ring, her chin was down and hands up, and her hair, drenched with sweat, whipped around her face as she slipped and punched. When her hand was raised in resounding victory, Martin was not only the winner of that night's match, she was the new face of women's boxing.

Martin is one of the most famous female boxers of the late twentieth century. After Don King signed her to fight in his legendary pay-per-view events, she competed on the same card as Mike Tyson and Evander Holyfield, earning money and attention from the international boxing community. But Christy Martin is a controversial figure. She helped put women's boxing on the map but also criticized her fellow athletes and claimed that none of her opponents were really able to compete with her. At a time when the sport needed support, especially from the inside, Martin seemed indifferent about advocating for women's boxing. Her personal career was tantamount to any desire for women's progress, and placing her career first, before any desire for helping other women in the sport, created tension amongst her cohorts in the emerging women's professional boxing circuit. Former welterweight champion Sugar Ray Leonard admired the female boxer, saying, "I've seen her work out, and she is quite impressive."[59] Leonard predicted that fans would also be impressed by Martin's skill in the ring, admitting, "She packs quite a punch."[60] Christy's fighting career is well-documented; she does not have to rely on her own assertions of victory and greatness to deserve her spot in the Boxing Hall of Fame.

In the middle of the 1990s, only a few years after women had become eligible to receive professional boxing licenses, Americans still had a difficult time accepting women's fighting in the limelight. In fact, many people seemed to question not only the necessity for women to box, but whether boxing, in general, had run its course in American culture. Most of the pieces published about Christy Martin, inarguably the most visible female boxer of the late twentieth century, either clearly supported the fighter in terms of gender equality in sports or criticized her incessantly about anything ranging from her fighting skills to her looks to her personal life.

The *San Diego Union-Tribune* published an article on Martin entitled "Is She Admirable or Abominable?" that questioned whether she was a "symbol of women's equality . . . or part of a freak show?"[61] The article claimed that the sight of women fighting is sickening and that the only reason Martin saw reasonable success in the media was because of her looks. Martin apparently agreed, responding, "I don't think I'd be as popular if I drove a Jeep and wore combat boots and a flannel shirt into the ring."[62] It was this type of comment, standard in Martin's interviews, that made her controversial to those who sought to support her as a figurehead for gender equality in sports. According to Don King, however, her success was dependent on three distinct points: "Christy Martin is attractive. She can fight, and she is a novelty," he said.[63] Throughout the history of women's fighting sports, we have seen that female fighters have been treated poorly by the media, but the coverage of Christy Martin is much more cutting than that regarding Hattie Leslie or Hattie Stewart one hundred years earlier.

When she retired in 2012, Martin claimed forty-nine victories (thirty-one of those ending with a knockout), seven losses, and three draws. Her last few years were marked by losses, including a devastating knockout by Holly Holm in 2005. But Martin's early career was marked by success and a number of "women's firsts." She is featured on the cover of the April 15, 1996, edition of *Sports Illustrated*, along with the headline, "The Lady Is a Champ: Boxing's New Sensation, Christy Martin." This was the first time a female boxer had appeared on the cover of a major magazine. The article, entitled "Gritty Woman," identifies the social climate in 1996, which does not feel like that long ago.[64] It was acceptable for women to leave the house to become doctors or lawyers, but it was unsettling to see women "appropriate the testosterone-driven sports that men have traditionally enjoyed."[65] Martin not only had the gall to fight brutally in her matches, she dressed like a woman, some said provocatively, in short skirts and makeup, outside the ring.

Martin's technical proficiency and indomitable attitude made her respected in the boxing world, especially when her matches were considered more action-packed and interesting than some of the main events on a fight card, but she refused to be the voice of feminism, often admitting her dislike for masculine-looking women. In "Gritty Woman," one photo features her vacuuming the carpet barefoot. The image is disconcerting and seems unnecessary, both on the part of the magazine for including it and Martin for posing. This particular article was a milestone in the history of women's fighting, because it literally put women at the forefront by using Martin's image on the cover of the magazine. Yet, the piece seems reluctant to consider a future for women's boxing "beyond the sideshow status is has sporadically enjoyed."[66] Granted, the article admits that boxing, in general, may see its demise in the coming years, but, as we have seen, boxing endures, and despite her controversial personal life and ideology, Christy Martin endured, fighting regularly for the next ten years.

OTHER FEMALE FIGHTERS

Christy Martin may have been on the cover of *Sports Illustrated*, but other female fighters deserved the attention as much as she did. As is often the case, the media chooses one woman to embody the spirit of a new sport even though there are plenty of other women competing, some of whom are more talented than the "face" of that particular sport. Bonnie Canino, a skilled martial artist with black belts in Kenpo, tae kwon do, and kung fu, was a champion in both kickboxing and boxing in the 1990s. She began her career in kickboxing and retired with an impressive record of thirty-two wins, four losses, and one draw.[67] But Canino did not leave the fight game entirely; instead, she fought as a professional boxer and

Figure 4.1.   Christy Martin (left) fighting Holly Holm (right). Courtesy of Mary Ann Owen.

retired in 2004, with fifteen wins and four losses.[68] In November 1996, she fought two professional fights in a four-day span, beginning with a Don King Production match on a Wednesday evening, followed by another fight on Saturday evening. Canino explained that she was in training for a world championship bout in January and was basically using the events as tune-ups. In her own words, which are perfectly quote-worthy, she stated, "I am a bad girl, but I need the work."[69] Canino retired in 2004, but she continues to be a part of the martial arts community, from running her own gym in Florida to coaching other women, including Ada Velez, who won the first International Boxing Association bantamweight title in January 2001.

Another kickboxer-turned-boxer in the 1990s was Lucia Rijker, the undefeated kickboxing champion from Holland. Rijker held four different

Figure 4.2. Bonnie Canino with her head coach, Burt Rodriquez. Courtesy of Mary Ann Owen.

world titles, and when she retired from kickboxing in the late 1980s, she had won all thirty-six of her matches, twenty-five of which had ended with a knockout. In her professional boxing career, she had seventeen wins and no losses, with fourteen of her victories ending with a knockout.[70] Often referred to as the "most dangerous woman in the world," Rijker could have been successful in any sport, and intense MMA fans may indulge in time-traveling fantasies in which she meets Cris "Cyborg" Justino in the cage. But like Justino, Rijker was sometimes criticized for her dominating performances and looks. When Rijker sought a fight with Christy Martin, Martin's camp claimed that they needed Rijker to take a DNA chromosome test to prove she was a woman. The two ended up in a scrap at a gym, but there is no substantiated story as to exactly what went down between the two champion female boxers. The fight never occurred, and the two women continued to exchange vitriolic and cruel comments.[71]

But Rijker became successful again when she turned to acting later in her career. She plays Hillary Swank's villainous opponent in *Million Dollar Baby* (2005), a film that rejuvenated interest in women's boxing, and she later went on to perform in other popular television programs and films. She may be the most dangerous woman alive, but she also successfully embodied the fighter-turned-actor for women that would later be emulated by MMA fighters Gina Carano and Ronda Rousey.

One of the most infamous battles of the 1990s was when Margaret MacGregor boxed Loi Chow, a male jockey, in 1999. MacGregor decisively won each round, but the fight nonetheless stirred up controversy. Many believed that Chow would easily defeat MacGregor, despite MacGregor's superior skill, simply because he was a man. Sadly, the critical slant created an environment that the fight would be ridiculous no matter what the outcome. If Chow were to viciously beat MacGregor, it would prove the unsuitability of women in the ring—and "teach her a lesson." If MacGregor defeated Chow, it would simply prove that he was not a real man. Although MacGregor easily won the match, her victory was clouded by these arguments. In a similar contest in 1973, twenty years earlier, Billy Jean King roundly shut down former tennis pro Bobby Riggs in the infamous "Battle of the Sexes." In the aftermath, people speculated that Riggs intentionally lost the match because he bet against himself. Even when women are victorious, they never truly win.

LAILA ALI FOLLOWS IN HER FATHER'S FOOTSTEPS

Women's boxing continued to flourish in the late 1990s and early 2000s, as Laila Ali, the daughter of Muhammad Ali, entered the ring. Laila was eighteen years old when she decided to compete in boxing, despite her father's initial efforts to talk her out of his own career ; however, the former champion quickly shifted his perspective to support his daughter.[72] Laila's professional career began with a bang in 1999, when she knocked out April Fowler in the first round. Eight years later, Laila fought in the first women's professional boxing match in South Africa, where she defeated Gwendolyn O'Neil in the presence of Nelson Mandela. After that fight, she officially retired, with an incredible record of twenty-four wins and zero losses, living up to her promise to end her fighting days undefeated.[73] One of her many victories was over Christy Martin in 2003, when she knocked out Martin, who was ten years her senior, six inches shorter, and twenty pounds lighter.[74] While the fight between Ali and Martin may have not been fair in terms of size, Ali demonstrated true skill and convinced many skeptics that she belonged in the ring.

In 2005, Ali defeated Erin Toughill, a prolific fighter who competed in professional MMA, professional boxing, and Brazilian jiu-jitsu, as well as on the television show *American Gladiators*. Toughill is one of the most famous faces of women's MMA. She fought for more than a decade before retiring in 2011, with ten wins, three loses, and one draw. Since the end of her boxing career, Laila Ali has remained in the limelight, appearing on a variety of television programs and contributing articles to lifestyle magazines about parenting and health. Although many of her contemporaries criticized her for never taking "difficult" fights and essentially padding her record, Ali retired undefeated, a feat that could incite jealously in anyone. Her arguably most famous match came in 2001, when she, the daughter of Muhammad Ali, fought Jacqui Frazier Lyde, the daughter of Joe Frazier. Ali defeated Lyde by a small margin, but the fight was, in a way, symbolic of the new generation of fighters. The children of boxing legends could follow in their parents' footsteps, whether they be sons or daughters.

Figure 4.3. Shelly Burton (left) versus Laila Ali (right). Courtesy of Mary Ann Owen.

THE 2012 OLYMPICS

The 2000s saw growth in women's boxing at both the amateur and professional levels, but the next milestone occurred in 2012. The 2012 Olympics in London featured female fighters for the first time in history. This historic proceeding was an exciting development in the fighting world and the lives of the young women who competed that summer, but before they could enter the ring, the joy of including female boxers in the Olympics was quickly overshadowed by the International Boxing Association's (AIBA) declaration that female fighters must wear skirts in the ring. From this odd declaration there ensued a furious debate about female athletes, as well as the institutions that govern both the sport and their bodies.

Outfitting Female Olympic Boxers

There is no doubt that the commercial success of a female athlete is heightened by an emphasis on her looks. Part of creating a look hinges on sartorial choices. Tennis stars Serena and Venus Williams incite controversy regarding their outlandish garments worn in tournaments. For most female athletes, clothing must be functional for the sport. Fight apparel is designed to stay in place, an important consideration for grapplers and MMA fighters. Boxing uniforms, meanwhile, tend to be universal for men and women, with boxing trunks and a sleeveless tank top being the standard for amateurs. Yet, the 2012 Olympics saw controversy when the AIBA insisted on creating a gender-specific uniform.

During World War II, women took to the field in their own professional baseball league. As popularized by the 1992 film *A League of Their Own*, the female athletes were forced to wear skirts in an effort to eroticize the players and promote the sport to the American public, which supposedly had little interest in watching women play. The outfits also emphasized the difference between the male and female ballplayers, although longer skirts would have had the same effect. Female baseball players were not just supposed to mark themselves as female by wearing skirts: The purpose of their outfits was to titillate the crowd.

Beyond the practice of sexualizing female athletes, notably practiced in nearly all forms of marketing, there is also perhaps the assertion of sexual difference in the AIBA's idea of making skirts part of the boxing uniform for women. Yes, the AIBA would allow women to fight, but female fighters can never forget that they are just women, subjugated by their bodies and marginalized by gender stereotypes.

Whether the intention was to increase the visibility of female fighters by sexualizing them or to mark the difference between men and women using fashion, the AIBA's pronouncement created an immediate controversy—perhaps not the type of reaction they had desired. Instead, female fighters expressed their distaste for the decree, and the association had to reconsider their mandate. Ireland's three-time world champion and eventual gold medalist, Katie Taylor, spoke with the BBC, saying, "I won't be wearing a miniskirt, I don't even wear miniskirts on a night out, so I definitely won't be wearing miniskirts in the ring."[75] Taylor's colleagues heartily agreed with her, and on March 1, 2012, the AIBA changed their ruling to allow women to choose whether to wear shorts or skirts. Although the association's retraction was quiet, it was obviously due to the loud protestations made by boxers and boxing fans throughout the world that women do not have to wear skirts to be women and certainly do not have to wear skirts to be boxers.

Glory

The 2012 London Olympics generated great excitement as women prepared to step into the ring for the first time. Marlen Esparza signed a contract with *CoverGirl* cosmetics and was featured in a commercial that aired during the Games. She also received a bronze medal, as did Chungneijang MeryKom Hmangte of Indonesia in the women's flyweight division. In the final, gold medalist Nicola Adams of Great Britain defeated silver medalist Cancan Ren of China. Katie Taylor of Ireland, who declared that she would never wear a miniskirt, earned gold in the female lightweight division, and in the women's middleweight division, seventeen-year-old Claressa Shields of the United States earned gold by defeating Russia's silver medalist, Nadezda Torlopova. Women's boxing established a strong profile that would help it grow in popularity and authority for future fighters.

WRESTLING IN THE MODERN ERA

By the 1960s, wrestling had begun to diverge into two distinct camps: "professional" wrestling for entertainment, and sport wrestling, primarily practiced in high schools and colleges. The "professional" style of wrestling simply meant that wrestlers earned money, but the fights were more theatrical than the matches seen in high school gyms. The entertainment style of wrestling may have primarily been a spectacle, although less so than today's professional wrestling, but practitioners still needed skill and strength to perform. Sport wrestling, also known as scholastic wrestling because it is chiefly practiced in schools, became more popular in the 1970s, with isolated instances of girls participating on boy's teams.

Even with the passage of Title IX, girls had to fight for access to wrestling teams in high schools, and some still seek that right today in the private and religious school sectors. The popularity of professional or entertainment-style wrestling increased in the late twentieth century, as large television promotions were featured on major cable networks. In the world of sport wrestling, two types dominated: freestyle and Greco-Roman. Women typically compete in freestyle wrestling, and, in 2004, women's wrestling became part of the Olympics. But prior to the Olympics, female wrestlers, like female boxers, had to push for the right to compete at the national and international levels.

Jerry Hunter was not the only woman to fight a legal battle to wrestle. In both 1987 and 1996, two high school students brought lawsuits against their school districts for refusing to allow them to wrestle on the all-boy teams. The courts ruled in the girls' favor in both instances. In the 1996 case, the court agreed that Tiffany Adams, the plaintiff, could wrestle on the team because "wrestling is an athletic activity and not a sexual activity."[76]

In 1987, Norway hosted the first all-woman wrestling tournament, and the United States sent no competitors. Three years later, the United States hosted its own national championships in San Francisco, although American women still had to pay their own way to compete internationally. USA Wrestling did not support women in 1991, so female wrestlers founded their own group, the U.S. Women's Amateur Wrestling Federation, to help support women competing at the national and international levels.[77] Finally, in 1995, USA Wrestling, the national organization in charge of the American Olympic wrestling team, sponsored the U.S. women's national team.

Although women could not yet compete in the Olympics, USA Wrestling saw the benefit of maintaining a team of women that was competitive on the world stage. Shannon Williams, a former high school cheerleader, started competing in 1989, amongst only a dozen women, but by 1995, more than 150 women showed up to compete for a spot on the national team.[78] In an article in the *San Diego Union-Tribune*, Williams correctly asserts that women's wrestling would be an Olympic sport within ten years. One of the headings of the article explains that, "it's no longer uncommon to see young girls compete" in wrestling.[79] In 1995, one coach explained, it was standard to see at least ten or fifteen girls for every four hundred boys at a wrestling tournament. The women on the U.S. national team were unquestionably products of Title IX, and while many schools reinforced the ban against girls in contact sports, some programs did not. The international wrestling community also supported the growth of women's wrestling; the Women's World Championship tournament was held in Moscow in 1995; however, many of these events continued to treat women differently than male competitors. The 2000 World Championships in Sofia, Bulgaria, presented an award to the most beautiful female wrestler. The woman refused to accept her "award," and the promoters ceased attempting to present this ignominious honor. [80]

Female wrestling initially gained wider cultural acceptance than boxing, perhaps because boxing already had a connotation of violence. Women participated in wrestling tournaments globally, and, in 2004, women's freestyle wrestling became an official sport in the Olympic Games in Athens. Sara McMann, future Ultimate Fighting Championship MMA fighter, earned a silver medal and was one of many women who participated in the first Olympic Games to include women's wrestling. Women continued to participate in the Olympics, although they received little media coverage. Nonetheless, it is not just female wrestlers who are ignored by the Olympic media. In 2012, the IOC decided to remove wrestling of all kinds from the Olympic roster. The enormous backlash and subsequent support for the sport persuaded the committee to rescind its decision, but whether that means wrestling will receive more media coverage in the future is unclear. Luckily, there are numerous prestigious competitions held worldwide for elite wrestlers of both sexes.

JUDO

Judo was the first fighting sport to include women in Olympic competitions. In 1992, female judo practitioners, referred to as judokas, competed in the Barcelona Olympic Games. The male and female divisions both consist of six weight-classes, and each class secures four medalists: one gold, one silver, and two bronze winners, due to the bracketing format. Other combat Olympic sports also follow this medaling format. As is mentioned in the introduction, judo has long been a popular martial art in the Western world.

Arguably, the most influential female judo practitioner in history is Rusty Stewart, who, in 1955, learned judo in New York City. She began to teach at the local YMCA and trained with a group of forty men. In 1956, when the team was invited to the state championship, Stewart passed herself off as a man by binding her breasts and wearing her hair short. She made it all the way to the finals, but when an official discovered she was a woman, he threatened to disqualify the entire team unless she returned her well-earned medal. In 1963, fifty-five women competed in the first women-only judo competition in New York City, at the instigation of Stewart. Stewart had recently returned from Japan, where she had obtained a second-degree black belt. It would be nearly a decade before the first national judo competition for women would occur in the United States, but judo was more accepting of female athletes than most combative sports in the 1970s.

Throughout the years, women have had a prominent role in judo as it has been practiced and contested in numerous countries. Female judo players have regularly participated in prominent events and tournaments. In 1992, women's judo was added to the Olympics, held in Barcelona. The most famous Olympic judo player in the United States is undoubtedly Ronda Rousey, who has become the most famous female MMA fighter in the world. As a martial artist, Rousey has followed in her mother's footsteps. AnnaMaria Waddell won first place in the 1984 World Judo Championships, making her the first American to win gold in that event. Rousey has made history as a MMA fighter, as chapter 5 reveals, but, as it turns out, she is simply following in a rather fantastic family tradition.

As the twentieth century came to a close, women saw historic gains in institutionalized equality. The governing bodies that had sprung up in the middle of the century and restricted females from competing in sports were suddenly forced to recognize equal rights for women under the law. It would be several more years before the IOC, perhaps the largest and most rigid sports governing body in the world, would acquiesce to admit female wrestlers, judo players, and boxers into the hallowed realm of the Olympic Games, but the momentum from the lawsuits and court decisions from the late twentieth century created a catalyst for women to compete in a number of sports that were supposedly reserved for men. The 1990s also popularized the sport of MMAs, and the fighting world was forever changed. As is detailed in the next chapter, women fought, and continue to fight, for equal opportunities and recognition as fighting sports continue to evolve.

5

MMA GOES MAINSTREAM

November 1993 was a banner month for the martial arts world. USA Boxing allowed women to compete in amateur events for the first time when sixteen-year-old Dallas Malloy defeated Heather Poyner in Lynwood, Washington. On November 12, 1993, the first fight card for the Ultimate Fighting Championship (UFC) aired in the United States. The UFC would swiftly become the largest mixed martial arts (MMA) promotion in the world, drawing viewers from a large demographic spectrum. But MMA and the UFC, as the largest provider of the sport, also drew harsh critiques and censure from numerous institutions and groups worldwide. Despite this, MMA, as a modern embodiment of the Pankration fought in the Roman Colosseum, became one of the fastest-growing sports in history.

The history of MMA is extensive and could be a book on its own, but since the purpose of this volume is to highlight the history of women's involvement in the sport, it will suffice to say that the significance of MMA is its rapid growth during the past two decades. Since the first UFC event in 1993, MMA has made headlines as the most violent sport in the world. Whether this is true remains to be seen. Injuries in MMA fights may not be any more prevalent than those in boxing, or even American football, but the visual spectacle of a MMA fight appears more violent than other sports.

One of the reasons MMA appears to be more violent is because of the types of attacks fighters are allowed to execute and the small amount of protective gear fighters don in the cage. In most MMA promotions fighters wear only a mouth guard, a groin protector (for men), and four-ounce gloves. When compared to the ten-ounce gloves in boxing and extensive padding of a professional football player, the paucity of protective gear worn by a MMA fighter seems to invite injury. Furthermore, fighters are able to carry out many more types of attacks than in boxing. Thus, many fighters are injured and sometimes defeated by kicks, knee, or elbow strikes. The submission portion of MMA allows fighters to do joint manipulations that could, and sometimes do, break arms and tear knee or ankle joints. Competitors can choke one another unconscious, which always includes a risk of brain injury. MMA fighters have a higher risk of injury than most athletes because they wear less protective gear and can sustain damage through a variety of submission techniques. Four-ounce gloves and elbow strikes often lead to bloody noses and split eyebrows, so most MMA bouts include some form of bloodshed; however, not all fights end with severe injury, as most end with no more bumps and bruises than a NFL player receives after a hard game. But MMA still contains a connotation of violence and brutality inherent in multidiscipline fight sports.

It is not just violence that makes MMA popular. There are numerous possible outcomes in this multidisciplinary sport, so fights are rarely predictable. Viewers tune in for a variety of reasons, from the violence, to the skill, to the narratives of fighters. Individual fighters draw attention from fans and the sports media industry for being controversial, likeable, or good-looking. Promotional machines advertising fight cards emphasize rivalries and underdog stories, just like any other sport medium. Throughout the past two decades, MMA has become a cultural zeitgeist, creating a new platform for the Pankration, a sport that, by all accounts, appears to have died out thousands of years ago.

MMA CONTROVERSY

MMA grew swiftly in popularity, although critics like Senator John McCain have denounced the sport as a spectacle of violence, rather than skill. Injunctions against MMA competitions sprung up throughout the United States, as groups from the USA Boxing Commission to state governments sought to eliminate MMA bouts. After its first show in 1993, the UFC promotion offered more frequent events, all of which were

Figure 5.1. Jocelyn Lybarger lands a heavy cross on Rosa Acevedo at RFA 14.
Courtesy of Bryan James Carr of Liquid Steel Photogs.

available on pay-per-view, occupying the same airwaves as professional boxing. Although the UFC was on its way to becoming a monopoly in the fight world, it still endured numerous roadblocks from opponents of the sport. Officials in Georgia tried to prevent the UFC from holding its twenty-first pay-per-view event in Atlanta in May 1997, because of disagreements regarding licensing.[1] The following month, the Ultimate Fighting Alliance, a now-defunct MMA promotion, agreed to create more stringent rules to govern the cage to position MMA alongside the sports of boxing, judo, and karate.[2] The new regulations, which were also implemented in other MMA venues, included glove size specifications, weight-class divisions, and defining such illegal techniques as groin strikes, hair-pulling, and small-joint manipulations. Even with these modifications, many individuals and groups, USA Boxing, in particular, hoped the sport of MMA would die as quickly as it had meteorically rose.

Conversely, MMA would prevail over its detractors, becoming the one of the fastest-growing sports in recent history. In the early days, the UFC and PRIDE Fighting Championships, the Japanese equivalent, were televised sporting events held several times per year that featured fighters from throughout the world in various martial art disciplines. But MMA also became popular at the local level; small shows with local fighters were held in dirty bars or amphitheaters in settings reminiscent of an underground fight in a B movie. Fighters would prepare for these events in wrestling schools, karate and tae kwon do dojos, boxing gyms, and kickboxing studios. Local shows would help grow some of the UFC's greatest fighters, as well as increase the popularity of MMA as a sport and not just a spectacle. MMA allowed fighters to hurt one another with an unprecedented number of techniques. Fighters were no longer constrained to one specific methodology; boxers could go to the ground, wrestlers could kick, and Brazilian jiu-jitsu fighters could punch. And as MMA grew internationally through pay-per-view events featuring such stars as Royce Gracie and Ken Shamrock, traditional fighting gyms began to offer cross-training opportunities to create well-rounded competitors for this new sport.

THE ORIGINS OF WOMEN'S MMA

Women's history in MMA has been largely underestimated. Several online articles that claim to outline the history of women's mixed martial arts (WMMA) begin their timeline as late as 2004 or 2009. Although both years were important for the sport, women participated in the new sport of MMA prior to those dates. While there are many discrepancies in online articles and websites, the website www.sherdog.com is a fantastic and accurate resource for anyone looking for MMA statistics and past-event information. Nearly all dates, fight records, and statistics in this chapter, unless otherwise stated, are from Sherdog's website.

In the early 1990s, Japan had two all-female professional wrestling promotions, both of which added no-holds-barred-style fights to their venues. The first all-female MMA fight card was held in Tokyo in 1995, by the Ladies Legends Professional Wrestling fighting promotion. There were seven bouts on the card featuring fighters from throughout the world. The headline event was between Russian Svetlana Goundarenko, a six-foot, three-inch, 330-pound fighter who retired in 2001, with six wins and two losses, and Shinobu Kandori of Japan, a much smaller opponent, at five feet, seven inches and 165 pounds, with a rear naked choke. The

Russian emerged victorious. The women fought again in 1998, but this time Shinobu defeated Svetlana with a submission.

The next Ladies Legends Pro Wrestling fight card took place in 2000, and included Marloes Coenen in her debut fight, which she won with an arm bar against Yuuki Kondo. The fight venue was reconfigured into Smackgirl, an all-women's promotion that ran from May 2001 to April 2008, and presented dozens of incredible fight cards in Japan. Women worldwide traveled to participate, including American Laura D'Auguste, who retired in 2008, with nine victories, one draw, and no losses. D'Auguste is a registered nurse who traveled to Japan to compete in Smackgirl, where she defeated France's Tevi Sai and Japan's Meguimi Yabushita.[3] In 2005, she was considered by many to be the best female MMA fighter in the world; however, the most famous fighter to emerge from Smackgirl was Megumi Fujii, a 115-pound Japanese native who dominated the strawweight class with twenty-six wins and three loses as of October 2013.

Although the first women to compete in a modern-day MMA fight in the United States remain unidentified, one of the earliest on record is Jennifer Howe, who defeated Terry Lukomski with a rear naked choke on November 21, 1998, in Utah. Howe was the longtime girlfriend of MMA great Jeremy Horn, and her training partner and boyfriend stood by her as she became one of the best fighters in the early days of WMMA. During her seven-year career, Howe won thirteen professional fights, her only two losses going to Roxanne Modafferi, a tough opponent who ended up competing on the UFC's *Ultimate Fighter* reality television competition series more than a decade later.

GLORIFIED BAR FIGHTS

While a lot of legitimate promotions sprang up in the wake of the UFC inaugural event's success, MMA fights also began appearing as entertainment in bars. It may be unfair to describe these events as MMA fights, although there were certainly rules and time restrictions in the spirit of professional MMA venues. One event, in Iowa, in 2002, included a bout between two young women, and although it was the shortest fight of the night, it was also the last, a position typically reserved for the main event.[4] Twenty-three-year-old state worker Misty Hytrek defeated twenty-one-year-old Janine Keptting, a karate instructor who lost within twenty seconds of the first round. Whether Hytrek was a trained fighter remains unknown, but she certainly made short work of Keptting with an abundance of punches, providing the latter with a broken nose. The fight night was apparently successful, but lawmakers quickly quashed these in-bar fights.

Unfortunately, these no-holds-barred fighting events were not regulated, which means that people who should not have been fighting entered the fray. On June 14, 2003, at the Sarasota County Fairgrounds in Sarasota, Florida, Stacy Young, a thirty-year-old mother of two, was killed in a fighting competition called Toughman.[5] Toughman competitions originated in 1979, under the auspices of being a legitimate amateur boxing event that allowed anyone to enter the ring; the only limitation was that no competitor could have more than five amateur bouts. Thus, many individuals, like Stacy Young, had no training or fight experience. Many people point to Toughman as part of the MMA origin story, but it is a tenuous connection. Toughman was reminiscent of the early catch-as-catch-can exhibition at American fairs in the early twentieth century, but with punching as part of the program. When Young entered the ring, she thought it would be fun. Instead, she was beaten unconscious in front of a crowd of cheering fans and later pronounced brain dead at the hospital. Three other competitors were taken to the hospital after their fights in Sarasota, but Young was the only one to die. Young's tragic death had a dramatic effect on fighting regulation in Florida. Sadly, Toughman remains linked to the sport of MMA in the minds of many. The death of the young mother instigated a media furor demanding the end of these extreme fighting sports, and MMA was grouped with this Toughman event. Fortunately, the UFC was already focusing on rebranding itself as a legitimate sport to continue to grow its business. ZUFFA, the company that owns the UFC tried to distance itself from its first fights, claiming that the sport and the athletes were safe now because of new rules and regulations.

HOOK-N-SHOOT

The success of the various Japanese female fighting promotions led Jeff Osbourne, UFC commentator and early supporter of all things MMA, to add women to his successful Hook-n-Shoot promotions in 2001. Hook-n-Shoot was an early MMA promotion that launched many famous fighters, including Frank Mir and Miesha Tate, into the UFC. But Osbourne did not just put women on his March 10, 2001, Hook-n-Shoot fight card; he had the two women featured as the main event of the evening. That night, bantamweight fighter Judy Neff defeated Jessica Ross with a technical knockout. The following year, on April 13, 2002, Hook-n-Shoot hosted the first all-female professional MMA fight card in the United States. There were seven bouts on the card, and the headliner, Debi "Whiplash" Purcell, choked Christine Van Fleet out in the first round. Hook-n-Shoot continued to feature all-female fight cards throughout the next decade, launching a number of big-name fighters into the spotlight. Debi Purcell, the headliner at the first Hook-n-Shoot event, would become one of the most active advocates for WMMA, even after she left the cage.

FIGHTERGIRLS

In 2001, bantamweight fighter Debi "Whiplash" Purcell fought her first professional MMA bout in Minnesota. She defeated Amber Mosely with a surfeit of punches for the technical knockout in the first minute of the first round. From there, Purcell went on to win three more times in her career, and she was the first woman to be named "King of the Cage" in 2002. King of the Cage was another early promotion, with its first show in 1999, which launched the careers of several top UFC fighters, including Frank Lister, Shaun Sherk, and Quentin "Rampage" Jackson. Purcell fought Nicole Albrect for two 5-minute rounds and was declared the winner by unanimous decision. Albrect weighted thirty pounds more than Purcell and stood several inches taller. Purcell used her Muay Thai background to throw leg kicks and knees from the clinch when standing and took Albrect to the ground with several strong wrestling shots. The video of the fight shows the many differences in the early days of MMA compared to today, because Albrect is wearing wrestling shoes in the cage. Purcell is well-respected in the MMA community, not just as a female fighter, but as a fighter in general.

Purcell is the only woman to act as coach for the short-lived International Fight League, an attempt to turn MMA into a semblance of a team sport. She also founded FighterGirls, a website designed to help match up female fighters from throughout the world and a place for women's fighting news and events. The website eventually expanded to include a store, also called FighterGirls, which produces fighting gear for women. The site contains an extensive database of female fighters and a list of schools that provide training for women. Purcell is a pioneer of WMMA and supporter of female fighters, but she retired from the fighting world in 2008, after a defeat by another early female fighter, Rosi Sexton.

Sexton began her professional career in 2002, and she continues to fight as of this writing in 2014. The fight against Purcell put Sexton on the map when she scored a victory by decision and became the new 130-pound female champion. She made headlines, however, not just for her victory in the cage, but for her fascinating and seemingly antithetical personal life. In addition to her career as a fighter, Sexton has a doctorate in theoretical computer science from the University of Manchester and runs a successful osteopathic practice in Manchester. People were baffled by her decision to fight in the cage, especially given her osteopathic practice. Sexton was also the mother of a two-year-old son at the time of her fight with Purcell, which, yet again, made her seem antithetical to the idea of first, a doctor, and second, a mother. But Sexton is all of these things—and more. In 2013, she was signed to the UFC bantamweight division, where she fought Alexis Davis at UFC 161. Although she lost the fight by unanimous decision, she continues to fight, as well as advocate for female MMA fighters.

WOMEN IN BRAZILIAN JIU-JITSU

WMMA began to take off worldwide in the mid-2000s. In 2005, Australia's first WMMA match took place at the Spartan MMA Showdown in March, between Fiona Attig and Mandy Stewart.[6] England already had WMMA bouts, as evidenced by Rosi Sexton's dominating performance on British soil starting in 2002. The popularity of the UFC led to an explosion of training centers in the United States and other countries. Some gyms, for example, the Reality Training Center in Charleston, South Carolina, offered multiple types of fighting disciplines—including kickboxing, wrestling, and grappling—to train members for MMA venues.[7]

Fourteen-year-old Kizma Button told reporters that she hoped to fight one day, despite the various injuries she received while training. Aside from gyms offering MMA training, the sport of Brazilian jiu-jitsu (BJJ) flourished, thanks to the dominating presence of the Gracie family in the UFC. BJJ had been taught in the United States since the mid-1970s, but the UFC made the Brazilian/Japanese sport increasingly popular and facilitated a surge in interest. BJJ had the added benefit of being a particularly good martial art for women, because the gi, or kimono, helps increase leverage. The Gracie family's own stock, Kyra Gracie, has remained one of the most popular female BJJ fighters, not only because of her black belt, but because she is quite attractive. In fact, Kyra's reputation often exceeds that of one of the best female BJJ fighters in history, Lana Stefanac, despite the latter's demonstrated dominance on the mat and in the cage.

Lana Stefanac

One of the first American women to make a name for herself in the international BJJ community was Lana Stefanac, who remains one of the greatest BJJ fighters of all time. Not just as a woman, or an American, but as an individual, her fight career rivals some of the most iconic names in the sport. Stefanac's enviable record reads as a tableau of a fighter's progression to greatness. In 2006, she won the Pan Ams in the blue belt division; that same year, she fought and won three consecutive professional MMA matches, all ending via submission in the first round. She won the Pan Ams in the purple belt division the following year and came in second at Worlds. Stefanac won three more MMA matches during the next two years, rounding out her MMA career in 2008, with an impressive 6–0 professional record. In 2009, she dominated the Abu Dhabi Combat Club (ADCC) World competition and came in first place in both her weight class and the absolute brown/black belt divisions, a first for an American woman. According to the ADCC, Stefanac has fought in nearly two hundred BJJ and no-gi matches and only lost a handful. In addition to her extraordinary personal fight record, she has also acted as a coach, manager, corner-woman, and advocate for numerous professional female fighters.

After receiving her blue belt in BJJ in 2006, Stefanac appeared in her first professional MMA fight, against champion boxer Martha Salazar.

California had previously hosted MMA bouts between women, but the fight between Stefanac and Salazar was the first WMMA match sanctioned by the California State Athletic Commission. Although Salazar was predicted to win via knockout, with 40–1 odds, Stefanac submitted her with a guillotine choke in the first round. Stefanac went on to fight five more times and retired from MMA undefeated in 2009.

In 2008, Stefanac took a group of American women to New Zealand to compete in the "Princesses of Pain" fight card against a team of Aussies. A documentary crew filmed them before and after the fights, and in the ensuing months, Stefanac found herself being bombarded by promoters and matchmakers who wanted her girls for their shows. At the time, her team of professional women was one of the best sources for scouting talented fighters. Working with her former partner, matchmaker Sam Wilson, Stefanac placed many of her fighters at the forefront of local and international MMA venues, but she always fought for the best representation for her girls. She revealed that people would call her and ask to book certain fighters, but instead of referring to them by name, they would ask for "George Lucas's daughter" or the "porn star." And she told them no. In an interview, she stated, "No, if you don't know their names, you don't get them. For me it wasn't about money, or promoting myself, it was about making [my girls] better people."[8] Stefanac did not just make her fighters better, she made the MMA community take notice of women for their skill and not just their looks.

WMMA GROWS

WMMA maintained popularity in Asia, where women first gained recognition as practitioners of the sport. Emily Kwok is a BJJ powerhouse who competed in MMA in Korea's Smackgirl promotion and was the first Canadian woman to receive a black belt in Brazilian jiu-jitsu. She competed in numerous BJJ world tournaments, winning a gold medal in the Absolute Division of the Pan Ams in 2007. Kwok won both of her amateur and professional bouts at Smackgirl, which presented WMMA until late 2008, when it closed its doors. Smackgirl is a memorable part of WMMA history, and its demise was sad. The promotion allowed many female fighters to get their feet wet and demonstrated the legitimacy of WMMA. Furthermore, many of the fighters, especially the Korean ladies, wore amazing costumes reminiscent of the outfits popular in professional wrestling. But while the costumes may have been similar to those worn by the "divas" in professional wrestling circuits, Smackgirl was more than a spectacle; it was a legitimate and important part of WMMA history.

The success of the UFC led to the creation of several other MMA promotions, although none would ever recreate the zeitgeist of the Ultimate Fighting Championships. On August 22, 2006, Bodog Fight held its first show in Costa Rica and featured Tara LaRosa defeating Amanda Buckner with a rear naked choke. LaRosa is another pioneer of WMMA, with an extensive MMA career spanning more than a decade. Her first professional victory, in 2002, at a Hook-n-Shoot bout, marked her in the forefront of the bantamweight division. Throughout the next ten years, LaRosa won bouts against such top-tier fighters as Roxanne Modafferi, Hitomi Akano, Julie Kedzie, Shayna Baszler, Alexis Davis, and Carina Damm. In 2013, she participated in the historic mixed-gender season of the *Ultimate Fighter*, the UFC's reality show competition that pits professional MMA fighters against one another in a tournament-style setting. The 2013 *Ultimate Fighter* season eighteen cohort consisted of both male and female fighters who were coached by either Ronda Rousey or Miesha Tate. The show is discussed more thoroughly later in this chapter, but the upset on the first night, when longtime veteran LaRosa lost to up-and-coming Sarah Moras, was, honestly, to be expected but still disappointing. LaRosa's lengthy career, however, is best remembered by her earlier days and dominating fight record of twenty-one wins and four losses.

In 2007, ZUFFA purchased Japan's PRIDE Fighting Championships and tightened its hold on the MMA entertainment market. Other rival MMA promotions would slowly decline and eventually die in the shadow of this martial arts monopoly; however, in 2007, the Showtime television network hopped on the MMA bandwagon and started its own promotion, Elite Xtreme Combat, or Elite XC. Elite XC's first show, dubbed "Destiny," was headlined by Renzo Gracie and Frank Shamrock on February 10, 2007. This was the first televised MMA event since the UFC had used pay-per-view to distribute its promotion. Shamrock was famously disqualified for kneeing Gracie when he was down, but the other fights were more straightforward. Two women, Gina Carano and Julie Kedzie, were also on the fight card, and their presence would catapult WMMA from the sidelines toward the center of the MMA phenomenon. The UFC had the monopoly on televised MMA events, and many MMA fans had never seen women in the cage. Showtime provided viewers with a WMMA bout, and both the women's skills and looks changed the way fans thought about female fighters.

Gina Carano: The "First Lady" of WMMA

Gina Carano stepped confidently into the cage, knowing that her unde-feated record was due to her skills as a kickboxer. She felt a bit unsure about what would happen if Julie Kedzie took her to the ground, but if she could remain standing, she would undoubtedly win. There were those who believed that Carano was not well-rounded enough to be considered the first great female MMA fighter in the larger fighting community. Until this point, women were on the periphery of a growing sport that was still fringe itself. But on this night, on the first televised show on the Showtime network, MMA would be available for fans to watch at home without purchasing a pay-per-view event. Among fighting legends Renzo Gracie, Frank Shamrock, and Antonio Silva, Gina Carano and Julie Ked-zie stood waiting as the cage door was shut and locked behind them.

Carano began her fighting career in the sport of Muay Thai and had a professional record of twelve wins, one loss, and one draw. She took her first professional MMA fight in 2006, and, within two years, had an undefeated record of seven wins. But her first big victory was in 2006, when she defeated Elaina Maxwell and became the first woman to appear in the Strikeforce lineup. Strikeforce was the second-largest MMA pro-motion in the United States, and beginning in 2009, its fights appeared on CBS and HBO in the United States. The first fight between Carano and Maxwell, however, was not televised, even though it was the first female fight on such a large fight card. Some critics suggested that Carano's victory over Maxwell was a poor decision, but the two fought again, this time in a professional Muay Thai bout, and Carano defeated Maxwell for a second time. Maxwell would go on to fight some of the rising stars in WMMA, including Miesha Tate, who was eager to get back in the cage after being defeated by Kaitlin Young at a Hook-n-Shoot tournament. Tate defeated Maxwell by unanimous decision. Carano, meanwhile, went to Elite XC on February 10, 2007, to compete in the first televised MMA match between two women.

Gina Carano and Julie Kedzie Make History

In the cage on that historic night were twenty-four-year-old Gina "Conviction" Carano and twenty-five-year-old Julie "Fireball" Kedzie. Like many other women, Kedzie began her professional MMA career at the Hook-n-Shoot promotion in 2004. Carano is often dubbed the first "face of WMMA," but she was certainly joined by another great pioneer of the sport. Kedzie, who has a long and storied career in MMA, is one of the more personable and funny women in the fighting world. In an interview with *Fightland* magazine, she gives several humorous anecdotes about her early fighting career, from not knowing how to cut weight to soiling her pants during a show and meeting Vladimir Putin moments thereafter. Kedzie already had a dozen fights before she met Carano in the cage and was ready to take on the newcomer. Carano had only three professional MMA fights before her Showtime debut. She competed in Strikeforce, another MMA promotion that would eventually be swallowed by ZUFFA, and won her first three fights. Carano was a Muay Thai champion who had trained extensively in Thailand, and Kedzie was a grappling expert who trained under catch wrestler Erik Paulson, so the matchup was perfect. Carano was already being praised for her beauty, even before commentators noted her superior striking skills.

As the referee called the women to the center of the ring, he told them to prepare for "three 5-minute rounds," but the announcer quickly explained that while that was standard for men, the women would only do "three 3-minute rounds."[9] The distinction is interesting; women may be able to compete amongst the men, but the time they were allotted in the cage was shortened significantly. Today, women in the UFC fight under the same conditions as their male colleagues, but in this first televised WMMA fight, the women were restricted to shorter rounds.

It was common knowledge that while Carano was an incredible Muay Thai fighter, she was uncomfortable fighting on the ground. During the fight, Kedzie desperately tried to take Carano to the ground, but she took a number of hard strikes in the process. By the end of the second round, the commentators and even Kedzie seemed surprised that she had been able to continue standing after receiving so many punches, knees, and kicks. When the fight came to an end, the girls both jumped up, grabbed one another's hands, and raised them in victory. They smiled, laughed, and repeatedly hugged, as the promoter of Elite XC congratulated them on their historic appearance on televised WMMA. The commentators noted that both women still needed work as fighters, which was a bit demeaning considering how many of the male fighters in the event could have used the same advice. Nevertheless, as the fight ended and the women received a standing ovation, it was a hallmark moment for the growing sport of WMMA. When interviewing Carano after her unanimous victory, the commentator asked what she felt the fight had done for WMMA. The victor smiled and asked the audience if they wanted to see more, and the crowd cheered with what was obviously a resounding "Yes!"

Carano went on to win her next three fights, which included a victory over Kaitlin Young, a fighter who would go on to compete in the all-female Invicta Fighting Championships and the UFC. In her final fight, she fought Cris "Cyborg" Justino as the main event on the August 15, 2009, Strikeforce card. This highly anticipated bout between the undefeated Carano and the 7–1 Justino was an incredible fight; however, it started long before they entered the cage.

Cris "Cyborg" Justino

The female body is historically described as soft and slight, as opposed to the hard, strong bodies of men. In her assessment of athletic women and bodybuilders, "Holding Back: Negotiating a Glass Ceiling on Women's Muscular Strength," Shari Dworkin contends that women who strength train find themselves constrained by "ideologies of emphasized femininity that structure the upper limit on women's bodily strength and musculature."[10] Women seeking to increase muscle mass are often described derogatively, with masculine characteristics. This critique is heightened when women participate in historically male sports, especially sports that have been denounced for excessive violence.

Gender ideals suggest that women should be passive and lack the strength of men, while men are aggressive and driven by sex. These ideals generate the many criticisms that female fighters behave in an "unfeminine" or "manly" manner because of their participation in an aggressive sport. This criticism grows when a woman's physique does not adhere to cultural expectations. Analyzed later in this chapter, the fight between Carano and Justino was centered on Justino's supposedly masculine appearance. Internet pundits ruthlessly criticized Justino for her well-developed musculature and created the narrative of Carano as the (beautiful) underdog by titling the fight "Beauty and the Beast."

Dworkin claims that many women who work out often feel that they are limited by society's idealization of them as female. In her interviews, many women stated that they wanted to be strong but did not want to look like a man. The majority of the contemporary martial arts community recognizes the validity of women participating and competing in combative sports. Female fighters work hard to increase strength and develop precise technique. Most professional athletes have bodies that differ greatly from runway models, although different sports require specific musculature development. Athletes tend to focus on creating the strongest version of their bodies to be competitive, rather than to try to adhere to some impossible, culturally idealized feminine body standard.

More than any other fighter in WMMA history, Justino's name has become synonymous with a "masculine" female body. In a basic Internet search of her name, the first suggestion to pop up is "Cris Cyborg Steroids," followed by "Cris Cyborg Is a Man." In 2011, Justino was stripped of her Strikeforce title when she tested positive for anabolic steroids. Following her one-year suspension, she reentered the fighting circuit with a renewed dedication to her sport and won her subsequent fights, but she continued to receive flack for her offense, which is understandable to many fans. It is interesting, however, to see a fighter like Sean Sherk bounce back from his steroid infraction, while Justino remains maligned by many in the MMA world. In 2013, she announced her intention to drop to the bantamweight class to fight Ronda Rousey, but the UFC seemed hesitant to sign her, despite the predictions from numerous fans and experts that she was the only woman able to defeat the champion Rousey. Cris Justino is one of the most famous female fighters today, and love her or hate her, as some people do with vitriolic vigor, in 2009, she roundly and decidedly defeated Gina Carano in what would be the most viewed WMMA fight to date.

Gina and Cris in the Cage

The matchup between Carano and Justino was the first female title fight for five rounds of five minutes each, with both women weighing in at 145 pounds. The cheers of the crowd were deafening when Justino came straight out of her corner and began striking Carano. Carano's conditioning, which was praised, was disrupted in the first round, when Justino repeatedly took her to the ground. The crowd screamed Carano's name, but in the last few seconds of the first round, Justino overwhelmed her with strikes from the mount position. The referee called the fight less than a second before the bell rang to end the round, as the crowd booed. Carano did not get up, and the fight was obviously over. In her postfight interview, tears streamed down Justino's face as she thanked her opponent and fans. She went on to defeat Marloes Coenen and Jan Finney, but her twelfth fight, against Hiroko Yamanaka, which ended in just sixteen seconds, initiated her fall from grace when she tested positive for anabolic steroids. But Justino worked hard to return to the sport, competing in the all-female MMA venue InVicta.

As for Carano, after the resounding defeat in the Strikeforce title match, she left the fighting world and entered Hollywood, starring in the 2012 Steven Soderbergh film *Haywire*, along with celebrated actors Ewan McGregor, Michael Douglas, and Michael Fassbender. Her performance received little praise, but her acting career has continued, and she initiated the idea that a particularly good-looking fighter could transition from the cage to the big screen. After Carano left MMA, the world was eager to find another "face" of the women's division, not knowing that the next big thing, Ronda Rousey, was fresh off winning a bronze medal at the 2008 Olympics and ready to enter the world of WMMA.

STRIKEFORCE BUILDS ITS RANKS

Strikeforce had become the dominant purveyor of professional WMMA in the United States and brought in fighters from throughout the world. Michelle Waterson, the 105-pound "Karate Hottie" from New Mexico, defeated Tyra Parker with a rear naked choke in October 2008, to become the first atomweight to win in a large American fight venue. After a rather spotty appearance of female fighters on Strikeforce cards, the women became a feature of most shows, and fighters like Kim Couture joined the promotion. In 2009, Strikeforce introduced several new weight classes and held more WMMA fights than ever before.

The 125-pound flyweights were introduced when Jeri Sitzes defeated Lacey Schuckman. Marloes Coenen, the much-loved Dutch featherweight fighter, arm barred Roxanne Modafferi, another longtime fighter, in the first minute of the first round of their November 2009 Strikeforce fight. A few months later, Coenen fell to Cris Justino in their first, but not last, meeting in the cage. In May 2009, Sarah Kaufman defeated Miesha Tate as part of the two-tiered main event and went on to beat Shayna Baszler the following month. Kaufman became the first Strikeforce women's welterweight champion after defeating Takayo Hashi by unanimous decision on February 26, 2009.

Kaufman has had a steady career as a bantamweight fighter, with sixteen wins, two losses, and one no contest. She became a subject of debate and some undeserved ridicule in 2011, however, when she was passed over for a shot at the Strikeforce belt against Miesha Tate, and Ronda Rousey was chosen instead. In the bantamweight division, Kaufman continued to remain supreme until she lost to Marloes Coenen in October 2010. Meanwhile, another fighter was rising through the Strikeforce ranks.

Miesha Tate, a former high school wrestler, defeated Coenen in July 2011, to become the new Strikeforce bantamweight champion. Kaufman was scheduled to be her next opponent, but another woman, Ronda Rousey, had a different idea. Strikeforce was an excellent proponent of WMMA and a platform for male fighters as well, but, in 2011, it was purchased by ZUFFA, the parent company of the UFC. The plan, according to UFC president Dana White, was for Strikeforce to continue to operate as a separate promotion, but in January 2013, it was officially closed, and fighters either went to the UFC or lost their contracts.

BELLATOR FIGHTING CHAMPIONSHIPS

One fight promotion in the United States that survived the ZUFFA monopoly is the Bellator Fighting Championships, or Bellator MMA, as it is currently named. Bellator takes a unique approach to MMA, because it is based on determining the best fighter in a weight class through a tournament, rather than the typical rise in ranks featured in most fight promotions. During each season, a cohort of fighters competes to win their weight-class championships. Bellator is the second-largest fight promotion in the United States, and it has no relationship with ZUFFA and the UFC, other than an occasional spat between the two organizations. On May 1, 2009, Bellator 5 presented their first WMMA bout, between Jessica Penne and Tammie Schneider, 105-pound atomweights. The fight did not last long; Penne overwhelmed Schneider with punches just a minute and a half into the first round. A few weeks later, Kerry Vera defeated Leslie Smith by unanimous decision in the bantamweight division.

On June 19, 2009, Bellator introduced its first featherweight fight, when Stefanie Guimaraes knocked out Yvonne Reis with knees with less than a minute remaining in the first round. Many other women signed on the Bellator roster. These included strawweight Felice Herrig, who defeated Jessica Rakoczy in her Bellator debut; Megumi Fujii, the Smackgirl strawweight champion; Lisa Ellis, another Smackgirl, Bodog, and Hook-n-Shoot alum; as well as Rosi Sexton, the British physician and MMA champion. Bellator began to collect a bevy of excellent female fighters from throughout the world, all of whom were searching for a place to compete in a televised platform. Strikeforce continued to be an excellent place for female fighters, but it featured only the 135-pound bantamweight and 145-pound featherweight classes. Women who did not compete in those particular weight classes were often limited to fighting in Asian MMA competitions, which offered more opportunity for a variety of sizes. But Bellator often featured fighters from some of the smaller weight classes and gave more women an opportunity to fight in the United States.

One of Bellator's drawbacks is that fighters compete with much greater frequency than in the UFC because of the tournament format. The seasons, which typically last about two months, include weekly fights and a large cohort of fighters. Women initially appeared intermittently in Bellator; it was not until season three, which took place August 12, 2010, through October 28, 2010, that Bellator introduced the first female championship division. The first weight-class competition that took place was between female strawweight fighters, who must weigh 115 pounds at the most. In the first round of the tournament, Jessica Aguilar defeated Lynn Alvarez with an arm triangle, Meguimi Fujii defeated Carla Esparza with an arm bar, Zoila Frausto won via unanimous decision over Jessica Penne, and Lisa Ward also won a unanimous decision against Aisling Daly. In the semifinals, held on September 30, 2010, Frausto scraped a win over Aguilar with a split decision, and Meguimi arm barred Lisa Ward. That placed Frausto and Meguimi in the final, which took place on October 28, and resulted in a win for the Japanese Meguimi, who defeated Frausto with a narrow split decision to become the first Bellator women's champion.

After season three, Bellator continued to sporadically include women on its fight cards, but there would never be another female championship tournament. On May 12, 2012, Jessica Aguilar, who continued to compete in Bellator and win her subsequent fights, defeated Megumi Fujii by unanimous decision. Aguilar remains the best strawweight fighter in the world, even though she decided not to sign with the UFC when they announced a strawweight season of the *Ultimate Fighter* for 2014, because she was already under contract with the World Series of Fighting promotion. The UFC is, at this point in MMA history, the elite fighting platform. Fighters who win championships in the UFC are considered the best in the world, despite whomever may hold the same title in other promotions. This is where Aguilar struggles to retain her title as the best strawweight. Statistically, as of this writing, she is still the best strawweight MMA fighter, but when her fellow 115-pound fighters enter the UFC and compete for the title, she may lose her standing in the eyes of many in the MMA community.

Bellator's occasional female bouts from 2010 through 2013, before it cut its female fighters, included appearances by Michelle Ould, Munah Holland, and Jessica Eye, who defeated the champion, Zoila Frausto, on December 12, 2012. In early 2013, professional boxer Holly Holm used her boxing skills to earn a technical knockout against Katie Merrill. Holm has a professional boxing record of thirty-three wins, two losses, and three draws. She transitioned into MMA in 2011, and has remained undefeated, with six wins and no losses, thanks to her striking skills, which earned her two knockouts, three technical knockouts, and one unanimous-decision victory. Fans have been clamoring to get Holm into the cage to face the undefeated champion, Ronda Rousey, but thus far, Dana White thinks she is unqualified to box in his promotion. Until she competes on a larger platform, the boxer will not be able to break into the UFC.

Holm was the last woman to win in the Bellator cage. After that fight, Bellator released its female fighters, explaining in an interview that the company wished to develop its men's division and simply could not provide its female fighters with enough opportunities.[11] With Bellator and Strikeforce out of the WMMA game in 2013, women needed a place to compete for the sport of WMMA to survive. While some people argue that Ronda Rousey saved WMMA, it seems more likely that the person who provided women with more opportunities to compete was not a fighter, but a promoter.

INVICTA FC

In 2012, Shannon Knapp, an executive who held high-level positions in several MMA promotions, saw the opportunity to create her own venue when Strikeforce closed its doors. Knapp gathered the contracts of numerous top female MMA fighters and created Invicta Fighting Championships, or Invicta FC, a professional all-female MMA venue. Invicta FC offered its first show, streamed live and free on the Web, on April 28, 2012. Headlining the fight was longtime veteran Marloes Coenen, who defeated Romy Ruyssen by decision. Other experienced and high-ranking fighters were featured in the lineup. These included atomweight Jessica Penne (winner over Lisa Ellis by technical knockout); Liz Carmouche (winner over Ashleigh Curry by technical knockout); and the fight of the night, if not the year, between Kaitlin Young and Leslie Smith, which ended in a draw. Invicta has held several events featuring some of the best female fighters in the world. After offering the fights through a free streaming platform for the first few shows, the organization switched to the pay-per-view formula used by the UFC, although at a fraction of the price.

One of the most fascinating aspects of Invicta FC for MMA aficionados are the "walkout" arrangements. In a typical UFC bout, fighters walk out with a large entourage of coaches, a medical crew, and security people while their song plays overhead. Between the music, the slow (or swift) swagger to the cage, checking in with medical personnel, hugging teammates, and then speaking to the official, each fighter may take as long as five minutes to enter the cage. During each walkout, commentators struggle to fill the void with pointless anecdotes and high-dollar advertisements. At Invicta events, each fighter walks out to her music by herself, having already parted with her team. Instead of traversing the distance of a large event center, fighters walk down a runway, disrobe, check in with officials, and then enter the cage. The process is much more streamlined and intimate than the typical walkout, even if the fighter is not surrounded by an entourage.

Shannon Knapp also implemented a protocol for weigh-ins for Invicta fighters. Women tend to have a more difficult time cutting weight than men because of hormones and other physiological factors. Knapp's extensive experience as a MMA executive promoter makes Invicta a highly organized event, with the focus on the fights, rather than any Sturm und Drang between fighters. The organization currently signs fighters ranging from 105-pound atomweights to 155-pound lightweights, although it seems likely that it will add some of the heavier weight classes in the future. Invicta continues to sign female fighters worldwide and now has title fights for all of its existing weight classes.

Invicta FC represents the future of professional WMMA. While the greatest bantamweight fighters in the world may be signed with ZUFFA, Invicta provides a platform where numerous women can fight at an elite level. The promotion does not always receive as much media attention as it deserves, but this is because the most talked about female fighter, perhaps in history, while a supporter of Invicta, remains firmly and inextricably linked to the UFC. In 2013, when the UFC introduced its first-ever female division, it named Ronda Rousey the champion bantamweight fighter, even before she entered the cage.

RONDA ROUSEY

In 2011, Ronda Rousey was swiftly becoming one of the most talked about women in the competitive martial arts world. Rousey was brought up practicing judo, a Japanese art that uses hip throws and leg trips to take opponents to the mat, where the goal is to finish them with a grappling submission. Rousey qualified for the 2004 Olympic Games as the youngest competitor, at seventeen years of age. Four years later, she went to Beijing and earned two bronze medals at the 2008 Olympics. Two years after that, she entered the world of MMA with the tenacity expected of a former Olympian. After three definitive wins as an amateur, Rousey became a professional MMA fighter, winning her next four fights with furiously applied arm bars. But all of Rousey's previous fights had been as a featherweight, at 145 pounds. Her new target, Miesha Tate, was the Strikeforce champion as a 135-pound bantamweight.

Tate started her martial arts career as a wrestler on her high school's all-male team. She won titles in multiple wrestling and grappling events before transitioning into her new career as a MMA fighter. Tate quickly dominated the bantamweight class and became the darling of WMMA, with an impressive record of twelve wins and two losses under the championship belt. Dubbed one of the "hottest women in MMA," she appeared in the men's magazines *Maxim* and *FHM*. Gina Carano's retirement left a void at the forefront of the sport. Tate was presumed the new "face of WMMA" and the perfect target for the up-and-coming Rousey. Only a few months after Tate defeated Marloes Coenen for the Strikeforce title, Rousey defeated Julia Budd with an arm bar thirty-nine seconds into their November 18, 2010, fight. After acknowledging Budd, who was lying on the mat with a dislocated elbow, Rousey shocked the MMA community by calling out the incumbent Strikeforce champion, Tate. Challenging other fighters is standard practice in the boxing and MMA realm, but Rousey's challenge raised eyebrows because although she was undefeated, four professional MMA fights were not enough to qualify her for the belt. More importantly, Rousey had won all of her fights in the 145-pound featherweight class and had yet to drop to 135 pounds.

Rousey pleaded with the Strikeforce executives, claiming she would "put on a good show" if given a "crack at Miesha first." While Rousey was making headlines by calling for a fight, Tate was anticipating a rematch with Sarah Kaufman, who was ranked second in the division. Rousey wanted to bypass Tate's expected opponent and fight in a weight class in which she had never participated. As an undefeated fighter and a former Olympian, she argued that she would generate more interest than Kaufman. Her challenge dominated the postfight media blitz and overwhelmed the news of her quick defeat of Budd. On November 29, 2010, Rousey and Tate met for a press conference to discuss an upcoming fight.

Ronda Rousey Challenges Miesha Tate and the Status Quo

The press conference between Strikeforce champion Miesha Tate and newbie Ronda Rousey was a discussion of female representation more than a negotiation between fighters. Tate felt that she should fight Sarah Kaufman next rather than give the upstart Rousey a chance. Rousey audaciously argued that she deserved the chance, not simply because of her impressive 4–0 record, but because a fight against her would be more marketable than a rematch against Kaufman. Rousey argued that Strikeforce had the tendency of setting up fights based on monetary potential and not according to any ranking system. Based on this premise, Rousey believed that Strikeforce would make more money from a Rousey–Tate bout, explaining,

> I really feel 100 percent that a fight between her and me needs to happen. It'll be great for women's MMA. It'll be the first highly anticipated fight in women's MMA for a long time. . . . We need to capitalize on the opportunity while we still have it. I don't want to risk her losing the title and us not being able to fight each other for the title. [12]

Tate's argument was simple: There is a hierarchy amongst female fighters, and Rousey had to qualify. Rousey had yet to fight at 135 pounds, so why should she get a title shot before the other women currently operating within that bracket? Rousey's response was also simple: She was more marketable than Kaufman because of the growing hype surrounding her skill—and looks. Rousey explains her stance in a *MMA Hour* interview:

> Sarah Kaufman kind of gives boring interviews, she's not a supermodel the way she fights, she doesn't finish matches in extraordinary fashion. It's just kind of being realistic. I'm sorry that I have to say things bluntly and offend some people. I just want there to be a highly marketable, exciting women's title fight, and I want to be part of that because I feel like I could do a really good job, and you could, too [speaking to Tate]. I think the two of us could do a better job of that than you and Sarah Kaufman. [13]

Rousey's comments certainly enraged many people, but she made the legitimate, albeit infuriating, argument that women's sports receive more recognition when the athletes are good-looking. When it comes to women and the sports media, the better looking an athlete is, the more media attention she will receive. Moreover, female athletes are discussed through a gendered framework because of the "female" qualifier. They are not just athletes; they are "female athletes." This notation of gender means that the body is the focus of any and all conversation involving the athlete.

WMMA JOURNALISM

Most MMA news outlets write about female fighters in a respectful and intelligent manner; however, there are always outliers who seek to create controversy (and increase clicks to their website) by writing demeaning and insulting articles about female fighters. The larger problem is when advertisements or articles use female sexuality to promote fights. In some cases, one fighter will be praised as attractive, while her opponent is promoted as the less attractive and, therefore, less popular fighter. Sexualizing female athletes occurs in every sport, but in a one-on-one contest like fighting, creating a difference between opponents based on looks alone is problematic in more ways than one.

Female fighters are still considered anomalies and are often viewed with both fear and fascination. The female fighter who does not adhere to normative beauty ideals is often ridiculed or scorned by some media outlets and fans. It is interesting to examine previous female champions, for instance, Hattie Leslie and Hattie Stewart, both of whom were described as handsome, Amazonian women. That type of nuanced and descriptive language is rarely heard today; fighters are either deemed hot or ugly. Although there are numerous individuals who love the sport of MMA despite the appearance of the fighter, they are vastly outweighed by the "fan" who is disgusted by the appearance of a fighter. The faces and bodies of male fighters, of course, are not treated with the same level of scrutiny as those of female fighters. This is not to say that a male fighter cannot have his appearance critiqued, but that the conversation is decidedly different than the one about the female fighter. The debate surrounding Ronda Rousey and Miesha Tate in 2011 was not about who was attractive and who was not. Instead, Rousey argued that she would be the best opponent for Tate because they were both conventionally attractive and could increase the ratings exponentially.

The promotion for the fight between Rousey and Tate hinged on eroticizing both women. Rousey argued that the sport must embrace the sexualization of the athletes and use the attention to promote WMMA. Tate argued against this, yet Tate herself is no stranger to cheesecake portraiture, having posed scantily clad for numerous photo shoots for various publications. But posing for a provocative photo shoot does not make these women victims. In fact, many feminists believe that this type of self-promotion is empowering.

THE MMA PINUP

Participation in sexualized, pinup photography does not mean that the models have lost agency. In her book *Pin-Up Grrrls: Feminism, Sexuality, Popular Culture*, scholar Maria Elena Buszek explains that pinup imagery is a source of power for women and third-wave feminists.[14] Second-wave feminism was a feminist movement in the Western world from the 1960s to the 1990s that sought social equality for women. In the 1990s, feminist ideology split into a third wave that primarily focused on the rights of individual women rather than women as a group. One of the primary differences between second- and third-wave feminists is the contentious subject of female sexuality and agency. While second wavers fought angrily for their sexuality to be free of any social context, third wavers "tend to feel their sex has much to explore and celebrate."[15] Third wavers look at representations of women in popular culture to see how they can use those images for their own powerful statements. Buszek believes that "by looking to theory and popular visual languages" that promote female power rather than commodifying women, "younger women who identity with feminism today have found tools for self-expression and a place for themselves in the continuum of feminist evolution."[16] Thus, new participants in the feminist culture can look to popular culture and find agency in the images that are represented, as long as they can use these images in a positive manner.

The icon of the pinup has, since its inception, been seen as an image of sexuality, individualism, and power. The pinup is typically a scantily clad or nude woman with extremely curvy proportions posing in a highly sexualized position and appearing to enjoy it. Although this image could be seen as merely a source of sexual visual pleasure for men, the pinup image reveals a woman who is comfortable and confident in her sexuality.

One of the first images of the pinup, first marketed by Alberto Vargas in *Esquire*, was imitated by women during World War II to create homemade cheesecake photographs that were sent to their lovers overseas. Although both Vargas's drawings and the DIY pinup pictures were used for men's pleasure, the women who reproduced the images in *Esquire* were exploring a sexuality in their own lives that had yet to be seen in the United States. Buszek explains,

The pin-up [*sic*] provided an outlet through which women might assert that their unconventional sexuality could coexist with conventional ideals of professionalism, patriotism, decency, and desirability—in other words, suggesting that a woman's sexuality could be expressed as part of her whole being.[17]

Buszek's book argues that this tradition of pinup imagery continues today and allows all women, regardless of age, race, and size (and, I would argue, athletic prowess) to celebrate femininity. Although the centerfold imperative may leave some female athletes feeling pressured to pose in pinup-style photo shoots, many women find the display empowering. In addition to creating a marketable image as an athlete, there is the simple pleasure of feeling beautiful. For highly visible sports like tennis or MMA, participating as a pinup is part of the lifestyle. In combat sports with high female participation but low media scrutiny, athletes do not have to adhere to the centerfold imperative, primarily because that necessity does not exist.

HYPING THE ROUSEY–TATE FIGHT

The Rousey–Tate fight was an exhausted subject for the MMA community; many claimed that the hype surrounding these two women had reached a saturation point. The bout was indeed promoted with daily interviews, projections, Twitter updates, and boasting from both women. Many WMMA supporters felt overwhelmed by the excessive publicity, declaring that there were other female fighters who deserved attention, which was absolutely true. There were plenty of women fighting in smaller venues and training diligently to reach the critical mass currently occupied by Rousey and Tate. Although Rousey's continual self-promotion and Tate's numerous attempts to exempt herself from the drama became overbearing, the buildup of this fight was an integral part of bringing women out of the margins and into the forefront of the sport of MMA.

The problem was not the hype surrounding the match, it was the constant insistence from multiple media outlets that Rousey or Tate must be the "face" of WMMA. Yet, the search for a singular representative of the sport had been ongoing since Debi Purcell first came onto the scene nearly a decade earlier. The popularity of the UFC and other MMA venues does not ride on the shoulders of one man, but the sport of

WMMA must, for some reason, be embodied by one woman. Gina Carano, now a B movie star, failed to uphold this monumental position after her loss to Cris "Cyborg" Justino, and Justino was never considered the "face" of WMMA because she was not deemed "beautiful" by American sports media outlets. The hype surrounding the fight between Rousey and Tate revealed that female fighters are promoted in the media as pageant contestants whose talents are punching and kicking rather than singing or dancing.

When Rousey and Tate finally met, Rousey did exactly what she claimed she would do: She threw Tate to the ground and applied her signature arm bar submission. Tate also did exactly what she promised she would do: Out of pure obstinacy, she refused to tap. Instead, Rousey applied the arm bar slowly, but fully, and Tate's arm, because of her refusal to submit, was broken. Six months later, Rousey fought Sarah Kaufman and defeated her with an arm bar as well. Within the following year, Strikeforce would close its doors, and its fighters would need a new place to call home.

THE UFC WOMEN'S DIVISION

By this time, Rousey had caught the eye of UFC president Dana White, who infamously told reporters in 2011, while stumbling out of the Mr. Chow restaurant in Beverly Hills, that women would never fight in the UFC. But White was fascinated by Rousey, not only because of her aggressive fighting style, but also because of her brashness and, undoubtedly, looks. So the UFC president changed his stance on female fighters in the UFC, and he did so with a rather sentimental gesture. White invited Rousey to dinner at Mr. Chow's restaurant and told her the reason that they were at this particular establishment was because this was where, two years prior, he had told TMZ reporters that women would never fight in the UFC. He informed her that women would indeed fight in the UFC and that he wanted her to be the first female fighter.[18] This rather charming exchange initiated what White would call the "Rousey show," as MMA fans and fighters speculated about who Rousey, the only woman signed to the UFC's new women's division, would fight in the first match.

White chose Liz "Girl-Rilla" Carmouche, a former U.S. Marine and outspoken lesbian fighter. Carmouche had just defeated Kaitlin Young in her second Invicta FC appearance and seemed primed to take on the undefeated Rousey. The fight was historic in many ways. Not only was it the first time women would appear in the UFC, it was the first time an openly gay fighter would participate in the promotion. Carmouche, known for wearing a rainbow-striped mouth guard, and Rousey showed a lot of respect for one another, but in the cage on February 23, 2013, Carmouche submitted to Rousey's arm bar just like her predecessors. The excitement about WMMA could be felt in the arena. Rousey and Carmouche were the main event of the evening, with major male fighters Urijah Faber, Lyoto Machida, and Dan Henderson appearing beneath them on the card.

THE *ULTIMATE FIGHTER* SEASON 18

WMMA would remain in the UFC. In fact, Ronda Rousey was so successful in the eyes of Dana White that he set up the next season of the *Ultimate Fighter* to feature not only female coaches (Rousey, of course, being one of them), but for the fighters themselves to be both male and female bantamweights. The only question was who would coach the other team. On April 13, 2013, Miesha Tate entered the cage with Cat Zingano for the second UFC WMMA fight. Zingano, a Colorado-based fighter who had just returned from an extensive training camp in Thailand, is considered a particularly well-rounded fighter as a former wrestler and BJJ player. On her way into the cage, she smiled widely in the bright lights as tears streamed down her cheeks. It was a moving moment for Zingano, who was realizing her dream of fighting in the UFC, where she would be the second female fight in UFC history. In the cage, however, her smile quickly disappeared, as she pummeled Tate to a technical knockout in the third round.

Zingano was slated to be the other coach for season 18 of the *Ultimate Fighter*, except that a knee injury and immediate surgery forced her to back out of the deal. White named Tate the new coach, and the rivalry between her and Rousey escalated, especially in the heightened drama of a reality television show. The show included numerous bantamweight fighters, including veterans Roxanne "Happy Warrior" Modafferi and

Shayna "Queen of Spades" Baszler, known for being the first person to pull off the twister submission in a fight, and was, of course, filled with drama, but the finale resulted in Julianna Pena defeating Jessica Rakoczy with a technical knockout out in the first round, making her the first female winner of the *Ultimate Fighter*. Sadly, Pena suffered a devastating knee injury in January 2014, and had to pull out of her forthcoming UFC debut fight.

Meanwhile, as is tradition on the *Ultimate Fighter*, the coaches faced off in the octagon a few weeks after their fighters had competed in the show's finale. The animosity between Rousey and Tate had grown to epic proportions, and after Rousey yet again submitted Tate with an arm bar (she tapped this time), the reigning champion refused to shake her opponent's hand, prompting boos from the crowd. Rousey explained in a press conference that Tate had insulted her family, but the rivalry and hostility between the two runs deeper than any one particular issue. The problem between Rousey and Tate is that Rousey is the face of WMMA, and according to some people, including Tate, she never paid her dues.

Rousey continued her winning streak in the bantamweight division, defeating Tate and Sarah Kaufman in Strikeforce, before defeating Liz Carmouche, Tate, and Sara McMann in the UFC. The second fight with Tate was punctuated in the media with vitriolic comments and signs of poor sportsmanship all around. Heightened by the dramatic editing of the *Ultimate Fighter* reality show, where Rousey and Tate were both coaches, the fight was almost shamefully dramatized. The promotion of Rousey's next fight with fellow Olympian Sara McMann was tame, and even boring, by MMA standards. Rousey and McMann approached one another as colleagues in a dysfunctional office, each declaring their own superiority, yet doing so in a polite manner. It was a welcome change for many MMA fans.

As we have seen, long before Ronda Rousey entered the octagon in the UFC, women were competing in MMA. On many occasions, exceptionally great female fighters the likes of Debi Purcell or Meguimi Fujii competed on fight undercards, although they should have been featured higher on the card roster. Female fighters had been underpaid and underappreciated; Ronda Rousey instantly received endorsements, magazine editorials, and a celebrity following. Even Gina Carano, the first internationally recognized and admired female fighter, did not receive the type of press Rousey has generated. Thus, many WMMA fans and some fighters believe that Rousey not only stepped on the shoulders of the great female fighters before her, but that she did so with an arrogance that was offensive and disrespectful. When Rousey called out Miesha Tate in 2011, to fight for the Strikeforce championship, Tate felt that she was speaking out of turn, but the etiquette of fighting sports is not dictated by Emily Post.

Muhammad Ali created an institution around self-aggrandizement, and modern MMA fighters Chael Sonnen and the Diaz brothers, Nick and Nate, followed in his footsteps. These fighters have received a great deal of press and, therefore, more fighting opportunities because of their self-promotion. What Rousey did was promote herself to an extent that no other professional female MMA fighter had accomplished, and she used all of her tools at hand—her good looks, winning record of submitting opponents with arm bars in the first round, and Olympic medals—to convince not just Dana White, but the MMA community as a whole, that she was worthy of the belt and the praise. Then she backed up her assertions. She continues to win her fights, and she does so without pretending to abide by the gender ideal that women should be passive, nurturing, and giving.

CONCLUSION

Past, Present, and Future Pugilism

After months of wild speculation surrounding Ronda Rousey's next opponent, the announcement that she would face Alexis Davis at UFC 175 felt anticlimactic, not because Davis is anything less than a fantastic fighter, but because the conjectured opponents had suddenly become absurd. Cat Zingano seemed the most logical fighter to receive a shot at Rousey, although she was still recovering from ACL surgery. Holly Holm, professional-boxer-turned-MMA-fighter, was also predicted to face Rousey, and, of course, numerous fans were dying to see Cris "Cyborg" Justino finally join the animated fighter in the cage. But the most talked about suggestion was that Gina Carano should come out of retirement after spending five years in Hollywood, which seems both ludicrous and strange given that she fought in a different weight class than Rousey and had not fought in years. The UFC and Dana White played up this debate, even allowing rumors to "slip out" that fans would be shocked by the choice of opponent. When Davis's name was announced, many people felt that the intense speculation and hype diminished the reality of the contest.

It is interesting to contemplate the arc of Ronda Rousey's career. In the beginning, she continually asserted the importance of manipulating the media to generate interest for fights. When arguing why she should be Strikeforce champion Miesha Tate's next opponent in 2011, she explained that the media would eagerly promote a bout between two beautiful, media-savvy women. During the next few years, she continued to use the media to her advantage, just like many of her male colleagues do. Yet, she was demonized by many people in the women's mixed martial arts (WMMA) community, who called her everything from an upstart to over-rated. By 2014, Rousey had fully established herself as the champion, especially when she defeated Sara McMann with a sharp knee to the liver and not with her signature arm bar. Her right to the bantamweight belt is undeniable, and so she can be less bombastic in her media appearances and instead indulge in spending more time with her girlfriends. By mid-2014, Rousey seemed more relaxed in her interviews and carefree with her roommates and training partners, Shayna Baszler, Marina Shafir, and Jessamyn Duke. Ronda's three roommates, all professional mixed martial arts (MMA) fighters known as the "Four Horsewomen," create an environment of love and support that may be just what the sport of MMA needed.

The history of female fights is often a mere footnote in most martial arts books, a few pages that mention Elizabeth Wilkinson Stokes or Christy Martin but quickly move on to other marginal issues in fighting. In her phenomenal text *On Boxing*, published in 1987, Joyce Carol Oates asserts that, "Boxing is a purely masculine activity and [*sic*] it inhabits a purely masculine World."[1] Oates was not a pessimist, but perhaps she was not cognizant of the rich history of female fighters. She recognizes the inherent masculinity within the sport of boxing. Even now, when we talk about women boxers, there is the necessity to qualify them as women, and not just boxers. Yet, this is not a phenomenon restricted to fighting sports.

I would like to return to Professor Michael Kimmel, whose quote in the introduction recognizes that those in the center of power do not have to be named: Men in sports are athletes, but women in sports are female athletes. The qualifier of female takes one away from the center of power, and that marginalization increases when other qualifiers are added, for instance, African American woman or Asian American woman. It can be disconcerting and disheartening as women when we see stark statistics, like those provided by Professor Michael Messner in the introduction, that reveal the ever-decreasing amount of coverage devoted to female athletes in the American media, but when we leave the realm of the professional athletes and take a look at athletics on the micro-scale, in schools and community centers throughout the United States and in Europe, we can see that girls are participating in sports in unprecedented numbers.

According to a recent study conducted by *ESPN* the magazine, by age six, 60 percent of boys and 47 percent of girls are already playing a team sport.[2] Of course, these numbers vary significantly depending on location (urban, suburban, or rural), economic status, and race. The study also reveals that girls are less likely to play sports when a family is in dire circumstances; in fact, 59 percent of girls from single-parent households do not play sports. While there is still a significant gap between the activities of young boys and young girls, the options for females have grown exponentially throughout the past few decades. As education and civil rights for women have increased during the past one hundred years, there has been concomitant growth in sports participation, but one drawback to our current situation is that we neglect to remember that women have always taken part in sports, although participation in those activities has been mired in social and gender stereotyping.

The history of women's sports is not perfectly linear; it has been a rollercoaster ride that continues, even today, to be marked by quick shifts and variable progress. In the late nineteenth century, the number of women participating in sports began to rise. In the United States and Europe, sports were primarily practiced by middle- and upper-class people who had free time. Most lower-income individuals did not have the time during a busy work day to play a sport, although there are tales of men wrestling and boxing after work for fun. Like today, certain sports had a connotation that marked them within society. Golf and tennis were seen as more upscale activities, while wrestling and boxing were, for some reason, considered lower-class endeavors. There continues to be a class divide between those who practice golf, tennis, skiing, or horseback riding and those who box, wrestle, or run. Moreover, the cultural conception of certain sports changes throughout time. Cheerleading is often considered a "female" sport today, but cheerleaders in the mid-twentieth century were often men. Such sports as golf, tennis, swimming, running, and gymnastics tend to be more gender-neutral, while American football remains a primarily masculine sport. Fighting sports are, of course, historically thought of as male-centric activities: Consider the early American name for boxing as the "manly art of self-defense."

The interesting thing about fighting sports is that the action and technique of each activity are no different between men and women. Fighters perform the same moves and techniques regardless of sex. There are, in effect, more differences between male fighters than there are between men and women in the ring. It takes courage to enter the ring no matter who you are; however, the women who fought in the eighteenth and nineteenth centuries were, in my opinion, the epitome of bravery and resiliency. Despite risks of social alienation and even scuffles with the law, these historic female fighters were relentless in their pursuit of the sports they loved. Their courage reminds us that as important as it is to look forward to the next fight, the next opponent, the next title shot, it is just as crucial that we look back and remember the women who gave us the audacity to fight today.

NOTES

PREFACE

1. Martha McCaughey, "The Fighting Spirit: Women's Self-Defense Training and the Discourse of Sexed Embodiment," *Gender and Society* 12, no. 3 (1998): 277.
2. McCaughey, "The Fighting Spirit," 279.
3. Martha McCaughey, *Real Knockouts: The Physical Feminism of Women's Self-Defense* (New York: New York University Press, 1997), 7.
4. Catherine Hodge McCoid and Yvonne J. Johnson, "The Women's Army of the Dahomey," in *Combat, Ritual, and Performance*, ed. David E. Jones (London: Praeger, 2002), 53–65.
5. Barbara Ehrenreich and Dierdre English, *For Her Own Good: Two Centuries of the Experts' Advice to Women* (New York: Random House, 1978).

INTRODUCTION

1. Cesar A. Torres, *Routledge Companion to Sports History*, ed. John Nauright Pope (London: Routledge, 2010), 553.
2. Michael Mandelbaum, *The Meaning of Sports* (New York: PublicAffairs, 2004).
3. Mandelbaum, *The Meaning of Sports*, 7.
4. Cheryl Cooky, Michael Messner, and Robin Hextrum, "Women Play Sport, but Not on TV," *Communication and Sport* 1, no. 3 (September 2013): 203–30.

5. Cooky, Messner, and Hextrum, "Women Play Sport, but Not on TV," 203–30.

6. Michael Kimmel, *The Gendered Society* (New York: Oxford University Press, 2004), 7.

7. Elizabeth Angell, "Sex and Female Politicians," *Allure*, 2010. Available online at http://www.allure.com/beauty-trends/blogs/daily-beauty-reporter/2010/09/sex-and-female-politicians-the-debate-rages.html (accessed 16 September 2010).

8. Lawrence Wenner, ed., *MediaSport* (New York: Routledge, 1998), 188.

9. Helene Elliot, "Marion Bartoli Overpowers Sabine Lisicki for 2013 Wimbledon Title," *Los Angeles Times*, 2013. Available online at http://articles.latimes.com/2013/jul/06/sports/la-sp-elliott-wimbledon-women-20130707 (accessed 6 July 2013).

10. Kasia Boddy, *Boxing: A Cultural History* (London: Reaktion Books, 2008), 7.

11. Homer, *The Iliad* (New York: Oxford University Press, 2014), 211.

12. Homer, *The Iliad*, 211.

13. Homer, *The Iliad*, 211–12.

14. Boddy, *Boxing*, 10.

15. Suetonius, "Augustus," in *The Twelve Caesers*, trans. Robert Graves (London: Penguin, 1962), 63.

16. Barratt O'Hara, *From Figg to Johnson: A Complete History of the Heavyweight Championship* (Charleston, S.C.: Nabu Press, 2013), 7.

17. William Hickey, *Memoirs of William Hickey*, ed. Alfred Spencer (London: Hurst and Blackett, 1913), 82.

18. *New York Post*, 14 December 1826.

19. Elliot J. Gorn, *The Manly Art: Bare-Knuckle Prize Fighting in America* (Ithaca, N.Y.: Cornell University Press, 1986), 75–76.

20. Homer, *The Iliad*, 212.

21. Thomas A. Green and Joseph R. Svinth, eds., *Martial Arts of the World: An Encyclopedia of History and Innovation*, Vol. 1 (Santa Barbara, Calif.: ABC-CLIO, 2010), 127.

22. Green and Svinth, *Martial Arts of the World*, 199.

23. Green and Svinth, *Martial Arts of the World*, 259–60.

24. Green and Svinth, *Martial Arts of the World*, 322.

25. Michael Poliakoff, *Combat Sports in the Ancient World* (New Haven, Conn.: Yale University Press, 1987), 54.

26. Douglas Booth and Holly Thorpe, eds., *Berkshire Encyclopedia of Extreme Sports* (Great Barrington, Mass.: Berkshire, 2007).

27. "'Judo' Gene LeBell vs. Boxer Milo Savage: America's First MMA Fight," *Black Belt*, 2011. Available online at http://www.blackbeltmag.com/

daily/mixed-martial-arts-training/boxing/judo-gene-lebell-vs-boxer-milo-savage-americas-first-mma-fight/ (accessed 14 October 2011).

28. Phil Pepe, "The Fight Hurt Nobody Except Fans Who Paid," *Hartford Courant*, 27 June 1976, 5C.

29. Pepe, "The Fight Hurt Nobody Except Fans Who Paid," 5C.

I. FIGHTING IN THE GEORGIAN AND VICTORIAN ERAS

1. William Hickey, *Memoirs of William Hickey*, ed. Alfred Spencer (London: Hurst and Blackett, 1913), 82.

2. Zacharias Conrad von Uffenbach, *London in 1710*, trans. W. H. Quarrell and Margaret Mare (London: Faber and Faber, 1934), 90–91.

3. *London Journal*, 23 June 1722, 3.

4. *London Journal*, 23 June 1722, 3.

5. Arthur L. Hayward, *Lives of the Most Remarkable Criminals Who Have Been Condemned and Executed for Murder, the Highway, Housebreaking, Street Robberies, Coining, or other Offenses* (Project Gutenberg, 2004).

6. Pierce Egan, *Boxiana*, Vol. 1 (London: G. Smeeton, 1830), 300.

7. Christopher Thrasher, "Disappearance: How Shifting Gendered Boundaries Motivated the Removal of Eighteenth-Century Boxing Champion Elizabeth Wilkinson from Historical Memory," *Past Imperfect*, 18 (2012), 53–75.

8. *British Gazetteer*, 1 October 1726.

9. *British Gazetteer*, 1 October 1726.

10. *British Gazetteer*, 1 July 1727.

11. *British Gazetteer*, 1 June 1728.

12. *Daily Post*, 12 November 1899, 27.

13. *Daily Post*, 16 June 1730.

14. *British Gazetteer*, 28 December 1728.

15. *British Gazetteer*, 24 May 1729.

16. *British Gazetteer*, 18 July 1730.

17. Tom Molyneux, *Pancratia* (London: W. Oxberry, 1812), 113.

18. Molyneux, *Pancratia*, 120.

19. Allen Guttmann, *Women's Sports: A History* (New York: Columbia University Press, 1991).

20. Guttmann, *Women's Sports*, 72.

21. *Observer*, 14 July 1973, 3.

22. Guttmann, *Women's Sports*.

23. William Hazlitt, "Of Great and Little Things," in *The Miscellaneous Works of William Hazlitt* (New York: R. Worthington, 18–?), 236.

24. Tom Paulin, "Spirit of the Age," *Guardian*, 4 April 2003. Available on-line at http://www.theguardian.com/books/2003/apr/05/society.history.

25. Mary Wollstonecraft, "A Vindication of the Rights of Woman," xiv.

26. Wollstonecraft, "A Vindication of the Rights of Woman," xiv.

27. *Essex Standard, and Colchester, Chelmsford, Maldon, Harwich, and General County Advertiser*, 2 September 1836.

28. *Times* (London, England), 25 September 1805, 3.

29. *Times*, 25 September 1805, 3.

30. *Times*, 25 September 1805, 3.

31. *Times* (London, England), 24 March 1807, 3.

32. Quoted in Barbara Ehrenreich and Dierdre English, *For Her Own Good: Two Centuries of the Experts' Advice to Women* (New York: Random House, 1978), 112.

33. Phyllis G. Tortora and Keith Eubank, *Survey of Historical Costume*, 4th ed. (New York: Fairchild, 2005), 281.

34. Valerie Steele, *The Corset: A Cultural History* (New York: Yale University Press, 2003), 51.

35. Quoted in Steele, *The Corset*, 51.

36. Quoted in Steele, *The Corset*, 57.

37. Jennifer Hargreaves, *Sporting Females: Critical Issues in the History and Sociology of Women's Sports* (London: Routledge, 1994), 66.

38. Paul Creswick, *Bruising Peg: Pages from the Journal of Margaret Molloy* (London: Downey, 1898), 5.

39. William Biggs Boulton, *The Amusements of Old London; being a survey of the sports and pastimes, tea gardens and parks, playhouses and other diversions of the people of London from the 17th to the beginning of the 19th century* (London: B. Blom, 1969), 30.

40. Creswick, *Bruising Peg*, 18.

41. Creswick, *Bruising Peg*, 18.

42. Creswick, *Bruising Peg*, 23.

43. Boulton, *The Amusements of Old London*, 234–35.

44. *Bell's Life in London, and Sporting Chronicle*, 7 April 1822, 48.

45. *Bell's Life in London*, 7 April 1822, 48.

46. *Bell's Life in London*, 7 April 1822, 48 .

47. *Bell's Life in London*, 7 April 1822, 48.

48. *Washington Post*, 21 June 1887, 1.

2. AMERICAN WOMEN JOIN THE FIGHT

1. *Detroit Daily Free Press*, 3 August 1856, 2.

2. *Little Rock Daily Gazette*, 31 October 1865, 6.

3. Elliot J. Gorn, *The Manly Art: Bare-Knuckle Prize Fighting in America* (Ithaca, N.Y.: Cornell University Press, 1986), 59.

4. Gorn, *The Manly Art*, 67.

5. *Daily Evening Bulletin*, 19 October 1866, 3.

6. *Chicago Tribune*, 12 March 1869, 2.

7. *Chicago Tribune*, 12 March 1869, 2.

8. *Chicago Tribune*, 12 March 1869, 2.

9. Linda Setnick, *Victorian Fashions for Women and Children* (Atglen, Pa.: Schiffer Publishing, 2012), 13.

10. Harvey Green, *The Light of the Home* (New York: Pantheon, 1983), 114.

11. *Cincinnati Enquirer*, 15 September 1874, 8.

12. *Cincinnati Enquirer*, 15 September 1874, 8.

13. *Cincinnati Enquirer*, 14 July 1880, 2.

14. Most websites point to this article as the originator of the (incorrect) information about the 1891 wrestling match between Alice Williams and Sadie Morgan. See http://www.fscclub.com/history/sonntag-pic2-e.shtml.

15. *Washington Post*, 28 April 1891, 4.

16. *Washington Post*, 28 April 1891, 4.

17. Gorn, *The Manly Art*, 67.

18. *National Police Gazette*. Available online at http://www.policegazette.us/ (accessed 30 May 2013).

19. *National Police Gazette*, 1 March 1884, 3.

20. *National Police Gazette*, 17 May 1884, 13.

21. *Georgia Weekly Telegraph, Journal and Messenger*, 31 March 1882, Col. G.

22. *Georgia Weekly Telegraph, Journal and Messenger*, 31 March 1882, Col. G.

23. *Georgia Weekly Telegraph, Journal and Messenger*, 31 March 1882, Col. G.

24. *Georgia Weekly Telegraph, Journal and Messenger*, 31 March 1882, Col. G.

25. *National Police Gazette*, 30 March 1895, 6.

26. *National Police Gazette*, 17 May 1884, 13.

27. *National Police Gazette*, 25 October 1884, 13.

28. *Atchison Daily Champion*, August 30, 1888, 1.

29. *Washington Post*, 24 October 1898, 8.

30. *Omaha Daily Bee*, 28 December 1887, 2.

31. *Omaha Daily Bee*, 28 December 1887, 2.

32. *Washington Post*, 24 October 1898, 8.

33. *Washington Post*, 24 October 1898, 8.

34. *Washington Post*, 24 October 1898, 8.

35. *Washington Post*, 24 October 1898, 8.

36. *Washington Post*, 24 October 1898, 8.

37. *Washington Post*, 24 October 1898, 8.

38. *Woman's Tribune*, 18 August 1888, 1.

39. *Washington Post*, 24 October 1898, 8.

40. *National Police Gazette*, 18 September 1890, 6.

41. *Cincinnati Enquirer*, 11 July 1888, 2.

42. *Cincinnati Enquirer*, 11 July 1888, 2.

43. *Cincinnati Enquirer*, 11 July 1888, 2.

44. *Cincinnati Enquirer*, 11 July 1888, 2.

45. *Daily Inter Ocean*, 17 September 1888, 2.

46. *National Police Gazette*, 3 October 1888, 10.

47. *Daily Inter Ocean*, 17 September 1888, 2.

48. *Cincinnati Enquirer*, 4 September 1888, 1.

49. *Chicago Tribune*, 6 October 1888, 9.

50. *National Police Gazette*, 18 September 1890, 2.

51. *Salt Lake Herald*, 28 December 1882, 7.

52. *Cincinnati Enquirer*, 19 December 1889, 2.

53. *Cincinnati Enquirer*, 19 December 1889, 2.

54. *Cincinnati Enquirer*, 19 December 1889, 2.

55. *Cincinnati Enquirer*, 29 December 1889, 2.

56. *Cincinnati Enquirer*, 29 December 1889, 4.

57. *Cincinnati Enquirer*, 29 December 1889, 4.

58. *Cincinnati Enquirer*, 5 January 1890, 2.

59. *Cincinnati Enquirer*, 5 January 1890, 2.

60. Jonathan C. Meakins, "Typhoid Fever in the 1890s and 1930s," *Canadian Medical Association Journal* 42, no. 1 (January 1940) : 81–82.

61. *Milwaukee Sentinel*, 25 September 1892, Col. B.

62. *New Hampshire Sentinel*, 2 December 1891, 3.

63. *New Hampshire Sentinel*, 2 December 1891, 3.

64. *Brooklyn Daily Eagle*, 22 November 1891, 20.

65. *Brooklyn Daily Eagle*, 22 November 1891, 20.

66. *Boston Herald*, 10 April 1894, 8.

67. *Brooklyn Daily Eagle*, 19 January 1941, 44.

68. *Boston Herald*, 10 April 1894, 7.

69. *National Police Gazette*, 28 October 1893, 10.

70. *National Police Gazette*, 27 January 1894, 10.

71. *Atchison Daily Globe*, 17 July 1893, 2.

72. *Atchison Daily Globe*, 17 July 1893, 2.

73. *National Police Gazette*, 24 September 1892, 11.

74. *National Police Gazette*, 24 September 1892, 11.
75. *Los Angeles Times*, 11 November 1894, 19.
76. *Los Angeles Times*, 11 November 1894, 19.
77. *Cincinnati Enquirer*, 11 February 1899, 13.
78. *Cincinnati Enquirer*, 11 February 1899, 13.
79. *Washington Post*, 17 January 1897, 24.
80. *Washington Post*, 17 January 1897, 24.
81. *Washington Post*, 17 January 1897, 24.
82. *National Police Gazette*, 21 August 1880, 6.
83. *San Francisco Chronicle*, 30 January 1897, 9.

3. FIGHTING AS SPECTACLE

1. *New York Times*, 25 September 1904, 34.
2. Lady Greville, ed., *Ladies in the Field* (London: Ward and Downey, 1894).
3. Greville, *Ladies in the Field*, 3.
4. Harvey Green, *The Light of the Home* (New York: Pantheon, 1983), 153–63.
5. Jennifer Hargreaves, *Sporting Females: Critical Issues in the History and Sociology of Women's Sports* (London: Routledge, 1994), 143.
6. "Polly Burns," *Women Boxing Archive Network*. Available online at http://www.womenboxing.com/Burns.htm (accessed 5 January 2014).
7. Donald K. Burleson, "Polly Burns (Polly Fairclough): World Champion Lady Boxer, 1900," *Travel Golf*, 1996. Available online at http://www.travel-golf.org/genealogy/burns_polly.htm (accessed 5 January 2014).
8. *Washington Post*, 1 March 1916, 4.
9. *Washington Post and Times Herald*, 3 January 1959, D2.
10. *Milwaukee Journal*, 17 August 1989, G1.
11. *Cincinnati Enquirer*, 29 September 1908, 1.
12. *Boston Globe*, 12 September 1909, SM3.
13. *Boston Globe*, 12 September 1909, SM3.
14. *Washington Post*, 15 July 1915, 1.
15. *Washington Post*, 15 July 1915, 1.
16. *Chicago Tribune*, 6 May 1921, 19.
17. *Hartford Courant*, 13 January 1931, 12.
18. *Manchester Guardian*, 28 January 1926, 9.
19. *Daily Mail*, 30 January 1926, 4.
20. *Daily Mail*, 30 January 1926, 2.
21. *Cincinnati Enquirer*, 16 June 1902, 3.

22. *Irish Times*, 30 January 1926, 7.

23. *Observer*, 30 July 1933, 8.

24. *Atlanta Journal-Constitution*, 9 December 1918, 5.

25. "Top Ten Old-Time Strongwomen," *Physical Culturalist*. Available online at http://physicalculturist.ca/top-10-oldtime-strongwomen/ (accessed 2 February 2014).

26. *Broadcasting, Telecasting*, 1 July 1946, 76.

27. *Times-Picayune*, 7 November 1938, 13.

28. *Miami News*, 22 March 1936, 17.

29. *Miami News*, 22 March 1936, 17.

30. *Evening Independent*, 5 October 1926, 18.

31. *Evening News*, 5 October 1926, 1.

32. *Washington Post*, 6 January 1933, 14.

33. *New York Times*, 6 January 1933, 26.

34. *Times-Picayune*, 7 November 1938, 13.

35. *Sunday Times-Advertiser* (Trenton, N.J.), 6 November 1938, 5.

36. The spelling of the word *jujutsu* in both titles reveals that the spelling has become more standardized today as *jiu-jitsu*.

37. *Cincinnati Enquirer*, 17 July 1910, B1.

38. *Health and Strength*, 8 April 1911, 339.

39. Dennis Brailsford, *Sport, Time, and Society* (London: Routledge, 1991), 133.

40. *Salt Lake Herald*, 20 July 1895, 8.

41. *Cincinnati Enquirer*, 18 July 1900, 6.

42. *Kansas City Star*, 4 November 1907, 10; *Washington Post*, 7 May 1961, C5.

43. *Detroit Free Press*, 9 January 1908, 8.

44. *Detroit Free Press*, 9 January 1908, 8.

45. *Cincinnati Enquirer*, 18 October 1908, 2.

46. *Cincinnati Enquirer*, 18 October 1908, 2.

47. *Detroit Free Press*, 4 November 1908, 11.

48. *Detroit Free Press*, 4 November 1908, 11.

49. *Chicago Tribune*, 5 March 1910, 3.

50. *Chicago Tribune*, 5 March 1910, 3.

51. *Denver Post*, 5 March 1910, 6.

52. *Richmond Times-Dispatch*, 27 December 1920, 3.

53. *Richmond Times-Dispatch*, 24 December 1920, 6.

54. *Richmond Times-Dispatch*, 24 December 1920, 6.

55. *Charlotte Observer*, 30 December 1920, 5.

56. *Grand Forks Daily Herald*, 24 November 1922, 7; *Kalamazoo Gazette*, 22 November 1922, 24.

57. Marilyn Morgan, "Aesthetic Athletics," in *Consuming Modernity*, eds. Cheryl Warsh and Dan Malleck (Vancouver: University of British Columbia Press, 2013), 137.

58. Hargreaves, *Sporting Females*, 122.

59. *Hartford Courant*, 3 September 1942, 13.

60. *Chicago Tribune*, 11 March 1943, 24.

61. *New York Times*, 28 July 1948, 25.

62. *New York Times*, 28 July 1948, 25.

63. *Philadelphia Tribune*, 7 June 1949, 11.

64. *Hartford Courant*, 17 November 1948, 13.

65. *Daily Mail*, 11 November 1948, 4.

66. *Daily Mail*, 26 March 1949, 1.

67. *Washington Post*, 15 February 1949, 17.

68. *Washington Post*, 30 January 1949, C3.

69. *Toronto Daily Star*, 26 October 1948, 12.

70. *Daily Mail*, 9 February 1949, 1.

71. *Daily Mirror*, 30 October 2010, 32.

72. *Daily Mirror*, 30 October 2010, 32.

73. *Dallas Morning News*, 29 May 1955, 4.

74. *Seattle Daily Times*, 4 November 1957, 22.

75. *South Bend Tribune*, 14 October 2005, 1.

76. Sue Fox, "Phyllis Kugler: The Boxer Named 'Phil,'" *Women Boxing Archive Network*, May 26, 2002. Available online at http://www.womenboxing.com/kugler.htm (accessed 4 January 2014).

77. *South Bend Tribune*, 19 September 2005, 1.

78. *South Bend Tribune*, 19 September 2005, 1.

79. *Globe and Mail*, 30 July 1958, 13.

4. THE FIGHT TO FIGHT

1. "American Women in the Olympics," *National Women's History Museum*. Available online at http://www.nwhm.org/online-exhibits/olympics/olympics3.htm (accessed 14 January 2014).

2. *Globe and Mail*, 10 October 1952, 23.

3. Mike Moneyham, "Remembering the Amazing Mae Young," *Post and Courier*, January 19, 2014. Available online at http://www.postandcourier.com/article/20140119/PC20/140119391 (accessed 30 March 2014).

4. "Lillian Ellison, Wrestled as Fabulous Moolah, 84," *South Florida Sun Sentinel*, 5 November 2007, B10.

5. "*State v. Hunter* 209 Or. 282 (1956)," *Justia US Law*, 2014. Available online at http://law.justia.com/cases/oregon/supreme-court/1956/208-or-282-3.html (accessed 4 April 2014).

6. "*State v. Hunter*."

7. "*State v. Hunter*."

8. "Wrestling and Boxing Headline Big Card at Auditorium Tonight," *Atlanta Daily World*, 26 August 1953, 5.

9. "Wrestling and Boxing Headline Big Card at Auditorium Tonight," 5.

10. "Ban Girl Wrestlers," *Globe and Mail*, 12 March 1959, 15.

11. "Woman New Head of Boxing Board," *Daily Defender*, 27 October 1958, A22.

12. "Woman New Head of Boxing Board," A22.

13. "New Boxing Referee in Sweden Always Right—She's a Woman," *New York Times*, 8 January 1958, 94.

14. Walter Ames, "Russ Hodges Finds Women Becoming Rabid Boxing Fans," *Los Angeles Times*, 2 May 1954, E11.

15. Ames, "Russ Hodges Finds Women Becoming Rabid Boxing Fans."

16. "Woman Scores Knockout on $64,000 Boxing Quiz," *Hartford Courant*, 7 December 1955, 1.

17. "Women's Boxing Bout," *Guardian*, 17 April 1961, 16.

18. "Battling Little Laura Ends Boxing Career," *Boston Globe*, 25 January 1969, 15.

19. Dick Beddoes, "Boxing with Belles On," *Globe and Mail*, 30 May 1967, 30.

20. Beddoes, "Boxing with Belles On," 30.

21. "Woman Practices on Husband for Boxing Opening," *Washington Post*, 17 January 1965, 49.

22. "Female Boxing," *Pittsburgh Courier*, 23 January 1965, 18.

23. Abigail Van Buren, "Dear Abby," *Log Angeles Times*, 30 November 1969, E7.

24. Iram Valentin, "Title IX: A Brief History," *WEEA Digest* (August 1997): 1–12.

25. Sarah Fields, *Female Gladiators* (Chicago: University of Illinois Press, 2005), 6–7.

26. Fields, *Female Gladiators*, 6–7.

27. "15-Year-Old Girl's a Whiz as a Boxer," *Augusta Chronicle*, 30 August 1973, E8.

28. "Kid Gloves Are Off for Girls in Dallas," *Washington Post*, 30 August 1973, E8.

29. "Girls Fight Sports Rule," *Hartford Courant*, 4 January 1973, 1.

30. Charles E. Price, "Wrestling School for Boys, Girls," *Atlanta Daily World*, 12 August 1975, 5.

31. "Lady Is a Fighter," *Hartford Courant*, 8 October 1974, 43B.

32. "Lady Is a Fighter," 43B.

33. "Lady Is a Fighter," 43B.

34. "Dooley Defends 'Manly' Image of Pro Boxing," *Hartford Courant*, 5 February 1975, 47B.

35. "Lady Is a Fighter," 43B.

36. "Woman Denied License to Box," *Hartford Courant*, 22 January 1975, 53.

37. "Woman Denied License to Box," 53.

38. William B. Hamilton, "Women Enter Ring—Swinging," *Boston Globe*, 8 January 1976, 1.

39. Nick Thimmesch, "Women 'Stage' First Fight in N.Y.," *Chicago Tribune*, 29 September 1978, D2.

40. "Girl Boxer Seeks License," *Hartford Courant*, 20 September 1977, 56.

41. "Woman Boxing Champ Thinks She's the Best," *Hartford Courant*, 15 March 1978, 66C.

42. "Put 'Em Up," *Hartford Courant*, 9 March 1978, 63.

43. Barbara Brotman, "Cat Davis Wanted a Fight—and Did She Get One," *Chicago Tribune*, 26 November 1978, M3.

44. "Fans Jeer Ref Pep at Women's Bout," *Hartford Courant*, 4 July 1979, 49.

45. "Fans Jeer Ref Pep at Women's Bout," 49.

46. Judy Kessler, "With Boxer Cat Davis, Cauliflower Doesn't Come to Mind—Tomato, Maybe?" *People*, 15 May 1978, 93–95.

47. Thimmesch, "Women 'Stage' First Fight in N.Y.," E3.

48. Thimmesch, "Women 'Stage' First Fight in N.Y.," E3.

49. Prentis Rogers, "Is Pro Boxing World's Next 'Great White Hope' a Lady?" *Atlanta Daily World*, 4 June 1978, 6.

50. Rogers, "Is Pro Boxing World's Next 'Great White Hope' a Lady?" 6.

51. *Cleveland Call and Post*, 10 December 1960, 5C.

52. *Washington Post*, 24 May 1979, D1.

53. Don King, "Is a Woman's Place in the Boxing Ring?" *WBB*, March 1980. Article reprinted by Women Boxing Archive Network. Available online at http://www.womenboxing.com/donking.htm (accessed 14 January 2014).

54. Ernestine Miller, *Making Her Mark* (New York: Contemporary Books, 2002), 67–68.

55. "Women Boxing," *Playboy* (December 1997): 117.

56. "Jill Matthews," *Women Boxing Archive Network*. Available online at http://www.wban.org/biog/jmatthews.htm (accessed 14 January 2014).

57. Katherine Dunn, "The Golden Girls," *Vogue* 185, no. 4 (April 1995): 260–62.

58. Katherine Dunn, "The Golden Girls," 260–62.

59. *Orlando Sentinel*, January 29, 1994, A1.

60. *Orlando Sentinel*, 29 January 1994, A1.

61. *San Diego Union-Tribune*, 6 November 1996, D3.

62. *San Diego Union-Tribune*, 6 November 1996, D3.

63. *San Diego Union-Tribune*, 6 November 1996, D3.

64. "Gritty Woman," *Sports Illustrated* (15 April 1996): 80–86.

65. "Gritty Woman," 80–86.

66. "Gritty Woman," 80–86.

67. "Bonnie Canino," *Canino's Karate and Boxing Studio*. Available online at http://caninoskarateandboxingstudio.com/kickboxing-program.html (accessed 31 March 2014).

68. "Bonnie Canino," *BoxRec*. Available online at http://boxrec.com/list_bouts.php?human_id=18479&cat=boxer (accessed 31 March 2014).

69. Sharon Robb, "Woman to Fight Twice in Four Days," *Sun Sentinel*, 20 November 1996, 3C.

70. "Lucia Rijker," *Women Boxing Archive Network*. Available online at http://www.wban.org/biog/lrijker.htm (accessed 2 April 2014).

71. Katherine Dunn, "Lucia Rijker—War with Christy Martin—War Rumors and More Rumors," *Cyber Boxing Zone*, 3 March 2000. Available online at http://www.cyberboxingzone.com/boxing/kd3300.htm (accessed 2 April 2014).

72. *Hindustan Times*, 18 June 2007.

73. Melody K. Hoffman, "On the Ropes with Laila Ali," *Jet* (12 September 2005): 54–58.

74. *Orlando Sentinel*, 25 August 2003, D9.

75. Jessica Creighton, "Women's Boxing Split as Governing Body Suggests Skirts," *BBC*, 26 October 2011. Available online at http://www.bbc.com/sport/0/boxing/1545259.

76. Thomas A. Green and Joseph R. Svinth, eds., *Martial Arts of the World : An Encyclopedia of History and Innovation*, Vol. 2 (Santa Barbara, Calif.: ABC-CLIO, 2010), 521–23.

77. *USA Today*, 5 June 1991, 2C.

78. *San Diego Union-Tribune*, 29 August 1995, D1.

79. *San Diego Union-Tribune*, 29 August 1995, D7.

80. Green and Svinth, eds., *Martial Arts of the World*, Vol. 2, 521–23.

5. MMA GOES MAINSTREAM

1. Matt Winkeljohn, "State to Seek Court Order to Prevent Ultimate Fighting," *Atlanta Journal-Constitution*, 29 May 1997, E8.

2. "Future Fights Will Feature New Rules," *Salt Lake Tribune*, 21 June 1997, C5.

3. "Long Island Mom Wins World Champion Martial Arts Title in Japan," *New Voice of New York*, 18 August 2005, 16.

4. Chris Clayton, "Midlands Lawmakers Seek to KO 'Extreme Fighting' Contests in Bars," *Omaha World Herald*, 23 February 2002, 1.

5. David Hackett, "County Plans Toughman Measure," *Sarasota Herald Tribune*, 24 July 2003, BS1.

6. "Women Add Punch to Fight Night," *Gold Coast Bulletin*, 26 March 2005, 183.

7. Rusty Marks, "Fight Club," *Sunday Gazette*, 1 September 2002, 6F.

8. Lana Stefanac, interview with L. A. Jennings, 29 August 2013.

9. "Gina Carano vs. Julie Kedzie," *YouTube*, 11 November 2012. Available online at http://www.youtube.com/watch?v=ngUOcReb-og&feature=player_embedded (accessed 3 March 2104).

10. Shari Dworkin, "Holding Back: Negotiating a Glass Ceiling on Women's Muscular Strength," *Sociological Perspectives* 44, no. 3 (2001): 337.

11. Michael Stets, "Meat on the Bone," *MMA Mania*, August 13, 2013. Available online at http://www.mmamania.com/2013/8/13/4615670/bellator-boss-bjorn-rebney-interview-rampage-vs-tito-ppv-tna-ben-askren-interview-mma (accessed 13 September 2013).

12. Mike Chiapetta, "Miesha Tate, Ronda Rousey Spar over Who Should Be Next Title Challenger," transcription from *MMA Hour* interview with Ariel Helwani, 28 November 2011. Available online at http://www.mmafighting.com/2011/11/28/miesha-tate-ronda-rousey-spar-over-who-should-be-next-title-cha (accessed 30 November 2011).

13. Chiapetta, "Miesha Tate, Ronda Rousey Spar over Who Should Be Next Title Challenger."

14. Maria Elena Buszek, *Pin-Up Grrrls: Feminism, Sexuality, Popular Culture* (Durham, N.C.: Duke University Press, 2006).

15. Buszek, *Pin-Up Grrrls*, 333.

16. Buszek, *Pin-Up Grrrls*, 334.

17. Buszek, *Pin-Up Grrrls*, 231.

18. Dan Wetzel, "Dana White's About-Face on Women's MMA Became Official One Historic Night Last August," *Yahoo Sports*, 19 February 2013. Available online at http://sports.yahoo.com/news/mma--dana-white-s-about-face-on-

women-s-mma-became-official-one-historic-night-last-august-045153399.html
(accessed 14 September 2013).

CONCLUSION

1. Joyce Carol Oates, *On Boxing* (New York: Dolphin/Doubleday, 1987), 72.

2. Bruce Kelley and Carla Carchia, "Hey, Data Data—Swing!" *ESPN*, 11 July 2013. Available online at http://espn.go.com/espn/story/_/id/9469252/hidden-demographics-youth-sports-espn-magazine (accessed 8 May 2014).

BIBLIOGRAPHY

"15-Year-Old Girl's a Whiz as a Boxer." *Augusta Chronicle*, 30 August 1973, E8.
Adelman, Melvin L. *A Sporting Time: New York City and the Rise of Modern Athletics, 1820–70*. Urbana: University of Illinois Press, 1986.
"American Women in the Olympics." *National Women's History Museum*. Available online at http://www.nwhm.org/online-exhibits/olympics/olympics3.htm (accessed 14 January 2014).
Ames, Walter. "Russ Hodges Finds Women Becoming Rabid Boxing Fans." *Los Angeles Times*, 2 May 1954, E11.
Angell, Elizabeth. "Sex and Female Politicians." *Allure*, 2010. Available online at http://www.allure.com/beauty-trends/blogs/daily-beauty-reporter/2010/09/sex-and-female-politicians-the-debate-rages.html (accessed 16 September 2010).
Atchison Daily Champion, August 30, 1888–17 July 1893.
Atlanta Journal-Constitution, 9 December 1918, 5.
"Ban Girl Wrestlers." *Globe and Mail*, 12 March 1959, 15.
"Battling Little Laura Ends Boxing Career." *Boston Globe*, 25 January 1969, 15.
Beddoes, Dick. "Boxing with Belles On." *Globe and Mail*, 30 May 1967, 30.
Beekman, Scott M. *Ringside: A History of Professional Wrestling in America*. London: Praeger, 2006.
Bell's Life in London, and Sporting Chronicle, 7 April 1822, 48.
Boddy, Kasia. *Boxing: A Cultural History*. London: Reaktion Books, 2008.
"Bonnie Canino." *BoxRec*. Available online at http://boxrec.com/list_bouts.php?human_id=18479&cat=boxer (accessed 31 March 2014).
"Bonnie Canino." *Canino's Karate and Boxing Studio*. Available online at http://caninoskarateandboxingstudio.com/kickboxing-program.html (accessed 31 March 2014).
Booth, Douglas, and Holly Thorpe, eds. *Berkshire Encyclopedia of Extreme Sports*. Great Barrington, Mass.: Berkshire, 2007.
Boston Globe, 12 September 1909–8 January 1976.
Boston Herald, 10 April 1894, 7.
Boulton, William Biggs, *The Amusements of Old London; being a survey of the sports and pastimes, tea gardens and parks, playhouses and other diversions of the people of London from the 17th to the beginning of the 19th century*. London: B. Blom, 1969.
Brailsford, Dennis. *Sport, Time, and Society*. London: Routledge, 1991.
British Gazetteer , 1 October 1726–18 July 1730.
Broadcasting, Telecasting, 1 July 1946, 76.
Brotman, Barbara. "Cat Davis Wanted a Fight—and Did She Get One." *Chicago Tribune*, 26 November 1978, M3.

Burleson, Donald K. "Polly Burns (Polly Fairclough): World Champion Lady Boxer, 1900." *Travel Golf*, 1996. Available online at http://www.travel-golf.org/genealogy/burns_polly.htm (accessed 5 January 2014).

Buszek, Maria Elena. *Pin-Up Grrrls: Feminism, Sexuality, Popular Culture* (Durham, N.C.: Duke University Press, 2006).

Charlotte Observer, 30 December 1920, 5.

Chiapetta, Mike. "Miesha Tate, Ronda Rousey Spar over Who Should Be Next Title Challenger." Transcription from *MMA Hour* interview with Ariel Helwani, 28 November 2011. Available online at http://www.mmafighting.com/2011/11/28/miesha-tate-ronda-rousey-spar-over-who-should-be-next-title-cha (accessed 30 November 2011).

Chicago Daily Tribune, 6 May 1921, 19.

Chicago Tribune, 12 March 1869–26 November 1978.

Cincinnati Enquirer, 15 September 1874–17 July 1910.

Clayton, Chris. "Midlands Lawmakers Seek to KO 'Extreme Fighting' Contests in Bars." *Omaha World Herald*, 23 February 2002, 1.

Cleveland Call and Post, 10 December 1960, 5C.

Cooky, Cheryl, Michael Messner, and Robin Hextrum. "Women Play Sport, but Not on TV." *Communication and Sport* 1, no. 3 (September 2013): 203–30.

Costa, D. Margaret, and Sharon R. Guthrie, eds. *Women and Sport: Interdisciplinary Perspectives*. Champaign, Ill.: Human Kinetics, 1994.

Creswick, Paul. *Bruising Peg: Pages from the Journal of Margaret Molloy*. London: Downey, 1898.

Daily Evening Bulletin, 19 October 1866, 3.

Daily Mail, 30 January 1926–26 March 1949.

Daily Mirror, 30 October 2010, 32.

Daily Post, 12 November 1899– 16 June 1930.

Dallas Morning News, 29 May 1955, 4.

Denver Post, 5 March 1910, 6.

Detroit Free Press, 3 August 1856–4 November 1908.

"Dooley Defends 'Manly' Image of Pro Boxing." *Hartford Courant*, 5 February 1975, 47B.

Dunn, Katherine. "The Golden Girls." *Vogue* 185, no. 4 (April 1995): 260–62.

————. "Lucia Rijker—War with Christy Martin—War Rumors and More Rumors." *Cyber Boxing Zone*, 3 March 2000. Available online at http://www.cyberboxingzone.com/boxing/kd3300.htm (accessed 2 April 2014).

Dworkin, Shari. "Holding Back: Negotiating a Glass Ceiling on Women's Muscular Strength." *Sociological Perspectives* 44, no. 3 (2001): 333–50.

Egan, Pierce. *Boxiana*, Vol. 1. London: G. Smeeton, 1830.

Ehrenreich, Barbara, and Dierdre English. *For Her Own Good: Two Centuries of the Experts' Advice to Women*. New York: Random House, 1978.

Elliot, Helene. "Marion Bartoli Overpowers Sabine Lisicki for 2013 Wimbledon Title." *Los Angeles Times*, 2013. Available online at http://articles.latimes.com/2013/jul/06/sports/la-sp-elliott-wimbledon-women-20130707 (accessed 6 July 2013).

Essex Standard, and Colchester, Chelmsford, Maldon, Harwich, and General County Advertiser, 2 September 1836.

Evening Independent, 5 October 1926, 18.

Evening News, 5 October 1926, 1.

"Fans Jeer Ref Pep at Women's Bout." *Hartford Courant*, 4 July 1979, 49.

"Female Boxing." *Pittsburgh Courier*, 23 January 1965, 18.

Fields, Sarah. *Female Gladiators*. Chicago: University of Illinois Press, 2005.

Fisher, Sue. *In the Patient's Best Interest: Women and the Politics of Medical Decisions*. New Brunswick, N.J.: Rutgers University Press, 1986.

Fox, Sue. "Phyllis Kugler: The Boxer Named 'Phil.'" *Women Boxing Archive Network*, May 26, 2002. Available online at http://www.womenboxing.com/kugler.htm (accessed 4 January 2014).

"Future Fights Will Feature New Rules." *Salt Lake Tribune*, 21 June 1997, C5.

Georgia Weekly Telegraph, Journal, and Messenger, 31 March 1882, Col. G.

"Gina Carano vs. Julie Kedzie." *YouTube*, 11 November 2012. Available online at http://www. youtube.com/watch?v=ngUOcReb-og&feature=player_embedded (accessed 3 March 2104).
"Girl Boxer Seeks License." *Hartford Courant*, 20 September 1977, 56.
"Girls Fight Sports Rule." *Hartford Courant*, 4 January 1973, 1.
Globe and Mail, 10 October 1952–30 May 1967.
Gorn, Elliot J. *The Manly Art: Bare-Knuckle Prize Fighting in America*. Ithaca, N.Y.: Cornell University Press, 1986.
Grand Forks Daily Herald, 24 November 1922, 7.
Green, Harvey. *The Light of the Home*. New York: Pantheon, 1983.
Green, Thomas A., and Joseph R. Svinth, eds. *Martial Arts of the World: An Encyclopedia of History and Innovation*, Vol. 1. Santa Barbara, Calif.: ABC-CLIO, 2010.
———. *Martial Arts of the World: An Encyclopedia of History and Innovation*, Vol. 2. Santa Barbara, Calif.: ABC-CLIO, 2010.
Greville, Lady, ed. *Ladies in the Field*. London: Ward and Downey, 1894.
"Gritty Woman." *Sports Illustrated* (15 April 1996): 80–86.
Guttmann, Allen. *Women's Sports: A History*. New York: Columbia University Press, 1991.
Hackett, David. "County Plans Toughman Measure." *Sarasota Herald Tribune*, 24 July 2003, BS1.
Hamilton, William B. "Women Enter Ring—Swinging." *Boston Globe*, 8 January 1976, 1, 53.
Hargreaves, Jennifer. *Sporting Females: Critical Issues in the History and Sociology of Women's Sports*. London: Routledge, 1994.
Hartford Courant, 13 January 1931–4 July 1979.
Hayward, Arthur L. *Lives of the Most Remarkable Criminals Who Have Been Condemned and Executed for Murder, the Highway, Housebreaking, Street Robberies, Coining, or other Offenses*. Project Gutenberg, 2004.
Hazlitt, William. "Of Great and Little Things." In *The Miscellaneous Works of William Hazlitt*. New York: R. Worthington, 18–?.
Health and Strength, 8 April 1911, 339.
Hickey, William. *Memoirs of William Hickey*, ed. Alfred Spencer. London: Hurst and Blackett, 1913.
Hindustan Times, 18 June 2007.
Hodge McCoid, Catherine, and Yvonne J. Johnson. "The Women's Army of the Dahomey." In *Combat, Ritual, and Performance*, ed. David E. Jones, 53–65. London: Praeger, 2002.
Hoffman, Melody K. "On the Ropes with Laila Ali." *Jet* (12 September 2005): 54–58.
Homer. *The Iliad*. New York: Oxford University Press, 2014.
Irish Times, 30 January 1926, 7.
"Jill Matthews." *Women Boxing Archive Network*. Available online at http://www.wban.org/biog/jmatthews.htm (accessed 14 January 2014).
"'Judo' Gene LeBell vs. Boxer Milo Savage: America's First MMA Fight." *Black Belt*, 2011. Available online at http://www.blackbeltmag.com/daily/mixed-martial-arts-training/boxing/judo-gene-lebell-vs-boxer-milo-savage-americas-first-mma-fight/ (accessed 14 October 2011).
Kalamazoo Gazette, 22 November 1922, 24.
Kansas City Star, 4 November 1907, 10.
Kelley, Bruce, and Carla Carchia. "Hey, Data Data—Swing!" *ESPN*, 11 July 2013. Available online at http://espn.go.com/espn/story/_/id/9469252/hidden-demographics-youth-sports-espn-magazine (accessed 8 May 2014).
Kessler, Judy. "With Boxer Cat Davis, Cauliflower Doesn't Come to Mind—Tomato, Maybe?" *People*, 15 May 1978, 93–95.
Kimmel, Michael. *The Gendered Society*. New York: Oxford University Press, 2004.
King, Don. "Is a Woman's Place in the Boxing Ring?" *WBB*, March 1980. Article reprinted by Women Boxing Archive Network. Available online at http://www.womenboxing.com/donking.htm (accessed 14 January 2014).
"Lady Is a Fighter." *Hartford Courant*, 8 October 1974, 43B.
Lana Stefanac, interview with L. A. Jennings, 29 August 2013.
Leen, Jeff. *The Queen of the Ring*. New York: Atlantic Monthly Press, 2009.

"Lillian Ellison, Wrestled as Fabulous Moolah, 84." *South Florida Sun Sentinel*, 5 November 2007, B10.
Little Rock Daily Gazette, 31 October 1865, 6.
London Journal, 23 June 1722, 3.
"Long Island Mom Wins World Champion Martial Arts Title in Japan." *New Voice of New York*, 18 August 2005, 16.
Los Angeles Times, 11 November 1894–30 November 1969.
"Lucia Rijker." *Women Boxing Archive Network*. Available online at http://www.wban.org/biog/lrijker.htm (accessed 2 April 2014).
Manchester Guardian, 28 January 1926, 9.
Mandelbaum, Michael. *The Meaning of Sports*. New York: PublicAffairs, 2004.
Mangham, Andrew, and Greta Depledge, eds. *The Female Body in Medicine and Literature*. Liverpool, U.K.: Liverpool University Press, 2011.
Marks, Rusty. "Fight Club." *Sunday Gazette*, 1 September 2002, 6F.
McCaughey, Martha. "The Fighting Spirit: Women's Self-Defense Training and the Discourse of Sexed Embodiment." *Gender and Society* 12, no. 3 (1998): 277–300.
———. *Real Knockouts: The Physical Feminism of Women's Self-Defense*. New York: New York University Press, 1997.
Meakins, Jonathan C. "Typhoid Fever in the 1890s and 1930s." *Canadian Medical Association Journal* 42, no. 1 (January 1940) : 81–82.
Miami News, 22 March 1936, 17.
Miller, Ernestine. *Making Her Mark*. New York: Contemporafis a champry Books, 2002.
Milwaukee Journal, 17 August 1989, G1.
Milwaukee Sentinel, 25 September 1892, Col. B.
Molyneux, Tom. *Pancratia*. London: W. Oxberry, 1812.
Moneyham, Mike. "Remembering the Amazing Mae Young." *Post and Courier*, January 19, 2014. Available online at http://www.postandcourier.com/article/20140119/PC20/140119391 (accessed 30 March 2014).
Morgan, Marilyn. "Aesthetic Athletics." In *Consuming Modernity*, eds. Cheryl Warsh and Dan Malleck, 136–60. Vancouver: University of British Columbia Press, 2013.
National Police Gazette, 1 March 1884–30 March 1895.
"New Boxing Referee in Sweden Always Right—She's a Woman." *New York Times*, 8 January 1958, 94.
New Hampshire Sentinel, 2 December 1891, 3.
New York Post, 14 December 1826.
New York Times, 25 September 1904–8 January 1958.
O'Hara, Barratt. *From Figg to Johnson: A Complete History of the Heavyweight Championship*. Charleston, S.C.: Nabu Press, 2013.
Oates, Joyce Carol. *On Boxing*. New York: Dolphin/Doubleday, 1987.
Observer, 30 July 1933–14 July 1973.
Omaha Daily Bee, 28 December 1887, 2.
Orlando Sentinel, 29 January 1994–25 August 2003.
Paulin, Tom. "Spirit of the Age." *Guardian*, 4 April 2003.
Pepe, Phil. "The Fight Hurt Nobody Except Fans Who Paid." *Hartford Courant*, 27 June 1976, 5C.
Philadelphia Tribune, 7 June 1949, 11.
Poliakoff, Michael. *Combat Sports in the Ancient World*. New Haven, Conn.: Yale University Press, 1987.
"Polly Burns." *Women Boxing Archive Network*. Available online at http://www.womenboxing.com/Burns.htm (accessed 5 January 2014).
Price, Charles E. "Wrestling School for Boys, Girls." *Atlanta Daily World*, 12 August 1975, 5.
"Put 'Em Up." *Hartford Courant*, 9 March 1978, 63.
Richmond Times-Dispatch, 24 December 1920–27 December 1920.
Robb, Sharon. "Woman to Fight Twice in Four Days." *Sun Sentinel*, 20 November 1996, 3C.
Rogers, Prentis. "Is Pro Boxing World's Next 'Great White Hope' a Lady?" *Atlanta Daily World*, 4 June 1978, 6.

175

Salt Lake Herald, 28 December 1882–20 July 1895.
San Diego Union-Tribune, 29 August 1995–6 November 1996.
San Francisco Chronicle, 30 January 1897, 9.
Seattle Daily Times, 4 November 1957–29 August 1995.
Setnick, Linda. *Victorian Fashions for Women and Children*. Atglen, Pa.: Schiffer Publishing, 2012.
South Bend Tribune, 19 September 2005–14 October 2005.
"*State v. Hunter* 209 Or. 282 (1956)." *Justia US Law*, 2014. Available online at http://law.justia.com/cases/oregon/supreme-court/1956/208-or-282-3.html (accessed 4 April 2014).
Steele, Valerie. *The Corset: A Cultural History*. New York: Yale University Press, 2003.
Stets, Michael. "Meat on the Bone." *MMA Mania*, August 13, 2013. Available online at http://www.mmamania.com/2013/8/13/4615670/bellator-boss-bjorn-rebney-interview-rampage-vs-tito-ppv-tna-ben-askren-interview-mma (accessed 13 September 2013).
Suetonius. "Augustus." In *The Twelve Caesers*, trans. Robert Graves. London: Penguin, 1962.
Sunday Times-Advertiser (Trenton, N.J.), 6 November 1938, 5.
Thimmesch, Nick. "Women 'Stage' First Fight in N.Y." *Chicago Tribune*, 29 September 1978, D2, E3.
Thrasher, Christopher, "Disappearance: How Shifting Gendered Boundaries Motivated the Removal of Eighteenth-Century Boxing Champion Elizabeth Wilkinson from Historical Memory." *Past Imperfect*, 18 (2012), 53–75.
Times (London, England), 25 September 1805–24 March 1807.
Times-Picayune, 7 November 1938, 13.
"Top Ten Old-Time Strongwomen." *Physical Culturalist*. Available online at http://physicalculturist.ca/top-10-oldtime-strongwomen/(accessed 2 February 2014).
Toronto Daily Star, 26 October 1948, 12.
Torres, Cesar A. *Routledge Companion to Sports History*, ed. John Nauright Pope. London: Routledge, 2010.
Tortora, Phyllis G., and Keith Eubank. *Survey of Historical Costume*, 4th ed. New York: Fairchild, 2005.
Uffenbach, Zacharias Conrad von. *London in 1710*, trans. W. H. Quarrell and Margaret Mare. London: Faber and Faber, 1934.
USA Today, 5 June 1991, 2C.
Valentin, Iram. "Title IX: A Brief History." *WEEA Digest* (August 1997): 1–12.
Van Buren, Abigail. "Dear Abby." *Los Angeles Times*, 30 November 1969, E7.
Washington Post, 21 June 1887–24 May 1979.
Washington Post and Times Herald, 3 January 1959, D2.
Weekly Journal or British Gazetteer, 1 October 1726–18 July 1730.
Wenner, Lawrence, ed. *MediaSport*. New York: Routledge, 1998.
Wetzel, Dan. "Dana White's About-Face on Women's MMA Became Official One Historic Night Last August." *Yahoo Sports*, 19 February 2013. Available online at http://sports.yahoo.com/news/mma--dana-white-s-about-face-on-women-s-mma-became-official-one-historic-night-last-august-045153399.html (accessed 14 September 2013).
Winkeljohn, Matt. "State to Seek Court Order to Prevent Ultimate Fighting." *Atlanta Journal-Constitution*, 29 May 1997, E8.
"Woman Boxing Champ Thinks She's the Best." *Hartford Courant*, 15 March 1978, 66C.
"Woman Denied License to Box." *Hartford Courant*, 22 January 1975, 53.
"Woman New Head of Boxing Board." *Daily Defender*, 27 October 1958, A22.
"Woman Practices on Husband for Boxing Opening." *Washington Post*, 17 January 1965, 49.
"Woman Scores Knockout on $64,000 Boxing Quiz." *Hartford Courant*, 7 December 1955, 1.
Woman's Tribune, 18 August 1888, 1.
"Women Add Punch to Fight Night." *Gold Coast Bulletin*, 26 March 2005, 183.
"Women Boxing." *Playboy* (December 1997): 117.
"Women's Boxing Bout." *Guardian*, 17 April 1961, 16.
"Wrestling and Boxing Headline Big Card at Auditorium Tonight." *Atlanta Daily World*, 26 August 1953, 5.

INDEX

ABOUT THE AUTHOR

L. A. Jennings is a fighter and scholar specializing in feminism, popular culture studies, and American history. She lives in Denver, Colorado, with her husband, Mike, where they run their MMA gym, Train.Fight.Win.